CAREERS IN ONE HEALTH

Social workers play a critical role in the wellbeing of communities – trained to help individuals, families, and groups effect positive change and address barriers that stand in the way of optimal life and wellbeing. In addition to a focus on people, many social workers include animals in their definition of systems and family units, leading to endless ways they have successfully incorporated animals into their work.

This book offers insights from pioneers as well as practitioners in the field who have created their niche within this growing area. Coming from the philosophy that we cannot work towards what we do not know exists, this book offers knowledge, pathways, and advice from those who have succeeded in including their love for animals into their careers, shining a light on the path for those who share similar passions.

This book can be used as a supplemental textbook in undergraduate and graduate social work academic programs as well as a resource for social workers in the field looking for ways to expand their work.

Lori R. Kogan, PhD, is a professor of Clinical Sciences at Colorado State University. She is the chair of the Human-Animal Interaction section of the American Psychological Association and Editor-in-Chief of the *Human-Animal Interaction* journal, an open-access, online publication published by CABI. She has published numerous journal articles and books, including *Pet Loss, Grief, and Therapeutic Interventions: Practitioners Navigating the Human-Animal Bond* and *Clinician's Guide to Treating Companion Animal Issues: Addressing Human-Animal Interaction*. She is currently engaged in research pertaining to the intersection of the human-animal interaction and veterinary medicine.

Skills for Social Work Practice

This textbook series is ideal for all students studying to be qualified social workers, whether at undergraduate or postgraduate level. Covering key elements of the social work curriculum, the books are accessible, interactive and thought-provoking.

Case Examples in Child Welfare and Family Services for Social Workers
Tyrone Cheng

Careers in One Health
Social Workers' Roles in Caring for Humans and Their Animal Companions
Edited by Lori R. Kogan

For more information about this series, please visit: https://www.routledge.com/Skills-for-Social-Work-Practice/book-series/SSW

CAREERS IN ONE HEALTH

Social Workers' Roles in Caring for Humans and Their Animal Companions

Edited by Lori R. Kogan

LONDON AND NEW YORK

Designed cover image: © Getty Images

First published 2024
by Routledge
4 Park Square, Milton Park, Abingdon, Oxon OX14 4RN

and by Routledge
605 Third Avenue, New York, NY 10158

Routledge is an imprint of the Taylor & Francis Group, an informa business

© 2024 selection and editorial matter, Lori R. Kogan; individual chapters, the contributors

The right of Lori R. Kogan to be identified as the author of the editorial material, and of the authors for their individual chapters, has been asserted in accordance with sections 77 and 78 of the Copyright, Designs and Patents Act 1988.

All rights reserved. No part of this book may be reprinted or reproduced or utilised in any form or by any electronic, mechanical, or other means, now known or hereafter invented, including photocopying and recording, or in any information storage or retrieval system, without permission in writing from the publishers.

Trademark notice: Product or corporate names may be trademarks or registered trademarks, and are used only for identification and explanation without intent to infringe.

British Library Cataloguing-in-Publication Data
A catalogue record for this book is available from the British Library

Library of Congress Cataloging-in-Publication Data
Names: Kogan, Lori, editor.
Title: Careers in one health : social workers' roles in caring for humans and their animal companions / edited by Lori R. Kogan.
Description: Abingdon, Oxon ; New York, NY : Routledge, 2024. | Series: Skills for social work practice | Includes bibliographical references and index.
Identifiers: LCCN 2023030872 (print) | LCCN 2023030873 (ebook) | ISBN 9781032371467 (hardback) | ISBN 9781032371436 (paperback) | ISBN 9781003335528 (ebook)
Subjects: LCSH: Social service. | Pets—Social aspects.
Classification: LCC HV41 .C285 2024 (print) | LCC HV41 (ebook) | DDC 361.3—dc23/eng/20230817
LC record available at https://lccn.loc.gov/2023030872
LC ebook record available at https://lccn.loc.gov/2023030873

ISBN: 978-1-032-37146-7 (hbk)
ISBN: 978-1-032-37143-6 (pbk)
ISBN: 978-1-003-33552-8 (ebk)

DOI: 10.4324/9781003335528

Typeset in Sabon
by codeMantra

CONTENTS

List of contributors   *xiii*

SECTION I
Veterinary Social Work   **1**

1 The Interprofessional Practice Space of Veterinary Social Work: A Social Worker's Perspective   3
Elizabeth Strand

2 Embedded Social Work in a School of Veterinary Medicine   8
Page Walker Buck

3 The Cherished Pets Model of Veterinary Social Work   11
Judy Wookey and Alicia Kennedy

4 Veterinary Social Work Journey   14
Erin Allen

5 Kaleidoscope of a Veterinary Social Worker   17
Jacquelyn Rebekah James

6 Grief Led Me Here   20
Michelle Mezansky

7   Veterinary Social Work: Becoming the Best Version of
    Your Professional Self   23
    Lisa Hacker

8   Hospital-Based Veterinary Social Work: A Brief Primer   26
    Judith Harbour

9   Partnering with Therapy Animal Handler Volunteers in
    Healthcare: An Introduction to Volunteer Management
    for Social Workers   29
    Whitney Romine

10 My Journey from Human Medicine to
    Veterinary Medicine   32
    Robin Lehrhoff

11 A Horse of a Different Color   35
    Tom Favale

SECTION II
Human-Animal Interactions Focused Program
Development and Policy Advocacy   **39**

12 Programs and Policies   41
    Susan P. Cohen and Anne-Elizabeth Straub

13 Policy Advocacy and Program Evaluation: The
    External Link of Practice Work in One-Health   46
    Bailey Fullwiler

14 "Puffy's Pet Boarding": A Second Home for Your Dog   51
    Rachel Nallathamby

15 Addressing the Link between Violence toward People
    and Animals as a Generalist Social Worker   53
    Kathryn Ford

16 Chasing Impact: Take That Leap of Faith   56
    Urvashi Shobhna Kachari

17 Sprout: Companion Animal to Service
   Dog to Career Inspiration 59
   Kristen Cudmore

18 On Canines, Conflicts, and Community: Reflections
   on One Health 62
   Rajlakshmi Kanjilal

19 Equine-Assisted Social Work: A Perfect Match 65
   Dana Spett

SECTION III
Animal-Assisted Interventions 69

20 The Power of Paws: Working Full-Time in
   Animal-Assisted Interactions 71
   Katherine Compitus

21 Animal-Assisted Psychotherapy: Integrating "Canine
   Co-Therapists" into Clinical Social Work Outpatient
   Treatment Settings 76
   Laurel Gray Robbins

22 Animal-Assisted Therapy in Clinical Work within the
   Disability Community 79
   Tiffany Banks

23 Paws in Play: The Power of Integrating Animals into
   Play Therapy Practice 82
   Michelle Pliske

24 "The World Is Best Viewed through the Ears of a
   Horse" My Career in Equine-Assisted Services 85
   Mary Acri

25 Paws for Play: Dogs in Play Therapy 88
   Lucy Llewellyn

26 Finding Your HAI Niche 91
   April Lang

27 Bear Is My Bridge   94
    Janus Moncur

28 Pandemic Pups: Research and Clinical Implications   97
    Jessica Wriedt

29 Shelter Pets and Sheltered Kids: Animal-Assisted
    Therapy in Juvenile Justice   100
    Stacy L. Mendell

30 When Psychology and Social Work Meet: A Clinician's
    Experiences in the Mental Health Field   103
    Emily Breitenbach

31 Animal-Assisted Psychotherapy: The Golden Standard   106
    Elizabeth Ruegg

SECTION IV
The Inclusion of Human-Animal Interactions within Social Work Practice — 109

32 HAI in Social Work Practice   111
    Janet Hoy-Gerlach and Lisa Townsend

33 Pursuing a Career in Veterinary Social Work   117
    Angie Arora

34 The Integrated Approach: One Social Worker's
    Roundabout Career Journey Incorporating
    Veterinary Social Work and One Health   120
    Christina Carr

35 Careers in One Health: Social Workers' Roles in
    Caring for Humans and Their Companion Animals   123
    Lizett Justa Gutierrez

36 Animals Are My Teachers   126
    Maureen MacNamara

37 A Social Work Path to Teaching in Higher Education   129
    Kristie Abbs

38 Providing Effective Supervision for Veterinary Social
    Workers in Practice   132
    Rebecca Stephens and Tracey Harris

39 Social Work outside the Box   135
    Emilie Evans

40 Advocacy and Pawprints: How a
    Dog Changed My Career   138
    Amber Depuydt-Goodlock

41 True Joy: Animal-Assisted Play Therapy   141
    Jacqueline George

42 A One Health Path to Support Health and Wellbeing   144
    Debbie Stoewen

43 Weaving Humane Education into Social Work   147
    Maggie Lantzy and Sarah M. Bexell

SECTION V
Human-Animal Interactions Focus within Human and Animal Organizations   **151**

44 Emerging Practices in Animal Welfare   153
    Doug Plant

45 Lessons from Horses Led My Career   157
    Aviva Vincent

46 A Social Worker's Learnings from the Human-Animal
    Bond: Animals as Family, Healers, and Colleagues   160
    Dillon Dodson

47 Elevating the Lives of Animals and Our Relationships
    with Them   163
    Molly Jenkins

48 The Best Way to Help Pets Is to Help People   166
    Elina Alterman

49 Centering Racialized Lived Experiences for Human
and Animal Well-Being 169
Mueni Rudd

50 Unexpected Implementation of AAI in Crisis Work 172
Denna Hays

51 Law Enforcement, Social Work, and Therapy Dogs 175
Angela Kenbok

52 Police Social Work: Partnering with Animals to Help
Heal Communities 178
Alyssa Peters

53 Serving People and Animals: A Worthy Career 181
Christine Kim

54 Social Workers' Roles in Caring for Humans and Their
Companion Animals 184
Adeline Wong

55 Animal-Assisted Therapy in an Israeli Psychiatric Hospital 186
Patricia Tiram

SECTION VI
Human-Animal Interactions Focus within Academia **189**

56 Finding Professional and Personal Meaning through
Human-Animal Interaction Academic Research 191
Jen Currin-McCulloch

57 The Professor and "the Pit Bull Lady" 196
Yvonne Smith

58 How I Became the "Dog Person" at Work 199
Ashley O'Connor

59 Social Workers' Roles in Creating Inclusive
Communities for All Animals: Human and Non-Human 201
Jedediah Bragg

60	Designing a Diverse Social Work Career *Meghan Morrissey*	204
61	Human-Animal-Environment Interactions in Social Work at the University of Denver *Jaci Gandenberger and Nina Ekholm Fry*	207
62	Supreme Dogs, Dream Jobs *Yvonne Eaton-Stull*	210
63	How I Got Here *Kayla Holland Baudoin*	213
64	Paw and Hoofprints on My Career Path *Angela Lavery*	216
65	Critical Animal Studies and One Health in Social Work *Atsuko Matsuoka*	219
66	Hospital Veterinary Social Work in the Canadian Context *Sarah Bernardi*	222
67	Bringing Veterinary Social Work into a One-Health Model *Augusta O'Reilly*	225
68	Social Work and Human-Animal Interaction in an Academic Setting *Lisa Townsend*	228
	Index	*231*

CONTRIBUTORS

Kristie Abbs, DSW, MSW, MEd, is an assistant professor and director of MSW Field Experience at Slippery Rock University. Dr. Abbs's research focus has been on social-emotional learning in college students, test-anxiety, and mental health.

Mary Acri is a mental health services researcher at NYU Grossman School of Medicine within the Department of Child and Adolescent Psychiatry, and currently holds the titles of Research Associate Professor within the Department as well as Faculty Member within The Center for Implementation and Dissemination Science in States for Children, Adolescents, and Families (PI: K. Hoagwood). Her research portfolio centers on reducing mental health inequities through developing and examining innovative programs and interventions to detect unmet mental health need and to improve mental health and functional outcomes for youth.

Erin Allen, MSSW, is currently the clinical support service associate director of the Argus Institute at Colorado State University Veterinary Teaching Hospital. Her research interests include self-care and resiliency within the veterinary profession, compassionate communication in veterinary medicine, and the human-animal bond and grief recovery.

Elina Alterman, MSW, MPH is the director of Development and Communications at the Lawrence Humane Society in Lawrence, Kansas. Previously, Alterman was the first ever Senior Manager of Social Work at Lawrence Humane. Her areas of interest are demonstrating how animal shelters can become integral social service agencies in a community and true collaborators in the fight for equity and justice and creating a future in which barriers don't exist in pet ownership.

Angie Arora is a social worker specializing in veterinary mental health and wellbeing, pet loss support, and equity issues within veterinary medicine. She is a professor with Seneca College's School of Community Services, where she developed and teaches a self-care course for veterinary professionals and led an applied research study which created guidelines for veterinary teams to support clients through their pets' end of life. In her private practice as a certified compassion fatigue specialist and wellbeing coach, Angie coaches and trains animal-care providers to foster self and community connection. She served on the inaugural Board of Directors for the International Association of Veterinary Social Work and is actively involved in wellbeing and equity-related veterinary initiatives.

Tiffany Banks (she/her), PhD, is an assistant professor in the School of Social Work at the University of Maryland Baltimore County. Her research interests include critical disability studies, the experience of the human-animal bond, and family-centered policy reform.

Kayla Holland Baudoin, MSW, LCSW, is the wellbeing manager at the Louisiana State University School of Veterinary Medicine in Baton Rouge, Louisiana. Her primary focuses are overseeing wellbeing initiatives at the veterinary school and providing mental health support, crisis intervention, grief education, referrals, and resources to clinical doctorate of veterinary medicine students, interns, residents, faculty, staff, and clients of the Best Friend Gone Project. Additionally, Mrs. Baudoin conducts workshops, small-group learning, and clinical rounds on professional development, communication skills, conflict resolution, and stress management. Mrs. Baudoin's research interests include moral distress in veterinary medicine, wellbeing, grief and loss, and older adults.

Sarah Bernardi is a registered social worker with her master's from the University of Toronto. Sarah is currently the veterinary social worker at the Ontario Veterinary College and Health Sciences Centre, where she provides clinical support services, resources, and continuing education to the OVC's Companion Animal Hospital, Large Animal Hospital, and Animal Cancer Centre. She is well-versed in supporting the human components of veterinary medicine and routinely collaborates with pet owners, animal-care staff, and mental health professionals around issues including animal care worker mental health, anticipatory and after loss grief, quality of life, end of life, and decision-making. Sarah is an executive board member for the International

Association of Veterinary Social Workers and a board member for Safepet Ontario, and facilitates two peer groups that bring mental health practitioners working in veterinary hospitals together to share their insights.

Sarah M. Bexell, PhD, is Faculty Director at the Center for Sustainability, Clinical Associate Professor with the Graduate School of Social Work, and Director of Humane Education with the Institute for Human-Animal Connection all at the University of Denver, Denver, Colorado, USA. She teaches and does research in the areas of ecological justice, regenerative education, and animal protection.

Jedediah Bragg is an assistant professor of Social Work at New Mexico Highlands University. His focus has mainly been on community social work, which has been combined with his passion for all things dog related. He has aided in growing animal-assisted programming at universities and within communities and is now working on implementing animal-assisted programming in New Mexico.

Emily Breitenbach's current position is an outpatient therapist at Winchester Community Mental Health Center. Emily attended Slippery Rock University for her bachelor's in psychology and master's in social work. She meets with children, adolescents, and adults and is working to implement animal-assisted interventions in her practice.

Page Walker Buck, PhD, is a social worker at the University of Pennsylvania's School of Veterinary Medicine and a professor of graduate social work at West Chester University. She is committed to developing ways that social workers can partner with the veterinary community to support all individuals involved in the care of non-human animals.

Christina Carr, LMSW, is currently a grief counselor at a non-profit grief center in Tennessee. Her current scope of practice focuses on grief and loss work as well as strengths-based whole person support – which includes human-animal bond work. Christina holds a certificate in Veterinary Social Work, is an editorial board member with CABI's *Human-Animal Interactions* Journal, is a member of the National Association of Social Workers, and is a board member of the American Psychological Association's Human-Animal Interaction Section.

Susan P. Cohen, DSW, is a self-employed social worker who has worked in the field of veterinary medicine and human-animal interaction for more than 40 years. Today, she leads support groups for Veterinary Information Systems, the VIN Foundation, and Downtown Veterinary Medical Hospitals. In addition, she writes and lectures about veterinary stress, pet loss, and communication techniques.

Katherine Compitus, DSW, LCSW-R, C-AAIS, is Clinical Assistant Professor of Social Work at New York University's Silver School of Social Work. She is a licensed clinical social worker with more than 20 years of experience in anti-oppressive relational work with children, families, and adults and is a certified animal-assisted interaction specialist. She is the director of the post-master's certificate program in Animal-Assisted Interactions at New York University and is the author of *The Human-Animal Bond and Clinical Social Work* (Springer) and *Animal House: A Clinician's Guide to Animal Hoarding* (Oxford University Press).

Kristen Cudmore MSW, RSW-C is a clinical therapist/healthcare social worker for the Nova Scotia Health Authority on Canada's East Coast. Kristen has co-founded an NGO, Maritime Service Dogs, which helps people navigate attaining a service dog teammate, educates the public on dis/ability rights and animal liberation, and safeguards force-free training practices to prepare assistance animals. Currently, Kristen is submitting her AAT curricula for accreditation through the ISAAT (International Society of Animal-Assisted Therapy). Kristen's research interests include ethical canine training methods, canine sentience when working with humans, and applications of animal-assisted therapy and its efficacy.

Jen Currin-McCulloch, PhD, is an assistant professor in the School of Social Work at Colorado State University. Her research focuses on understanding the experiences of those who have experienced a significant relational loss and factors that promote existential wellbeing during their grief integration.

Amber Depuydt-Goodlock, LMSW, is currently a child advocacy center program supervisor with over 20 years of experience providing counseling services to children, teens, and adults as well as conducting forensic interviews with youth. In 2013, Amber implemented Michigan's first Facility Dog Program at a hospital-based victim services organization. Professional affiliations include Michigan State Coordinator for Justice Facility Dogs, United States, Board Member for Children's Advocacy Centers of Michigan, and a volunteer with Canine Companions, North Central Region. Research interests include sexual violence and trauma, human-animal interaction bond, and the utilization of testimonial accommodations for child victim witnesses.

Dillon Dodson, MSW, joined Toronto Humane Society in early 2020 to head up the expansion of the Urgent Care program. Drawing on over 15 years of experience working as a professional social worker (Masters of Social Work from the University of Toronto and Bachelor of Social Work from McMaster University), Dillon utilized her experience in community mental health and private practice to inform every step of the UC program creation and associated training manual. Dillon was elected to the board of the International Association of Veterinary Social Workers in 2023 and received an award of Distinction from the Ontario Association of Social Workers in the same year. In January 2023, Dillon transitioned to fulltime as Senior Manager of social work to expand Toronto Humane Society's research and work on the importance of preserving the human-animal bond and how social work is integral to animal care.

Yvonne Eaton-Stull, DSW, LCSW, is an associate professor of Social Work at Slippery Rock University in Pennsylvania. She specializes in animal-assisted social work, forensic social work, and crisis intervention. She is also a canine handler with HOPE Animal-Assisted Crisis Response, where she has provided animal-assisted crisis intervention following crises and disasters throughout the United States. Her research has included numerous studies implementing animal-assisted therapy in state prisons and jails.

Nina Ekholm Fry is the director of Equine Programs at the Institute for Human-Animal Connection at the University of Denver and a faculty member in the Graduate School of Social Work and the Graduate School of Professional Psychology. She is the coordinator of the Human-Animal-Environment Interactions in Social Work MSW specialization and leads the post-master's Equine-Assisted Mental Health Practitioner Certificate program. For the past 15 years, she has focused on animals in human services, specializing in the inclusion of equine interactions in psychotherapy and counseling. She has a particular interest in applied ethics and social justice perspectives within human-animal interactions and is actively engaged in national and international organizations for both human and equine wellbeing.

Emilie Evans, MSW, serves as the veterinary research manager for the Golden Retriever Lifetime Study at Morris Animal Foundation. Her research interests include the human-companion animal bond, attachment theory, and veterinary medicine.

Tom Favale DVM, LMSW is an assistant professor of professional life skills at Lincoln Memorial University's College of Veterinary Medicine. He received his BS in psychology and DVM from Iowa State University. After practicing as an associate veterinarian for 22 years at a small animal hospital, he went on to purchase his own one doctor animal hospital. After five years of ownership, he sold the practice. For the next several years, Tom did relief work as a small animal veterinarian. During this time, he enrolled at Loyola University

Chicago to earn a master's in social work. His area of interest is around loss and grief working with pet owners and supporting those in the veterinary profession, in particular, veterinary students.

Kathryn Ford, MPH, LCSW, is the Clinical and Managing Director at Cobb Psychotherapy in New York City. Until recently, she was the Director of Clinical Supervision and Child Witness Initiatives at the Center for Justice Innovation, where she provided national training and technical assistance to tribal and state justice practitioners on strengthening system responses to violence and victimization. She was also a trauma therapist for children and teens for nine years through the Center's Bronx Child Trauma Support Program.

Bailey Fullwiler, MSSW, LSW, is a community social worker and independent ecological grief consultant. As a consultant, she works with environmental groups to navigate ecoanxiety, ecological grief, and burnout through strategic planning, collective care initiatives, and education. In addition, Bailey is a trauma-responsive 200-hour registered yoga teacher who teaches yoga for resilience for those in recovery.

Jaci Gandenberger, MSW, MAIS, is a research associate and faculty member with the Institute for Human-Animal Connection at the University of Denver. Her research focuses on the impacts of dogs on human stress and trauma. She also examines how canine wellbeing is impacted by human-canine interactions.

Jacqueline George has a private practice in York, PA. She is a licensed clinical social worker, a registered play therapist supervisor through the Association for Play Therapy, and a certified animal-assisted play therapist supervisor and instructor through the International Institute for Animal Assisted Play Therapy®, has a diploma in Animal Behavior Science and Technology through Companion Animal Sciences Institute, and is a member of the Association of Animal Behavior Professionals. Additionally, Jacque is certified as a diplomate of Clinical Forensic Counseling in the field of domestic violence through The National Association of Forensic Counselors. Research involving AAPT and clients of domestic violence is of particular interest to Jacque.

Lizett Justa Gutierrez, LCSW, LAC, VSW, is a bilingual therapist who serves a range of ages, using trauma-informed and culturally responsive modalities. Lizett has a deep appreciation for the human-animal bond and holds certificates in veterinary social work and animal-assisted social work. For the past five years, she has served on the National Latino Behavioral Health Association (NLBHA) Board of Directors, where she supports efforts to expand access to mental health resources and increasing awareness of issues affecting the Latinx community.

Lisa Hacker is a licensed social worker in the states of Arizona and Wisconsin, United States. She earned her master's degree in Social Work from the University of Wisconsin-Milwaukee in 2009. Lisa currently is the social work program manager for 1st Pet Veterinary Centers in Arizona, US. She has presented and published on topics related to human-animal relationships and veterinary social work in veterinary medicine spaces.

Judith Harbour, LCSW, is the veterinary social worker at Schwarzman Animal Medical Center in New York City. She supports clients in coping with the practical and emotional challenges that come with the illness or loss of a pet, and she provides education and support to AMC staff to reduce stress and promote mental wellbeing. She holds a Master of Social Work (MSW) from Fordham University and a Bachelor of Arts (BA) from Rice University. Judith has completed the post-graduate Veterinary Social Work Certificate Program from the University of Tennessee and is a member of the International Association of Veterinary Social Work (IAVSW).

Tracey Harris is CEO of Amovita International, and international author and speaker on organizational excellence. With a career spanning over 25 years, she has specialized in organizational design, supervision, and performance. Having an interest in leadership, supervision, and coaching, Tracey has developed a series of supervision models to support staff and leaders maintain high performance in the workplace. Tracey is currently in the process of completing her PhD on leadership and supervision capability.

Denna Hays, DSW, LSW, is currently an assisted professor of social work at Slippery Rock University. Research interests include benefits of animal-assisted interventions with vulnerable populations, impact of child advocacy centers on investigations of child sexual abuse, realities of being an elite athlete and the impact on mental health and social skills, and concussion-related mental health.

Janet Hoy-Gerlach, PhD, is a clinical social worker, researcher, and lead author of *Human-Animal Interaction: A Social Work Guide* published by NASW Press. She is the founder of OneHealth People-Animal Wellness Services (OHPAWS), a social work consulting practice focusing on collaborative development and evaluation of programs and practices that support human-animal relationships for mutual wellbeing. Her research on Emotional Support Animals (ESAs) has been cited in national media such as *Discover* Magazine, Business Insider, and Psychology Today, and she serves as an expert witness for the U.S. Department of Justice Civil Rights Division on human benefits of ESAs.

Jacquelyn Rebekah James, DSW, MSW, VSW, CGP, LSW, is a veterinary social worker in a large emergency and specialty hospital. Jacquelyn has over 25 years of experience in the social work field. Jacquelyn specializes in grief and bereavement, and her research focus is on pet loss, support groups, and animal-assisted interventions. Jacquelyn is affiliated with the IAVSW, NASW, and IAAHPC.

Molly Jenkins, MSW, is an adjunct faculty member with the Graduate School of Social Work's Institute for Human-Animal Connection at the University of Denver. She is also the senior writer for the Dumb Friends League and a current board member for the Feline Fix. Molly's primary interests center on human-animal-environment relationships, expanding equitable access to resources that preserve and nurture these bonds, social and ecological justice, and promoting the ethical treatment and sentience of non-human animals.

Urvashi Shobhna Kachari is a public policy professional working in the animal protection movement of India. She studied Political Science at Lady Shri Ram College for Women, Delhi University and International Relations at Jawaharlal Nehru University, New Delhi. She has worked closely with diverse social impact organizations like The Hunger Project India, Ananta Aspen Centre, People for Animals, People for Animals Public Policy Foundation, and Humane Society International India.

Rajlakshmi Kanjilal serves as Project Manager at Amrita Center for Research in Analytics, Technologies and Education (Amrita CREATE), Amrita Vishwa Vidyapeetham, Amritapuri campus, India. She received a PhD in Visual Media and Communication in 2021. Her research interests include animal and media studies, popular culture, and neurodiversity.

Angela Kenbok is a police social worker who resides in Pittsburgh, Pennsylvania. She developed and implemented her current position as a police social worker in 2020, where she focused on building strong collaborations with law enforcement. Angela obtained both her bachelor's degree in social work and her master's degree in social work from Slippery Rock University in Slippery Rock, Pennsylvania. Angela plans on continuing to expand and implement police social work in various departments while focusing on the benefits of collaboration.

Alicia Kennedy, BSc BVMS, is a veterinary graduate of Murdoch University (1986). Through her 35 year career, she has acquired extensive experience in the human-animal bond. She is the founder of Cherished Pets and has supported the development of an innovative bond-centered veterinary service, and the introduction of a Veterinary Social Work model, co-designed with

Judy Wookey, into the organization. Cherished Pets continues to partner with research institutions to support vital study into this emerging field.

Christine Kim is the founder and a board member of My Dog Is My Home, as well as the employer partnerships advisor at the nonprofit organization New Women New Yorkers. Her practice interests revolve around the human-animal bond and concepts of "home," which encompass homelessness, housing, and immigration.

April Lang, LCSW, SEP, is a psychotherapist based in New York City and has been in private practice for almost 20 years. Part of her practice is devoted to working with ethical vegans and animal advocates, as well as people who are suffering from the loss of their animal family members. She is also an animal advocate, humane educator, and writer.

Maggie Lantzy is the assistant director of professional programs and adjunct faculty at the Institute for Human-Animal Connection (IHAC) at the University of Denver, Graduate School of Social Work. She leads the educational offerings and programs offered by IHAC, which provide professional development education for those interested in human-animal interaction work. Maggie is a certified humane education specialist and member of the Association of Professional Humane Educators.

Angela Lavery is an associate professor with the Graduate Social Work Department and the graduate coordinator of the interdisciplinary Graduate Certificate in Gerontology at West Chester University of Pennsylvania. She is a licensed clinical social worker and a fellow in Thanatology through the Association for Death Education and Counseling. Dr. Lavery earned a PhD in Social Work from the University of Denver, an MSW from the University of Wyoming, and her BS in Human Development and Family Studies from The Pennsylvania State University. Her research interests include ageism, animal-assisted interventions, end-of-life care/grief and bereavement, as well as elder abuse and neglect.

Robin Lehrhoff, LCSW, is presently working at Veterinary Referral and Emergency Center in Westbury NY. Following her lengthy career in human medicine, she is intrigued and challenged by working in veterinary medicine. She is continually learning new facets of the animal human bond and looks forward to contributing to the growth of Veterinary Social Work.

Lucy Llewellyn is a registered social worker, BAPT Registered Play Therapist, Certified Animal-Assisted Play Therapist™ - Supervisor & Instructor, Certified AutPlay Therapist® and is an associate member of the Pet Dog Trainers of Europe. She lives and works as a therapist and consultant in West Yorkshire, UK, with her dogs, Freya, Lykke, and Alfie.

Maureen MacNamara, PhD, MSW, is Retired Associate Professor of community and organizational social work. As a consultant to HAI organizations, she focuses on inter-professional relationships in organizational learning and change strategies and nonprofit service development and evaluation. She is a pioneer in the development, implementation, and evaluation of animal-assisted interventions (AAI). Maureen has 30 years of experience designing goal-directed human-animal activities that result in measurable client change and developing and delivering staff training to support these programs. She is the author of numerous articles and book chapters and has conducted research in the areas of the link between violence to people and violence to animals, factors influencing the place and consequence of human-animal relationships, and climate change and rural sustainability.

Atsuko Matsuoka is a professor at the School of Social Work, York University, Canada. Her research has addressed the importance of understanding the intersectionality of oppression among immigrants, ethnic older adults, and animals. She is promoting consideration for animal-human relationships in social work.

Stacy L. Mendell, MSW, LCSW, has been working in the field of Animal-Assisted Therapy since 2011 and is currently in private practice. Her research interests include creating animal-assisted programs that include shelter pets and support the human-animal bond.

Michelle Mezansky is a veterinary social worker based in the Boston area. Her research interests revolve around exploring the impact of the human-animal bond on mental health and incorporating evidence-based practices to improve the wellbeing of animal caregivers.

Janus Moncur is a licensed clinical social worker and qualified supervisor with her PhD and master of Social Work from Barry University, master's in psychology from the University of Phoenix, and certificate as a human-animal intervention specialist from Oakland University. She is an adjunct professor for Barry University. She specializes in Canine-Assisted Trauma Therapy (CATT), with her private clients and volunteers as an instructor and handler with National Canine Crisis Response with her canine partner, Bear.

Meghan Morrissey, LCSW, LAC, CTRI, currently works for the State of Colorado as the policy advisor for Behavioral Health Crisis Services and has a small private practice. She is also Research Faculty at New York University, Department of Child and Adolescent Psychiatry, where she studies human-equine interactions. Meghan's research interests include human-animal interactions, adjudicated populations, and behavioral health crisis response.

Rachel Nallathamby, PhD, was born and brought up in the city of Chennai, India. She lives there with her daughter and pets. She has a PhD in Computer Science and runs Puffys Pet Boarding, where she boards and fosters dogs of all sizes. Her research interests include animal interaction, mental health, and healthcare data science.

Ashley O'Connor, PhD, is currently a social worker at the Alaska VA. She is also an adjunct professor at the University of Alaska and University of Denver. Dr. O'Connor's main area of interest is exploring how to best employ animal-assisted therapies for veterans who have experienced trauma.

Augusta O'Reilly is a licensed clinical social worker (LCSW) and veterinary social worker (VSW) in Southern Maine, the current president of the International Association of Veterinary Social Work and the director of Veterinary Social Work for the Program for Pet Health Equity at the University of Tennessee-Knoxville. Her focus is providing mental health support to veterinary professionals and families that are facing access to veterinary care barriers in the communities she works with. Her research interest includes the impact the human-animal bond has on marginalized groups and the impact of moral distress and compassion fatigue within the animal welfare community.

Alyssa Peters is a police social worker for the Millvale Borough Police Department. She has been doing this work full time for a little over a year, mostly working with juveniles, families, in the areas of trauma, internet access with young children and technology, and controversies in/betterment of diagnosis and treatment modalities. She also fosters a strong interest in the mental health and wellbeing of first responders.

Doug Plant is the chief operating officer for Michigan Humane, the largest and oldest animal welfare organization in Michigan. Since 2017, Plant has established a robust community outreach program designed to divert shelter admissions of companion animals. His focus has been to deploy a social work framework to assisting families on a variety of human issues to ensure stability for their pets. He is particularly interested in measuring the impact of companion animals on human's physical and mental health.

Michelle Pliske, DSW, is a licensed clinical social worker and registered play therapy supervisor. She is an assistant professor of social work at Pacific University and clinical supervisor at the Firefly Institute. Dr. Pliske's research involves qualitative design to explore the effects of adversity, social determinants of health, psychological trauma, and relational-cultural theory in application to education, supervision, and direct clinical care.

Laurel Gray Robbins (She/They) is a licensed independent clinical social worker who provides Animal-Assisted Psychotherapy with Canine "Co-Therapists" in Northern Vermont. She wears multiple hats at Otter Creek Associates: Vermont Center for Resiliency – a Trauma-Focused Group Outpatient Practice, including Clinical Administrator, Supervisor, and Direct Practice Clinician (Therapist) roles. Laurel Gray specializes in supporting people living with anxiety, mood disorders, and co-occurring mental health/recovery needs. She works collaboratively with children, adolescents, and adults to develop strategies to help them feel more grounded, resilient, and connected to themselves and their communities.

Whitney Romine is the animal therapy activity coordinator at Mayo Clinic in Rochester, MN. She comes from a diverse background in hospital volunteer management, animal-assisted intervention program management, and therapy animal handler team evaluation. She received her master's degree in Public Health from Kent State University and is a certified animal-assisted intervention specialist. She also holds a canine-assisted intervention specialist certificate from the University of Denver Institute for Human-Animal Connection. Whitney's education, work, and volunteer service have focused on promoting the health of humans, animals, and the environment—also known as One Health. Her experience as a therapy dog handler, team evaluator, and program administrator has fueled her drive to innovate human-animal interaction programs.

Mueni Rudd is a Kenyan American scholar advocate with experience in racial justice, social activism, and evaluative research. She is a published writer and proud TEDx speaker committed to filling the gaps in current training and approaches that avoid issues of racial diversity and ethnic cultural differences. She prioritizes Black and other historically marginalized group liberation in all her professional and community contributions. Her work amplifies historically oppressed communities, promotes authentic multicultural dialogue, and creates cross-cultural communication which fosters awareness and healing.

Elizabeth Ruegg is a faculty member in the MSW program at Saint Leo University in Saint Leo, Florida. Her research interest is mechanisms of effectiveness in canine-assisted psychotherapy. She is on the Certification Commission of the Association for Animal-Assisted Intervention Professionals (AAAIP).

Yvonne Smith is an associate professor in the School of Social Work at Syracuse University. She teaches a wide range of courses on social work practice, human diversity, and human/animal interaction. Eevie studies therapeutic residential care for youth and is part of an NICHD-funded research partnership to develop a new approach to maximizing the therapeutic value of interactions between kids and their care workers. Eevie's newest project is an autoethnographic investigation of the affective impacts of rural development and exurban sprawl.

Dana Spett, DSW, MSW, is the founder and executive director at Pony Power Therapies, a nonprofit community-based center in Mahwah, New Jersey. With a passion for equine-assisted services, nature, and social work, Dana actively conducts research and aims to develop an ethical and competent model for Equine-Assisted Social Work (EASW).

Rebecca Stephens is a senior lecturer in Social Work at the University of Sussex, UK. She is a registered social worker with Social Work England, member of the National Organisation of Practice Teachers, UK, and member of the International Association of Veterinary Social Workers. Rebecca's research interests include effective supervision for veterinary social workers, interdisciplinary cross-reporting of human and animal violence, and animal-related bereavement.

Debbie Stoewen, PhD, is a renowned veterinary health and wellbeing educator and the wellness columnist for the *Canadian Veterinary Journal*. She volunteers with, and is a member of, several veterinary and social work associations, provincially, nationally, and internationally. Her primary research interest is in the development of veterinary social work as a subspecialty of the field of social work to increase the health and wellbeing of those who care for others in animal health and welfare.

Elizabeth Strand, PhD, is the founder of the Center for Veterinary Social Work at the University of Tennessee. Her professional mission is to (1) support the humane treatment of people and animals, (2) attend to mindfulness in all settings and situations, (3) develop methods for interprofessional work across human and animal welfare and science professionals, and (4) focus this work on cultivating individual and collective peace.

Anne-Elizabeth Straub is a licensed clinical social worker and chair of Social Workers Advancing Human-Animal Bond (SWAHAB). She has a private practice providing psychotherapy to individuals, support group facilitation, and consultation to nonprofits and businesses. She also develops and delivers workshops and trainings and is involved in advocacy work on Disability Rights and Justice, Voting Rights, Prison Reform, and Immigration as a member of several advocacy groups.

Patricia Tiram, MSW, an American social worker from Seattle, Washington, went to Israel in 1975 and began working at a large psychiatric hospital. In 1998, she became the social worker at a new unit for Holocaust survivors and began using animal-assisted therapy with her severely traumatized patients. After retirement from social work, she opened a small AAT-related business and worked in numerous hospital wards, serving a multi-cultural clientele. When Covid hit Israel, only essential workers remained at the hospital. Patricia is currently enjoying her retirement.

Lisa Townsend, PhD, is an associate professor in the Divisions of Adolescent Medicine and Psychiatry and a clinical and research associate in the Center for Human-Animal Interaction at Virginia Commonwealth University. Her clinical and research interests include animal-assisted therapy, psychiatric assessment, and dialectical behavior therapy. Additionally, she has a specialization in Human-Animal Interaction. She is particularly interested in understanding factors that impact the effectiveness of interventions such as the involvement of dogs as therapy partners to enhance engagement with treatment and improve patient outcomes.

Aviva Vincent, PhD, LMSW, is a veterinary social worker and co-owner of Healing Paws LLC. She is Social Work Faculty at Cleveland State University and Program Director at Fieldstone Farm Therapeutic Riding Center. Dr. Vincent is on the board for PATH International Board of Trustees/Diversity Equity and Inclusion Committee Chair. She has published extensively on human-animal interaction in peer-reviewed journals and chapters in *Career Paths in Human-Animal Interaction for Social and Behavioral Scientists*, *The Comprehensive Guide to Interdisciplinary Veterinary Social Work*, *The Handbook on Human Animal Interactions*, and *Anthrozoology and Integrating Horses Into Healing*.

Adeline Wong is a certified substance abuse counsellor and conducts in-prison sessions at Singapore Prisons. She is also a certified animal-assisted psychotherapist with further practical skills-based training completed in Australia. She graduated from the National University of Singapore with additional post-graduate training from TCA College (Graduate Diploma of Christian Studies), WSQ Advanced Certificate in Learning and Performance, and completed the ACE Capstone Leadership Programme for Non-Profits (Aalto University, Centre for Non-Profit Leadership and LIEN Centre for Social Innovation). She is also a pastoral member of the Association of Christian Counsellors Singapore and a council member and treasurer of Parochial Church Council in her church.

Judy Wookey has 40 years of experience as a social worker within both the child and family services and tertiary education sectors. She is currently employed by Deakin University as a social work field educator. Along with Alicia Kennedy, she has led the establishment of a unique veterinary social work program in Victoria, Australia. This has included starting a robust student social work field education program at Cherished Pets in 2020. Thirteen students have now been through this program and have brought much knowledge, skills, and professionalism with them!

Jessica Wriedt, PhD, works in a private practice as a clinical psychiatric social worker. She provides individual therapy to individuals of all ages with mental health concerns. While completing her doctorate dissertation, she completed research to formulate an understanding of the lived experiences of individuals who obtained a dog during the Covid-19 pandemic.

SECTION I
Veterinary Social Work

1
THE INTERPROFESSIONAL PRACTICE SPACE OF VETERINARY SOCIAL WORK

A Social Worker's Perspective

Elizabeth Strand

On May 2, 2002, I was posted at the front desk of the Small Animal Clinic at the University of Tennessee College of Veterinary Medicine (UTCVM). This was my first exposure to "in the back" of a veterinary clinic. Dr. Jim Brace, Academic Dean of UTCVM, decided that was the best starting place for me to understand the clinic. It was true; I learned a lot. Quickly the notion that veterinary medicine was different from human medicine dissipated. The harried phone calls, conversations filled with gravitas, and the emotional reactions of clients all reminded me of similar experiences I had encountered in human hospitals.

As I shadowed on the clinic floor, with two new social work field interns as my team, I learned how a specialty veterinary teaching hospital worked. I learned that the specialty clinic serves wealthier clients who are highly bonded to their very sick pets, as well as indigent pet owners hoping the state institution might be able to help them save their ill companions. I learned that once veterinary (DVM) students complete four years of training and pass the NAVLE (North American Veterinary Licensing Examination), unlike physicians, they can go directly into general practice. I learned that an "intern" is a new veterinary graduate pursuing one year of specialty training. These interns rotate among all specialties, gaining a breadth of experience and developing tough calluses on their professional identities. I learned that after internship, some interns choose to continue their specialty education with a three-year residency program before sitting for their stressful specialty exams.

During this time, I also learned how suicidal thinking manifests itself in the veterinary setting. It was not unusual to hear a client say, "if you euthanize my dog, you might as well euthanize me too." Moreover, since the lifespans

DOI: 10.4324/9781003335528-2

for most animals are shorter than human life spans, and since veterinarians perform euthanasia as a way to reduce animal suffering, I became acutely aware of the exposure veterinary professionals have to human suffering at the end of animal life. This, of course, often results in burnout, compassion fatigue, and psychological distress, especially among younger veterinary professionals. Since veterinarians perform euthanasia regularly, have access to means, and consider euthanasia as a way to end suffering, the prevalence of suicide in the veterinary profession has contextual meaning that is important to understand in caring for this population.

I found myself in this veterinary social work training environment drawing from my experience as a family therapist and my systems perspective approach to understanding the environment. Due to the vision of veterinarians and social workers at UTK, a new opportunity arose. The Deans of the College of Veterinary Medicine and College of Social Work both knew that the human-animal bond was powerful and needed the specialized attention of professional social work skills attending to the "human side of things." I was pursuing my PhD and studying the link between human-animal violence when I founded the veterinary social work program. Through my research, I was immersing myself in all the human-animal bond literature and one night, I woke up with the notion that what I was doing in the clinic was "veterinary social work." There were already numerous types of social work—school, gerontological, forensic, hospital—and so, I thought, there should be *veterinary*. At that point, based on my review of the literature and my lived experience on the clinic floor, the four areas of veterinary social work were established: the link between human and animal violence, animal-related grief and bereavement, animal-assisted interactions, and compassion fatigue and conflict management. Given the core values of social work that approach human problems within a person-in-environmental context, each of these four areas has micro and macro practice implications.

To this day, for me, every day of veterinary social work practice includes integration of these four areas in varying proportions and on the micromacro level continuum. An example of this could be how a veterinary social worker navigates attending to the needs of a low-income family who own a dog with advanced osteosarcoma. Perhaps the humans in this situation include two small children and two parents as well as the veterinary team, composed of a senior clinician, a resident, an intern, and a veterinary nurse. In this example, the family is overwhelmed by lifelong poverty and has failed to have their beloved dog medically treated. They knew a problem existed, but work schedules, lack of money, and anticipatory grief caused them to delay assessment and care. They present at the clinic asking for help, children in tow because no one is available for childcare. The veterinary nurse and intern experience distress due to the advanced stage of the disease. The experienced senior clinician, after hearing the veterinary nurse and intern report their findings, recommends leg amputation and chemotherapy or euthanasia and instructs the intern and resident to make the recommendation. The owners refuse euthanasia as well as amputation as they are worried about post-op care and cannot handle their children's distress when they hear that their pet may have to be "put to sleep." The family does not have money for treatment and expresses their anger toward the team that there are no income-based discounts. The nurse and intern deem the family's response to treatment recommendations a form of abuse since they will not make a decision to end the animal's suffering. This leads the team to be concerned about the parents' abilities to make good choices for their children. The senior clinician continues to expect the intern, resident, and nurse to reason and convince the family to pursue some form of treatment. This causes intra team conflict. Meanwhile, the children are crying and asking their parents to save their best friend, creating even more family distress. In this situation, all areas of veterinary social work are at play: (1) animal-related grief and bereavement as the family faces the mortality of their pet and the veterinary team focuses on treatment decisions, including end-of-life options, (2) the link between human and animal violence as the veterinary team considers animal abuse and wonders if a family that could be "this cruel" to an animal might behave similarly toward their children, (3) compassion fatigue and conflict management as the veterinary team manages the family distress as well as intra team conflict, and even (4) animal-assisted interactions as I include pet ownership as a form of human quality of life assistance. From a macro perspective, I would also consider whether the veterinary clinic has any formal policy about client "medical negligence" to help the veterinary team assert treatment boundaries in this case as well as a pro-bono fund for low-income pet owners.

The preceding example demonstrates the way a veterinary social worker would understand the human needs in veterinary medicine from a systems perspective. Here, the vet social worker would help the stressed family regulate emotions and grief to then be able to cognitively consider goals of care. The veterinary social worker may help the parents talk with and support their children as they make a difficult decision. The veterinary social worker would also help the veterinary team, not only communicate with the angry family but also communicate among themselves about the moral distress they are facing as they are exposed to the dog's suffering without having complete power to relieve it. The veterinary social worker may also explore a macro follow-up intervention by engaging in a hospital-wide discussion about policy development to handle cases where the veterinary team considers medical care negligence as a form of abuse. This policy could help clarify rights and responsibilities that the veterinary team has in handling cases like these in the future. The veterinary social worker may also explore policies to support a limited number of pro-bono cases per month.

This example is on the clinic floor, however similar case scenarios could be applied to more macro environments such as policies about emotional support animals, or even animals that are raised for food or sport and are deeply connected to people's livelihoods and/or cultures. Every scenario where veterinarians and social workers are together attending to human and animal needs is veterinary social work.

An important and yet challenging aspect of veterinary social work is operating within "scopes of practice." The vision for the program at the University of Tennessee is "attending to the welfare of all species through excellence in global interprofessional practice." This aspiration directly acknowledges and centers the importance of interprofessionality in this practice area. Social workers are not professionally trained to understand or attend to the needs of animals as a required part of the Council on Social Work Education (CSWE) standards or state licensing board requirements. Nowhere in our code of ethics are non-human species directly mentioned as a target for what we must address. Sometimes, social workers may be emotionally moved by the needs of an animal and begin to assert influence over what they believe an animal should have or how an animal should be treated. Although it is the right of any human being to have perspectives on animal care and stewardship, animal welfare advocacy is not within the direct scope of practice for social workers. A social worker in the previous case scenario who may have advised the owner about an alternative medical treatment would be operating outside their scope of practice. If a social worker prioritizes animal welfare over human welfare during the course of professional duties, they are operating outside their scope of practice. Likewise, veterinarians or veterinary nurses who try to unilaterally attend to the mental health needs of a highly depressed client without referring that client for care with a licensed mental health professional are also operating outside of their scope of practice. The interprofessional space of veterinary social work calls professionals with scopes of practice focusing on humans and non-human animals to collaborate through highly attuned and nuanced teamwork between social workers and veterinarians.

This interprofessional systems approach to the world's problems is an extremely rewarding part of practicing veterinary social work! It is exciting to observe a problem in a system and to determine who is the best professional to address what parts, at what point in the evolution of the problem, and from which micro/macro level. Animals evoke strong emotions in people. It is not unusual for people to say they cried more when their dog died than when their parents died. People may also say they cannot watch any animal suffering but can tolerate human suffering without becoming overwrought. Often, the reason given is that animals are "powerless and innocent" but people are not. Given the powerful emotions that animals can elicit in people, it provides a very volatile environment not only for animal-related conflict but also for emotional transformation, healing, and growth. I enjoy being in connections with individuals and systems attending to animals so that I can work with people who care deeply about their work and animal parts of life. Moreover, I enjoy using my social work skills in these settings to create conditions where social work core values can enhance human life. Promoting human to human connections, standing up for the dignity and worth of people, attending to power in ways that support those with less power, and standing up for social justice are tools that guide veterinary social workers in attending to the welfare of all species through attention to humans. There is a phrase from a poem by Rumi called The Wagon. It reads—"Out beyond ideas of wrongdoing and rightdoing, there is a field. I'll meet you there." For me as a veterinary social worker, this is what inspires me most. It is rewarding to be a human services professional, knowledgeable about the veterinary and other animal-related industries, who applies professional skills to create neutral and safe spaces for people experiencing animal-related challenges and opportunities to reach their highest potential.

That said, each person finds their own niche in veterinary social work—one that speaks to them the most. Some of you may really like working with assistance animals, some hospice and palliative care, others are inspired to help people convicted of animal cruelty heal from the childhood trauma that may have resulted in the abusive behavior. You may come to the practice area as a social worker, or you may have another health-related license. A One Health challenge is balancing the needs of different stakeholders for the welfare of all. I believe working in the space of veterinary social work provides a unique opportunity to use the power of human-animal relationships for the healing and empowerment of all.

2
EMBEDDED SOCIAL WORK IN A SCHOOL OF VETERINARY MEDICINE

Page Walker Buck

Background

The intersection of mental health and veterinary medicine is a remarkably rewarding professional space: one that has challenged me to grow in ways that I never imagined. My journey in this professional role formally began in 2017 when I took on a part-time position as a counselor for clinical-year students at a school of veterinary medicine. Students at the large animal hospital were 30 miles from the main campus and often did not have time to commute to meet with any of the university counselors.

In 2015, given my interest in the human-animal dynamic, I sought training in veterinary social work from the University of Tennessee. Growing up on a farmette surrounded by animals, I developed a deep bond with non-human animals from an early age. As I practiced and taught social work, I became increasingly interested in the ways that humans and animals interact while also becoming concerned about how little content on this topic was included in most curricula.

A Day in My Life

As an embedded social worker in a school of veterinary medicine, I typically am engaged in a range of activities focused on supporting the wellbeing of the humans who care for animal patients. The model that we currently use extends support to all human members of the veterinary school community, including house officers, staff, faculty, alumni, animal owners, and trainers.

My primary role is a mix of clinical work and case management. Much of the time, I am engaged in short-term counseling, consultation, conflict mediation, debriefing, assessment, referral, and crisis response. Community members can reach out to me by phone, email, or through the internal messaging system. My initial response to any inquiry is a quick assessment of the situation to determine the level of need. In urgent situations or crises, I work hard to meet as soon as possible. I meet with people in whatever format makes sense for them, including in person, over video conference, or by phone.

Most people who reach out to me are struggling with feelings of overwhelm given the demands of veterinary medicine or animal ownership. Sometimes, they are seeking consultation about a specific case that has caused them distress or about an ongoing work issue that they have been unable to resolve. Others meet with me to talk about things happening in their personal lives, including the wellbeing of family members. If I feel that I am the right person to support them, I offer to meet for short-term counseling. When I am not the best resource for the situation, I work hard to help the individual find appropriate care. This often includes referrals to local colleagues who have openings for new clients or psychiatrists who I know can see someone quickly. I also refer employees to our Employee Assistance Program (EAP) where they have up to eight free counseling sessions per year.

There are times when I use my case management skills. This might include helping a staff member who needs information about how to get their child evaluated for a mood disorder or how to apply for a leave of absence. Additionally, I work on advocacy initiatives such as access to food for overnight staff or assessments of complex team dynamics. I collaborate with the other social workers on the embedded team as well as the wellbeing and ethics committees and the ombudsperson. Our MSW interns run the pet loss support group.

Rewards and Challenges

As a veterinary social worker, one of the most rewarding parts of my job is seeing the tangible impact of my work on the wellbeing of the humans I support. Whether it is helping a client navigate a difficult situation, providing emotional support during an animal's illness or death, or working with a team to address complex cases, seeing positive outcomes from my interventions is incredibly gratifying. One of the biggest challenges I face is navigating ethical issues that arise from being embedded in a school community. Because I work closely with such a wide variety of individuals—including students and the faculty teaching their courses, staff and their immediate supervisors—I am mindful to maintain clear boundaries around my role.

Another challenge is managing the high demand for my time, which can often feel overwhelming. With so many people in need of support, especially following the global pandemic, it can be difficult to prioritize my workload and ensure that I can provide the quality of response and intervention that people deserve. Additionally, the nature of the work can be isolating at times, particularly when working remotely or with limited team support. Collaborating with other team members and having access to regular supervision is key.

Entering this Field

For those seeking a career as a social worker in a school of veterinary medicine, it is important to remember that the role is focused on the humans who care for animals and not the animals themselves. As such, it is essential to have a strong background in mental health, including experience with suicide assessment and prevention, as well as other forms of clinical intervention. It is also important to have a strong understanding of the culture and context of the veterinary and academic professions, as this will help you to effectively support community members, whether they are students, staff, or animal owners. Ideally, those entering this field will have experience in mental health treatment, particularly in grief and loss, trauma, and interpersonal conflict. In most cases, schools will want members of their social work team to be licensed. These positions are becoming increasingly common, so if this sounds like a good fit for you, I encourage you to follow your passion and work toward your goals.

3
THE CHERISHED PETS MODEL OF VETERINARY SOCIAL WORK

Judy Wookey and Alicia Kennedy

As a veterinarian of 35 years, Alicia has always been drawn to the people side of veterinary practice. Through years of observing human-animal interactions and connecting to her clients, Alicia recognised that as life goes through its stages, the importance of a companion animal often increases, and yet human capacity to keep a pet healthy and well can be compromised. What started as an intention to create a veterinary service to support pets of the elderly evolved into a wrap-around veterinary social service utilising a social work framework to support pets of people who may be elderly, living with a disability, suffering mental health crisis, fleeing domestic violence, and/or facing insecure housing. Cherished Pets (CP), partnering with CP Foundation (CPF), includes a volunteer program and also provides subsidised funding to help eligible pet owners with the cost of veterinary and pet care. The CP purpose is to enable the benefits of healthy companion pets and a thriving human-animal bond to be accessible to all people. The CP Vision is a world where the human-animal bond is recognised and valued for the role it plays in thriving and healthy communities and individuals.

When Judy joined CPF as its Chairperson, she brought sound social work knowledge, skills, and practice wisdom to the CP team. Judy was similarly committed to the health and wellbeing benefits of pets to people, having witnessed their impact on vulnerable children and families in her lengthy social work career. In 2020, Judy raised the possibility of social work interns at CP. This was a watershed moment in the development of the signature CP Veterinary Social Work (VSW) service.

The Deakin University Field Education placement program was subsequently established with Judy serving as the field educator and providing professional supervision in line with accreditation requirements of the Australian

Association of Social Workers. Since that time, CP has hosted more than ten social work students who have contributed greatly to the formation of the VSW service. In 2022, CP received a significant State Government of Victoria grant to further enable the development of the Crisis Care and VSW service. This has provided a mechanism for social work students to train in VSW practice and the opportunity for some to work in this emerging field in Australia following graduation. Others have chosen to take their knowledge and understanding of VSW into more traditional social work roles following graduation, yet still benefiting the wellbeing of people and their pets. We would strongly recommend anyone considering VSW to undertake at least one placement in this specialist field if possible. We are confident that more and more student placement opportunities will arise in the future as this practice area grows across Australia.

The CP VSW team coordinates the following community services: Crisis Pet Care, Home Pet Care Assistance, Financial Assistance, and End of Pet Life Support. The CP VSW Services are provided through a blended model of funded case management, volunteer support, and external contracts with approved suppliers. Referrals to the service come direct from human service agencies, veterinarians, clients and family/friends/community members. The service follows a social work framework including risk and intake assessments, case management planning, referral, closure, and professional supervision.

What We Like About Our Positions

Navigating a new service model in an emerging field brings complexity, challenges, and new opportunities. No two days are the same. As our VSW team at CP works with new cases, we are constantly reminded of the uniqueness of the human-animal bond: no two animals and no two humans are the same. We, therefore, have to be innovative, responsive, and open to new solutions. Yet, this is what we like: working as part of a team of committed social workers, alongside the veterinary team at CP, is exciting.

Challenges in Our Roles

Our challenges lie in meeting unexpected surges in demand and delivering our services while still developing and refining our systems and processes. Our biggest challenges often emerge when what is best for the animal and what is best for the human are not the same thing. As an example, we do have cases where after much consultation and consideration, the CP team feels that surrendering could be the best option for both parties, however this goes against our overall intention – to keep pet and person together, well and healthy.

Our day-to-day Work

One of the highlights of our weeks are our Monday team meetings, where we discuss, plan and review cases and critically reflect on our practice. The rest of the week is a mix of following up new referrals and enquiries, conducting intake assessments, coordinating veterinary behaviour and health assessments, arranging transfer of pets, and attending to ongoing week-to-week management of pets in our care. We also develop and support community engagement initiatives and develop information and resources to support our work. The best part of being an animal-loving social worker is that we often have pets in our office who are in transit (on their way to respite care), and we get to connect and interact with not only people but also their companion animals.

Advocacy and Systems Change

The role of social workers in HAI is an exciting and emerging field. We are actively advocating for the role of the human-animal bond in human health and wellbeing, across all sectors, and for the need to build interdisciplinary, community-based, and integrated systems of care.

4
VETERINARY SOCIAL WORK JOURNEY

Erin Allen

My Journey

I am a Veterinary Social Worker at the Veterinary Teaching Hospital at Colorado State University. I oversee the Clinic Support Service and provide care to the people within the hospital. In my role, I stand alongside a pet's family when an emergency suddenly alters the life they had with their pet. I am present for some of the most heartbreaking goodbyes and I am grateful to be a part of these experiences. I cry with people and I am comfortable with that expression. I step forward as a buffer when a pet owner's grief causes them to lash out in fear, frustration, and heartache. I'm here to help the veterinary professionals when they are in the crosshairs of those emotional explosions, to help them recognize what's at the base of the emotion. We brainstorm know how to communicate with and support a hurting and afraid pet owner without sacrificing oneself. I also help new as well as seasoned veterinary professionals cope with the strain of medically caring for many ill patients. I teach, both in the front of a classroom and alongside students, technicians and doctors about compassionate communication, gentle handling of sensitive situations, the importance of caring for oneself as much as for one's patients, of balancing the time and dedication given to the profession with living and enjoying life. This is my journey in the world of Veterinary Social Work.

Starting Down the Path

When I entered college, I had no clear direction of where my future would or could lead. That all changed with a job opening at my veterinarian's clinic. I'd always had a deep connection with animals and believed that veterinary

DOI: 10.4324/9781003335528-5

work could shine some light on a possible path for my future. So, my life began down the path of veterinary medicine. Throughout my many years at the veterinary clinic, my life evolved. I loved the medicine but I felt myself drawn to the mental health field. Still unsure about what I would do with that degree, I enrolled in the graduate program for a Master of Science in Social Work at the University of Tennessee. After a semester, my path clarified when I found the Veterinary Social Work program.

A day of Veterinary Social Work in the Hospital

Currently, I am the associate director of the Clinic Support Service for the veterinary teaching hospital. Every day presents new experiences, rarely planned, often emotional, and always significant in some way – thus making detailing a 'typical day' quite challenging.

Some days start with Support Rounds – team meetings to debrief and discuss cases, interactions, communication strategies, and self-care. I also check in privately with students and doctors who I've worked cases with recently. I may assess self-care or provide resources for more in depth mental health support. Some days begin with notes awaiting me about a pet owner who needs some additional support from me or my team. When I meet the client, my role is to 'be there' for them in many ways. I sit with them, listening and guiding as they make medical decisions for their pet. I act as a confidential conduit between them and the veterinary team. At times, I'm the deliverer of the heartbreaking news.

A day may also include phone calls from people throughout the region regarding pet loss, hospital committee meetings, planning a community outreach event, a class to teach, or another emergency. There is no predicting what will occur, but that is part of what I like about the job.

Challenges

With every career choice that requires high empathy, there are pitfalls of caring so much, so often. Maintain focus on your self-care equally with your dedication and compassion to clients. Separation of your work and your life is key to longevity in a care-giving field. Even minute, in-the-moment assessments are important to maintain an awareness of your own emotional vulnerability. It has taken a lot of mindfulness and practice for me to not absorb the experiences of those I work with.

Thinking about this Path?

To someone thinking about a career as a mental health professional in veterinary medicine, I would recommend talking with or shadowing as many people as possible to make sure it is the right field. Many pet owners say their grief for a pet runs deeper and more intense than grief they experienced over a person. It's often attributed to the unconditional love pets give, the unique relationship and the roles pets play in their person's life. The physical aspect of this job can be difficult as well. Being comfortable around a deceased body, petting or holding it, is essential for normalizing the experience for your client. Recognizing the emotions of grief and being comfortable in their presence, no matter how they are displayed, is important. Balancing assertiveness and compassion when attempting to protect the relationship of the medical team and the pet owner is something you will likely do. You must also be willing to ask difficult questions to assess someone's own safety when the throes of their grief or their job becomes too heavy to bear. All of these things, along with a developed ability of reflection as well as a keen sense of self-awareness, are invaluable in protecting yourself through the emotional rollercoasters of this type of position.

Yet, as emotionally taxing as this work can be, it pales in comparison to how rewarding it feels to have a positive impact on someone during a heartbreaking time of their life. When a veterinary student graduates or pet owner returns and thanks me for my support, I am humbled and grateful. I recognize that each day, I get the chance to meet and work with amazing people and incredible animals, and hopefully help in a way that ripples out beyond what I will ever know. That's what keeps me coming back, day after day. This is definitely my labor of love.

5
KALEIDOSCOPE OF A VETERINARY SOCIAL WORKER

Jacquelyn Rebekah James

I have worked in the social service field for over 28 years. Most of my career has been in the medical field; however, I also have experience in early childhood education and residential treatment for youth. I have worked in home health care and hospice, dialysis, and entered the veterinary medicine industry in 2022. I obtained my veterinary social work certificate in 2022 from the University of Tennessee, Knoxville. To obtain a position like mine, you need to have a minimum of a master's in social work (MSW), be licensed in the state where you reside/work, have or be willing to obtain a certificate in veterinary social work, and have experience working in social work, healthcare, or the animal field. Passion for working with animals and providing social work skills and tools with clients is helpful. I believe in the benefits of patients nearing the end of their lives being able to remain with their pets. In my experience, I have witnessed the amazing benefits of animal-assisted interventions with many of my patients.

I have been around animals my entire life. Growing up, my mother worked at a veterinary clinic, I would accompany her to the veterinarian clinic and help take care of the animals. When the opportunity presented for me to work as a veterinary social worker for my current employer, I was excited to utilize my social work skills and love for animals.

I have worked at a veterinary owned and operated emergency and specialty veterinary hospital for over a year. The hospital where I work is large, containing 14 different specialties. Veterinary social work is not predictable; there are many opportunities to help both veterinary team members and clients bringing their pets into the hospital. As part of my role, I provide:

- Support and short-term crisis intervention for clients
- Consultation to the veterinary healthcare team regarding animal-related grief and bereavement services
- Act as a liaison between the client and healthcare team by assisting with communication and ensuring the healthcare team's information is presented in a manner the client can understand
- Provide crisis intervention
- Provide support during testing and treatment
- Help with family discussions related to their animal's illness and death
- Provide information about community resources (i.e., pet cemeteries, cremation companies, grief support sessions, mental health services)
- Support during euthanasia consultation support to team members for team debriefings, including wellness, departmental case reviews

On an average day in the hospital, I begin by:

- Checking our electronic management system for referrals and information to provide phone calls to the clients
- Working alongside the teams to assist with "in the moment" referrals with the teams
- Consulting with the departments and teams to provide education and guidance on proceeding with complex cases
- Supervising BSW and MSW interns
- Attending meetings as scheduled
- Providing intervention logs and documentation

Since the social work program is new at my agency, it requires program management activities such as administrative duties and developing new services within the program such as client pet loss support groups and internship programs.

In a position like mine, you must have a passion for social work and a commitment to building and growing a veterinary social work program. Social work is a broad field with many opportunities, especially in the veterinary field. There are also different models of veterinary social work in the veterinary field. Some agencies want a veterinary social worker to assist with helping team members with compassion fatigue and therapy. In contrast, others want a social worker to provide animal-assisted interventions or interact with clients. It is helpful, in addition to obtaining a certificate in veterinary social work, to have experience as a social worker before entering the veterinary social work field, have knowledge of community work and grief, and be aware of your state laws regarding animal abuse and neglect.

My job offers many rewards. It is incredible to see the healing of participants in our pet loss support groups. Seeing grieving pet owners learn tools to move through their grief journey is a rewarding experience. It also provides rewards of assisting the teams learn how to improve their interactions with clients and see teams process difficult cases positively. With any job or field, there are challenges. Some of the challenges include not enough hours in the day to manage all the needs of the hospital, budget concerns, and veterinarians buying into the program.

If you are enthusiastic about collaborating with clients and animals and want to use your skills and tools as a social worker, working in veterinary medicine is the position for you.

Working as a veterinary social worker has been a dream come true and has challenged me professionally and personally.

6
GRIEF LED ME HERE

Michelle Mezansky

My Background

In January 2014, I began working in an emergency and specialty veterinary hospital in a client services role. I was inspired to work in the veterinary field after Meowme, the cat that I grew up with, passed away from cancer. The grief I felt from losing him was monumental; I had never experienced something so painful. Little did I know that it would be the catalyst for my career as a veterinary social work (VSW).

My client services position entailed liaising between staff and clients, and it allowed me to gain an understanding of how caring for animals impacts both the staff member and the pet owner. It also helped sharpen my interpersonal skills and become comfortable helping people in crisis. I realized how much I valued the role of helping people in emotionally difficult situations and wanted to continue growing as a professional; so, after several years in this role, I decided to go back to school and pursue a Bachelor of Social Work degree. Later that year, the hospital coincidentally introduced its first VSW.

The more I learned about the role of a VSW, the more I felt like it was what I was meant to do. I was fortunate to have the opportunity to intern with the VSW at my job. Working with the same staff and clients in this new capacity solidified my desire to make this my goal. After graduation, I immediately went on to graduate school and obtain my Master of Social Work (MSW) degree. Several months after finishing the program, I saw an open VSW position in my area and went for it. Up until this point, I remained in the client care position as a per-diem employee to keep an ear to the ground and I am so glad that I did. It was not easy juggling that with my other obligations, but it paid off.

My Role

While VSWs can be utilized in all levels of social work, the work that I do mainly occurs on the micro and mezzo levels. At the start of my day, I typically go through my emails and usually see a few inquiries about our service made by clients or referrals from staff. Sometimes, these include a request to meet with a client who is bringing their pet into the hospital that day to make a quality-of-life decision and could use emotional support. The request might also come from a distraught staff member wishing to debrief on an emotionally challenging case. Due to the nature of working in an emergency room, I will occasionally be asked to assess and support clients who appear to be in crisis. In addition to this, I typically have a few individual appointments as well, so I plan my day accordingly. I am fortunate to be one of two VSWs in my organization, and we work closely together to make sure that we are prepared for unplanned situations. We also facilitate several monthly groups like our Pet Loss Support Group and a Wellness Group for Veterinary Interns.

The Good and the Challenging

It is incredibly fulfilling to work in an environment that aligns with both my personal and professional values. The veterinary staff works tirelessly to provide compassionate care to animals, and I am grateful to be in a position that supports their emotional needs. I also value the relationships I foster with pet owners, whether that means pet loss counseling, helping to make quality-of-life decisions, or accompanying them as they say goodbye to their beloved companion. Having such a strong connection to animals and the humans who love them has helped me grow in my role, but it is also what can make this job challenging. I have to remind myself that I am responsible for practicing the self-care that I preach to those I help, but I recognize that it is not always easy to do.

Advice

If you are interested in becoming a VSW, my first piece of advice is to do as much research about the role as possible so that you have appropriate expectations. If you work in an area with a VSW, reach out to them and ask questions to help you decide if the role is something you could see yourself doing. Ask about the possibility of an internship far in advance as there is most likely a scarcity of available placements. In the meantime, improve your qualifications by taking courses that focus on grief and loss, end-of-life, palliative care, etc. I recommend testing the waters by working or volunteering in an area of social work with overlapping responsibilities. I volunteered with a hospice for a year and found it to be an invaluable learning experience.

I also encourage you to think about the skills required of a VSW; many are inherent to the social work profession, but there are a few that are unique to this role. For example, it is essential to have a deep understanding of the human-animal bond and its significance on the well-being of both humans and their animal companions. Additionally, due to veterinary professionals' increased risk, you must have a comprehensive understanding of compassion fatigue and burnout, including evidence-based means of prevention and treatment.

In closing, I want to underscore that VSW positions are popping up everywhere. If there are no available positions, try not to become discouraged. Social workers have so much to offer the animal care community. Remember that if your heart is in it, it will happen for you.

7
VETERINARY SOCIAL WORK

Becoming the Best Version of Your Professional Self

Lisa Hacker

Background

I received my MSW from the University of Wisconsin – Milwaukee in 2009 and was subsequently licensed as an Advanced Practice Social Worker. I then spent almost a decade at a local pediatric hospital working with the families of ill, injured, or dying patients. In 2018, a unique opportunity arose in the greater Milwaukee area to implement a social work program at a private, three-hospital veterinary emergency and specialty practice. Combining my passion for animals and helping people, I found it similar to the work that I had been doing and developed a successful program. There I learned about the strengths and challenges of the veterinary profession and also gained valuable knowledge from the leadership team on becoming a mentor who inspires great culture and employee engagement. This motivated me to pursue additional training in conflict resolution, communication, grief support, team dynamics, and leadership. In 2021, I brought my experience to Arizona where I obtained additional licensure and established a similar veterinary social work program at an employee-owned, three-hospital emergency and primary care practice in the Phoenix metro area.

The Role of a VSW

Given the expansive role, I have broken down the responsibilities into the following groupings:

Client Support: Provide emotional support during emergency medical treatment of a family's pet, quality-of-life or end-of-life conversations, grief support during and after humane euthanasia procedures, and additional community resource information as needed.

Employee Support: Offer mental health and crisis support, a safe space to talk about personal or work-related challenges, conflict resolution with peers, case consultation or debriefings, referrals for ongoing community support, and advocacy to ensure workplace satisfaction. Additionally, a VSW will train employees on psychosocial topics such as grief, self-care and compassion, imposter phenomenon, stress management, suicide awareness, healthy boundaries for work/life integration, and de-escalation techniques. If the practice has a veterinary mentorship or training program for interns and/or residents, a VSW will want to ensure that they are providing additional support to these doctors as this can be a vulnerable time in their early careers.

Leadership Support: Collaborate when team challenges arise, assist with policies and procedures within our area of expertise, offer recruitment/retention suggestions, help with employee appreciation ideas, and advise leaders on information such as empathetic communication, psychological safety, emotional intelligence, conflict resolution, and team building to enhance morale and culture. Additionally, implement initiatives that boost overall team health and wellness.

Community Support: Develop and facilitate pet loss support groups (typically free of charge and open to all members of the community). Participate in advocating for policy changes or legislation that positively impact the veterinary profession for employees, pets, and their people.

Internship Program: If able in the geographic location, a VSW can serve as a field instructor for local universities that have graduate students in need of fulfilling internship hours prior to graduation. While this can be time-consuming as there are supervision, teaching, and administrative requirements, it is important to note that there are benefits of being a field placement site. One of these is the ability to maximize social work coverage available to clients and employees at no additional cost to the practice, which enhances the hospital's reputation in the community as well as value for recruiting new doctors. Having students focus on client support to build their direct practice skills allows more time for a VSW to focus on team and leadership support.

Challenges within VSW

Like most industries in the post-pandemic workforce, veterinary medicine has staffing shortages and is working without enough doctors and technicians for the patient demand which increases the team members' workload and stress. Veterinary staff are exposed regularly to crisis situations, death, moral dilemmas, and emotionally charged clients – all contributing to higher rates of compassion fatigue and burnout. Furthermore, in current economic times of high inflation and rising prices, increasing numbers of clients are struggling with the cost of services, resulting in families having to make medical decisions based on financial limitations. This has a direct negative impact on team members' strain and well-being. It is important to remember that self-care remains essential in this position to ensure you are available to emotionally support both clients and veterinary staff.

Rewarding Aspects of VSW

Veterinary social work has truly allowed me to become the best version of my professional self by routinely calling on me to utilize and sharpen a wide skillset which has resulted in a level of autonomy and career satisfaction I had not experienced before. The gratitude expressed by clients, whom we are often meeting on one of their worst days, is astounding, as well as team members and leadership conveying appreciation and respect for our role, definitely fills my bucket. And, of course, I cannot leave out the opportunity to interact with animals on a regular basis.

Concluding Words of Wisdom

If you are someone who is inspired after reading about the extensive functions of a VSW and not apprehensive of challenging work, then you may be the perfect person for the job. Veterinary practices are looking for social workers who have experience in trauma-informed care as well as working within multidisciplinary teams in settings such as medical social work, hospice, or mental health. However, more important is a social worker with passion, drive, independence, authenticity, and a persistent pursuit of making a difference in the lives of people who love and care for companion animals.

8
HOSPITAL-BASED VETERINARY SOCIAL WORK

A Brief Primer

Judith Harbour

I was interested in veterinary social work before I even knew the field existed. As a young person, I often found myself in helping roles for people and animals. Through high school and college, I explored interests and career paths in hippotherapy, animal-assisted therapy, and special education. After college, I found myself working at the front desk of a neighborhood veterinary hospital. After several years, I settled on social work as a career path, yet I had developed an affinity for the veterinary field. I saw how social work could meet needs in veterinary medicine, both for the staff and for the clients.

I felt impatient to move into veterinary social work practice, although it was some years before I was able to do so. I now reflect on my early years as a social worker in community social service agencies and hospitals with gratitude. In these jobs, I learned foundational clinical skills that I draw on everyday as a veterinary social worker. Working in a mental health clinic, a hospital or an agency will prepare you to be able to respond effectively to the myriad of situations and diverse populations that veterinary social workers encounter. Additional training in veterinary social work (e.g. the University of Tennessee certificate program) or relevant modalities such as mindfulness-based stress reduction, Cognitive Behavioral Therapy, narrative therapy, solutions-focused brief therapy, and motivational interviewing can also be valuable before starting or during your career as a veterinary social worker.

For a hospital-based veterinary social worker, each day looks a little different. For example, a typical day could include any combination of the following:

- Fielding calls from clients inquiring about low-cost veterinary care.
- Giving out stickers to veterinary staff members to brighten their day.

DOI: 10.4324/9781003335528-9

- Offering grief counseling for a client.
- Meeting with a client whose pet is in intensive care to help them make treatment or end-of-life decisions.
- Updating resource lists (e.g. home euthanasia providers, local therapists).
- Planning or hosting an event (e.g. wellness day or staff appreciation day).
- Helping a client or staff member find a therapist.
- Supporting a client whose pet unexpectedly died during a procedure.
- Facilitating a pet loss support group.
- Counseling a client with a paralyzed dog who is experiencing caregiver stress.

I am always intrigued, but not surprised, when previously unencountered situations come across my desk: a client wishing to mummify his deceased dog, a client in an abusive relationship trying to euthanize her sick cat without the knowledge of her partner, an unhoused client with a substance abuse disorder seeking care for his sick hamster. A hospital-based veterinary social worker has never "seen it all."

For all the richness and intellectual stimulation, there are notable challenges in this job.

The Dual Relationship

Most hospital-based veterinary social workers serve both the clients of the hospital and the staff. This can be challenging to negotiate because, in any given situation, your "client" may be a member of the medical team or a pet owner – or both! The social worker must be able to support the interests and wellbeing of both parties at the same time. Peer supervision can be immensely valuable in navigating these situations.

Isolation

Most hospital-based veterinary social workers are the sole social worker at their hospital. This is very atypical in the field of social work, where clinicians who work in more traditional settings are usually part of a team. In these settings, peer supervision and case consultation happen formally and spontaneously. VSWs who work alone must seek supervision and consultation from colleagues outside of their workplace. Fortunately, the VSW community is collegial, but the lack of peer support on a day-to-day basis can be a burden. To further complicate matters, as discussed above, the staff in the hospital are also the VSW's "clients," so the social worker must be circumspect about engaging in typical coworker interactions or friendships. These ethically mandated boundaries can further deepen a VSW's sense of isolation.

Portfolio Expansion

Hospital administration or staff may not understand your scope of practice, and depending on needs, the role may look a little different at each hospital. VSWs may be asked to take on projects or tasks that go beyond their job description – or their ability to manage as a single person. To avoid burnout and to make sure the VSW is able to complete their core job duties, it is vital that they are clear about the boundaries of their scope of practice and advocate to maintain those boundaries. That said, sometimes, flexibility is necessary and regular needs-assessments and strategic planning can ensure that the social worker is continuing to meet the needs of the hospital.

These challenges are part of the job but can be navigated effectively with good supervision, reflective practice, and supportive hospital administration. There is also deep professional fulfillment in hospital-based veterinary social work. Here is a glimpse into the most rewarding aspects of working in this field:

1 Clients and coworkers welcome your assistance. You have skills that no one else in the hospital has.
2 The scope of practice is incredibly broad (also a challenge, see above). You become a nimble, flexible, and open-minded practitioner.
3 You have independence as a clinician and program developer. You have freedom to set your hours, to set your program's priorities, and to make clinical decisions.
4 You bear witness to many stories and the love between people and their animals.
5 You are part of the network of smart, energetic, and generous VSW colleagues across the world. This is a growing field with many opportunities for research, advancement, and collaboration.
6 You are an "animal person." You get to work with animal people!

If you feel motivated to join this field, do not shy away from that goal. If you're in school, get a job at a veterinary clinic. If you're already practicing, start a pet loss support group in your community or offer counseling or training to veterinary professionals and practices. With a solid foundation, you'll be a highly qualified candidate for the next veterinary social work position that opens in your area.

9
PARTNERING WITH THERAPY ANIMAL HANDLER VOLUNTEERS IN HEALTHCARE

An Introduction to Volunteer Management for Social Workers

Whitney Romine

Never say never. The universe is always listening. I once said I would never work in a hospital, go back to school, or do research. Since then, I've spent the entirety of my career in hospitals, I've been back to school for a master's degree and several certificates, and dipped my toes in the waters of research. My early career was a lot of guess work and trying things out. I closed my eyes and picked an undergraduate degree by random finger point. I had never heard of volunteer services until I met with a hospital human resources recruiter who suggested a volunteer coordinator position after graduation. Little did I know that accepting that job would lead me to where I am today.

I have worked in hospital volunteer management for a little over a decade, dabbling in a variety of programs as all volunteer coordinators do, but specialize in animal-assisted interventions (AAI) program administration. My first exposure to animal-assisted activities (AAA) was in helping to facilitate a Pet Partners—then Delta Society—therapy dog handler team evaluation. Our hospital's licensed evaluator was a Recreational Therapist. She served as subject matter expert and guide for new teams integrating into the hospital setting. She taught me how to bridge the gap between therapy animal organizations and the facility when onboarding new teams, how to welcome handlers and answer the fundamental question of any new team: "I passed the test, now what do I do with my dog?"

Inspired by this experience, I became a Pet Partners therapy animal handler team with my first canine partner, Roxie, and visited patients at a local pediatric hospital. Not long after this, our regional hospitals collaborated to host a Pet Partners team evaluator workshop and I was invited to attend. Becoming an evaluator was probably one of the best decisions I ever made. That training and continued experience has become the foundation

DOI: 10.4324/9781003335528-10

of my knowledge and skills. I began to see AAI in a new light, with a deeper understanding of the traits and experience needed for successful canine handler teams and environments. I began to develop a systems-view of AAA programs, seeing them more like a puzzle and working together with teams to figure out where everyone best fits.

I sought educational programs and began to piece together my own education, starting with the University of Denver Institute for Human-Animal Connection's Animals & Human Health and later Canine-Assisted Intervention Specialist certificate programs. Through these experiences, I discovered the field of One Health—the connection between the health of humans, animals, and the environment. I then chose to pursue a Master's in Public Health from Kent State University, focusing as many of my assignments as I could on one health-related topics. Shortly after graduating, I took a year off to seek out roles focusing exclusively on AAI. After applying for a diverse range of AAI-related jobs, I eventually found and accepted the animal therapy activity coordinator position at Mayo Clinic in Rochester, Minnesota.

In healthcare, jobs like mine can be housed in a variety of departments such as volunteer services, integrative medicine, complementary medicine, child life, or patient experience. My primary responsibility is the coordination of AAI programs and oversight of regulatory compliance requirements, such as veterinary and behavior screening. My average day is mostly in-person volunteer engagement, evaluation, coaching, training new therapy dog handler teams, and connecting teams with appropriate patient, staff, and event requests. In between shadowing teams on the floors, I also do administrative tasks such as checking patient requests in EPIC—an electronic health record system—and communicating requests to teams, fielding email and phone questions or requests from staff, entering data, and updating schedules in a volunteer management database. I am also consulted on animal-related programming issues including policies and procedures, public relations materials, developing new programs, and collaborating with research teams studying AAI.

What I love about this job is the sheer diversity of people, animals, and projects I interact with. There are some routines that ensure everyone's safety such as therapy animal handler team evaluation and onboarding, but meeting new teams makes each day feel like I've been given a new puzzle piece and I get to try and find where it fits best. I enjoy watching the big picture come together, the constant growing and changing of tasks keeps me engaged. One of the hardest challenges of this job is falling in love with, and eventually having to say goodbye to, sometimes several therapy animals each year. Helping hospital staff, patients, and the therapy animal's handler navigate loss and grief, in addition to my own grief, is another challenge in my job.

Social workers pursuing AAI may find themselves coordinating or partnering with volunteer therapy animal handler teams as part of their role.

It may be helpful to find out if your organization has a Volunteer Services department and reach out to connect with their staff to explore AAI opportunities. Volunteer coordinators and managers can help with recruitment, screening, and onboarding of candidates based on organization policies, procedures, and a customized volunteer service description.

For anyone seeking a career working with volunteers and volunteer therapy animal handler teams, I highly recommend signing up to volunteer for a cause that interests you. Take note of what you enjoy about volunteering and what you wish was better. This kind of experience will help you connect with the motivation and needs of volunteers. If you don't have a qualified therapy animal to volunteer with, start by volunteering at a local humane society or rescue or contact a local chapter of a national therapy animal organization such as Pet Partners or Alliance of Therapy Dogs and volunteer to help with evaluation events. Networking organizations such as the Society for Healthcare Volunteer Leaders (SHVL), the American Psychological Association Human-Animal-Interaction Division (APA-HAI), and the Association of Animal-Assisted Interventions Professionals (AAAIP) are also great places to find colleagues for benchmarking and mentoring.

Volunteer managers, like social workers, wear many different hats. Curiosity, compassion, and flexibility are probably the most important traits for this work.

10

MY JOURNEY FROM HUMAN MEDICINE TO VETERINARY MEDICINE

Robin Lehrhoff

The COVID-19 epidemic was something I could have never imagined. Working on the front lines of inpatient hospital units was like working in a war zone. With 30+ years as a medical social worker, I was used to working around death, but the amount I witnessed left me feeling depleted and unsure if I could work in a hospital setting any longer. I desperately needed to be rejuvenated!

I casually began to look at job sites and a few short weeks later, received an email from Indeed listing a veterinary social work position. I was initially confused and thought there might be an error in the listing. As I read further, I began to smile as my dream job was unfolding right in front of me. The job description was so appealing, and I met all of the requirements! I had years of experience working as part of an interdisciplinary team, supporting caregivers, providing grief counseling, and had familiarity with a hospital setting. I have been an animal lover my entire life, and the thought of being surrounded by animals all day warmed my heart! I shouted out to the universe, "I want to be a Veterinary Social Worker."

My wish was granted, and I was hired as a Licensed Clinical Social Worker for a large veterinary corporation. I was excited to start this journey and help create the social work position at my new hospital in New York. I was greeted with open arms by a dedicated veterinary staff who were so excited to have me aboard. They were on overload due to COVID-19 and had been longing for assistance with clients and emotional support for themselves well before the epidemic.

My first days on the job were fascinating! I remember describing to my family and friends that, "I felt like I was on a movie set." To be in the Emergency Room/Critical Care unit and to see things up close and personal was

DOI: 10.4324/9781003335528-11

so different from the human hospital setting. When human patients take a turn for the worse or "crash," they are whisked away to procedure rooms or operating rooms and support staff are left behind – not so in veterinary medicine. I was so excited to wear scrubs and be in the midst of patient care and feel like an integral part of the hospital's daily mission, even the emergencies. I knew how important it would be for my hospital staff to see me as "one of the team" before they would turn to me for supportive counseling.

I love being able to support my associates while they are working with animals and their owners. I also find great satisfaction in helping to distract frightened or uncomfortable animals during medical procedures. Being part of the veterinary team in this way enables me to get to know my associates and in return, they get to know me.

Having a social worker on staff has benefitted my hospital tremendously. My biggest impact has been assisting the veterinarians with euthanasia cases. Veterinary professionals are exposed to death at much higher rates than human medicine professionals. My presence affords doctors the ability to move fluidly from one patient to the next without getting side-tracked with lengthy emotional discussions. Another great impact has been providing my hospital associates with proven stress management techniques that help them work with clients as well as their own feelings of pain and grief. In addition, I have had a tremendous direct impact on the clients. Having a sick animal or losing your furry family member is extraordinarily emotional. Having to euthanize a pet is often described as "the hardest decision I've ever had to make," or "the worst day of my life." Having had to euthanize my own animals, I can attest to the hardship and trauma. It's difficult to believe that veterinary hospitals have not had social workers all these years, and that roles like mine are relatively new in this field. One of the joys of this role is that each day looks a bit different, and I am afforded an opportunity to lend my talents on a variety of levels. A typical day can include everything from being the support as a client is confronted with an end-of-life decision, acting as a liaison between clients and a medical team, de-escalating angry clients, referring clients to outside resources, providing support to caregivers with ill pets, being present for euthanasias, providing both individual and group pet loss support, and even cleaning up poop when an extra hand is needed.

Some are surprised to learn that working in veterinary medicine can be just as intense as human medicine. Veterinary practices, like human hospitals, place great emphasis on minimizing stress in their patients and everyone is dedicated to supporting their patients' physical and emotional needs. The primary difference in veterinary medicine is that our patients can't directly communicate with us, making our job, at times, more challenging.

It has also been my experience that many clients have a harder time dealing with pet illness and loss than with human illness and loss, as shocking as it sounds. An early challenge was seeing men break down and sob over their unwell pets. By comparison, this was not my experience in human hospitals. Of course, men would become emotional and shed a tear but there is an appreciable difference in the way in which men show emotion over their furry best friends. I have a new found understanding of, "Man's Best Friend."

I am very excited about the growing opportunities for social workers in veterinary medicine. This is a much overdue and an important tool in combating compassion fatigue and changing hospitals' culture. I believe that employing veterinary social workers will soon become a best practice as this role is a *need* versus *nice* to have. Veterinary professionals as well as pet owners can benefit from onsite psychological support. Just as in human medicine, a veterinary social worker is dedicated to finding solutions to problems and advocating on behalf of their many clients, ideally with a cuddly outcome.

11
A HORSE OF A DIFFERENT COLOR

Tom Favale

My Story

It's still so vivid in my memory from several years ago arriving on a crisp, early March morning at the red brick ranch-style home and parking next to the extended and remodeled garage that is now a small animal clinic. Walking up to the entrance and jingling my set of keys, searching for the new one to unlock the door: "This is my place" I say to myself, turning the key in the deadbolt and opening the door. How proud I was: the new, experienced veterinarian in town. It was just the day before that I closed on the small animal clinic. "Wow, it's finally mine. It's been 22 years since I graduated from veterinary school, and I now own my one doctor animal hospital" were words repeated throughout the following days and months. However, as months turned to years, the thrill and excitement I once felt faded into dread and despair. I realized my active client list was not as robust as I was told, expenses were more than I had figured, and even though I was not physically present every day in the clinic, it was essentially a 24/7 job.

Within three short years of owning my practice, I became discouraged, fatigued, dispassionate, consumed with financial worry, and lonely. As a result of pure serendipity, a nearby, younger veterinarian asked about purchasing my clinic. With a heavy heart, yet little hesitation, I negotiated a contract to sell my clinic and with a "See you later" to my staff, like a fading whisper, I quietly walked away five years after first turning my key in the deadbolt on that crisp, early March morning.

Working as a relief veterinarian was far less stressful, allowed me to pay my bills, rejuvenated my sense of purpose, and gave me time to ponder my next move. I recognized I needed to help myself and felt the desire to help others in my profession. Two years after selling my practice, I enrolled in graduate school at Loyola University Chicago to earn a master's degree in social work. This new profession would allow me to learn about mental health and provide me with the education to not only help myself but to expand my opportunities to help others in the field of veterinary medicine. After graduating with my MSW, I became licensed and started working at my local health department as a crisis counselor in addition to fulfilling my responsibilities as a relief veterinarian at surrounding animal hospitals.

Within a few months of earning my master's degree, a position for social worker and faculty veterinarian opened at a college of veterinary medicine (CVM) in the Southeast United States for which I applied and was accepted. I was ecstatic: practicing both of my professions under one roof became a reality!

A Day in the Life

In my position, each day is different which adds to my enjoyment. I essentially fill two different roles, or in social work parlance, have dual professional roles. As a clinical assistant professor in the Community Practice service, I enjoy assisting clinical students as they work up cases. Each clinical service repeats itself every two weeks, so essentially my general schedule repeats itself that often.

In my larger role as a social worker, one of my favorite responsibilities involve facilitating social work rounds/debriefing sessions for clinical students. In the Community Practice service, I fulfill not only the role of a clinical teaching veterinarian but also the role of a social worker. Communication rounds are held weekly which consist of watching students' recorded interactions with their clients. As the social worker, I lead these sessions and facilitate peer feedback regarding the students' client communication skills. Of course, one of my main social work responsibilities is to provide counseling to those within the CVM, those in the veterinary field outside the CVM, and any individuals seeking counseling after the death of their animal. Other tasks include putting together presentations on various mental health topics, including compassion fatigue, mindfulness, and perfectionism as well as revising current and developing new programs around social work topics in the CVM. Community outreach for our underserved pet owner population and being a part of different research projects fill my days, too.

Rewards and Challenges

One of the most rewarding aspects of my position is working with students. They are bright, excited about their futures, and all share a genuine concern for animal welfare. Of course, they have their struggles, too. When they seek me out for counseling sessions, after hearing their stories, both achievements and challenges, I can provide them with the support they do not always find in others within their circle. Offering them new coping skills, a different perspective, and validating their experiences and feelings are just a few of the ways I can make a difference for them. Similarly, but on a different plane, being able to support those grieving in our community who have experienced the death of an animal is also a very rewarding experience.

There are also several challenges to this position. As a social worker, one of our ethical duties is to avoid dual relationships. As a veterinarian and social worker in the same building, that has proved to be a challenge, personally and professionally. Professionally, it is a matter of explaining and then receiving consent from a CVM student who seeks me out for counseling sessions as I may also be the clinical veterinarian helping them in Community Practice. On a personal level, to maintain clear boundaries around being a social worker, I have declined multiple invitations to social events with CVM personnel to avoid any chance of having a previous, current, or potential client see me in a different role. This has been particularly difficult for me since I moved to this position in 2020, relocating from a different state, during the pandemic. Being able to establish a personal support system and sense of community outside the CVM was essentially unattainable due to the necessity of social distancing guidelines during that time.

Advice

For those of you interested in helping at the intersection of veterinary medicine and social work, particularly while working in a CVM, I humbly offer this advice:

- If moving to a different state/location, be sure to explore, identify, and then diligently strive to establish a sense of community and source of support for yourself outside of your professional life. This is essential. Do not expect your colleagues to fill this need. Work hard to establish and maintain a life outside of work.
- Integrate and collaborate with others in the CVM who are also involved with wellness to maintain efficiency and provide the needed support for all stakeholders, including yourself.
- If filling a new position, establish protocols, expectations, and responsibilities early on and get those decisions in writing so they are clear to everyone. Expect learning moments and request tolerance navigating those times. Determine how you will be evaluated in your role.

SECTION II

Human-Animal Interactions Focused Program Development and Policy Advocacy

12
PROGRAMS AND POLICIES

Susan P. Cohen and Anne-Elizabeth Straub

At the risk of a spoiler alert, while there has been progress in the recognition of human-animal interaction (HAI) within the social work profession and a number of graduate-level programs now exist and resources and support are more available, the job path is still not clearly delineated.

To do that, we'll begin in the here and now, see where we've been and extract some possible hints on process.

First, let's visit the land of "what if?"

Wouldn't it be nice if there were an established path for social workers to find jobs in the field of HAI? First, they'd take courses in one of many graduate programs, then enter placements that touch on a range of HAI services, and at the end, walk into established careers with generous pay and benefits.

Unfortunately, that is not the case.

Historically, social workers with an interest in HAI have had to plot their own career courses. This was universally true 40 or more years ago and is still generally the case. In case of discussions with other social workers, HAI-related concerns are treated as unimportant or even frivolous.

In the past, students who discussed their plans to integrate HAI into their practice were frequently told they would never be able to find a placement or a job. Other students who were assigned to a "veterinary social work" placement struggled to see how they would be able to complete papers on clinical topics or in community organization classes reflecting their placement work.

Fortunately, there were social workers and students who didn't allow themselves to be discouraged. They managed to find the support they needed to make their way, regardless of the naysayers.

Social workers in agencies who proffer an idea to incorporate the benefits of connection with an animal into part of their work or to advocate for a

DOI: 10.4324/9781003335528-14

change in policy or procedure are still met with either outright dismissal of the idea or objections about the perceived difficulty of the project. An HAI-oriented social worker will often be the first in the agency to suggest involving animals. When they propose the inclusion of companion animals, farm residents, or wildlife as an option, anxious administrators call it cute, unnecessary, or even dangerous. However, a crucial piece is missing in that exchange. When the emphasis is placed on the animals, and not the relationships or systems involved, it reduces the discussion to a dichotomy: animals or people.

There is another way of framing the issue. We can apply the skills we learn in social work school and practice every day on the micro, mezzo, or macro levels to the programs and services that assist the people who see their animals as family members. There is no need to wonder how to apply the basic social work principles; they are the same whether animals are involved or not.

Being on the receiving end of the barrage of objections can be challenging. The HAI practitioner may feel isolated, but remember, others have been there. There is support available, if you know where to look.

One place to look is at the work that has already been done in the field. Skeptical agency directors and professors may be surprised to learn that numerous animal-oriented programs already exist. Social work practitioners offer animal-assisted therapy in psychiatric units, facilitate group support for grieving pet lovers, teach veterinary staff to manage stress, help mothers and children escape from domestic violence where threats to animals are used to control other family members, assist individuals with disabilities to learn skills of independent living by caring for resident animals, create opportunities for children with literacy problems to read to shelter animals, help traumatized veterans obtain service animals, intervene for those who would benefit from a live-in animal companion to find pet-friendly housing, provide psychotherapy with those who find it easier to talk about animals than people, handle specially trained dogs to comfort children who need to testify in court, improve the environment of older adults who will eat more in the presence of goldfish in a tank, help troubled teens view the effect of their behavior on others by working with shy donkeys, and encourage children with balance problems to develop strength and confidence through therapeutic riding. These programs are highly successful, have existed for more than 40 years, and have substantiated their effectiveness through research.

The basic approach to making change through programs, advocacy, or policy is "If you see something, do something". Here are two examples of social workers who saw a problem and did something about it. The Dean of the University of Pennsylvania School of Social Work, Dr. Louise Shoemaker, happened to walk through the waiting room of the School of Veterinary Medicine's clinic and noticed pet lovers looked as scared and sad as parents of sick children. After coming back several more times to confirm her impression and collaborating with the veterinary Dean, in 1978, she assigned doctoral student, Jamie Quackenbush, to work with veterinary clients and students. This led to a service that is now nearly universal at veterinary schools and some large veterinary practices.

Another example of an animal-oriented program involved social workers who regularly encountered families experiencing domestic violence. They needed to escape those situations, only to be required by policy to leave their pets behind in order to enter a shelter. Those workers researched, networked with others, and created alliances across agencies and disciplines, keeping at it through years of consistent work and advocacy on many levels. Their efforts bore fruit.

In 2018, a demonstration shelter project in New York City, run by the Urban Resource Institute (URI), was finally opened. It allowed families to enter a shelter along with their pet, providing a safe haven while keeping all its members together. Because of its success and with the support of national companies, URI has opened several more pet-friendly shelters.

So, how does one propose or begin a new HAI service, especially if the authorities who must approve it have doubts?

Step 1. Identify a need.

- What problem does your program or policy solve? Here are examples.
  - Does having a dog in the room ensure a better turnout to therapy groups?
  - Are people who need surgery more willing to get it if they know someone will take care of their pets while they are away?
  - Are mentally ill, homeless men willing to leave the streets for shelter if they can bring their cat or dog?
  - Do prospective clients have significant connections to animals that no one knows about because the intake form has no place to write it?

Step 2. Back up your proposal with research and examples of similar programs.

- If you are not connected to a university where you have access to academic material, do a search on Google Scholar and PubMed, both of which are free.
- Pull up the articles, read them carefully, and review their list of sources.

Step 3. Even if you are the only social worker you know with these interests, you don't have to go it alone.

- Reach out to others in the field who have similar programs or who have changed protocols or regulations in their agency or government.
- The HAI field is full of professionals who have created these changes from scratch. Most of them are delighted to share their experience.
  - You can get names of practitioners from direct contact, as well as the scholarly sources you've searched.
  - You can also find connections and ongoing support and information by joining a group of like-minded professionals.
    - One such group is our own Social Workers Advancing the Human Animal Bond (SWAHAB), a network developed in New York City in 2001 by social workers who experienced the same issues described earlier. The group functions primarily as a self-education and support group.
- Many of the examples given above, particularly those involving advocacy for large system policy or legislative change, were long-term projects that involved shared leadership from multiple sources and input from many others.
- When people who must approve your proposal feel anxious about a new idea, evidence that research supports it and other places have successfully implemented something like it can overcome their objections.

Step 4. Find allies.

- In addition to clinicians, veterinarians, animal-assisted therapists, social work school deans, or others in the HAI field, which individuals within the organization might support this idea?
- Is there a potential donor or board member who has influence with those who need to approve the plan?
- If you can secure funding in advance, the chances your idea will be approved increase exponentially.

Step 5. Develop a detailed proposal.

- What community will this serve?
- What kinds of animals will be involved?
- What measures will protect clients, staff, visitors, the agency, and the animal partners when this regulation or program comes to be?
- What is the point of the change and how will it be implemented, exactly?

- Is there an opportunity to make the organization look good? (To paraphrase a lesson from one of the authors' graduate classes, the two biggest motivators for organizational change are money and scandal.). If that applies to your idea, show how adopting it will increase one or prevent the other.

Step 6. Remember the magic words, "Pilot Program".

- It's a way to try out a new idea without making a lifelong commitment.
- Explain how long the idea will be tested, specify what measurements will show results, and describe what methods will be in place to tweak the program in case changes can make it more effective.

In summary, your basic social work skills, as well as your concern for your clients and the community, have given you a tool kit. You can add (or create) whatever additional tools, as well as any new skills you might discover that you need, along the way.

As you read the following personal stories, you will see how these steps play out in many different situations. You'll also see the role played by the free flow of ideas within networks of support developed and maintained by social workers themselves.

13
POLICY ADVOCACY AND PROGRAM EVALUATION

The External Link of Practice Work in One-Health

Bailey Fullwiler

Program evaluation and policy advocacy are foundational practices of macro social work. Macro social work looks at how clients are impacted by systems typically at the community, local, and national levels. Their work centers on modifying these systems to better serve clients through a wide range of activities, including conducting research and influencing public policy. However, all social workers, regardless of practice area, play a role in engaging in these professional activities. These twin pillars serve as an opportunity to share our work, knowledge base, and values to external stakeholders to address the systemic challenges our clients navigate that reduce the effectiveness of individual interventions. Particularly, in social workers' role within the emerging and growing field of One-Health, program evaluation and policy advocacy serve as key opportunities to connect our profession with interdisciplinary partners and external stakeholders to grow our impact and ability to be of service. In addition, our areas of research and professional history of community organizing and policy advocacy are unique and can add value to our interdisciplinary partners within One-Health settings.

In the era of evidence-based practice, program evaluation is the most powerful tool to bring social work interventions within the One-Health approach into the larger public sector. By conducting evaluations and sharing the findings, social workers build the narrative and data to demonstrate the need, effect, and impact of their work. These skills help tell the story of why social workers are so well positioned to advance the principles of One-Health and how interventions can benefit not only the individual receiving services but also the larger community. The areas of our research on social determinants of human health are not a focus or area of expertise of other related professions, making social workers' role in this work invaluable. Conducting

DOI: 10.4324/9781003335528-15

program evaluations increases our capacity to scale interventions and build more conclusive evidence to guide our practice recommendations within the field, as well as our policy recommendations.

Program Evaluation Example – While earning my bachelor's degree in social work in the mid-2010s, a professor introduced the notion of including questions regarding pets in client intake surveys. This recommendation came from the growing research field of the human-animal bond. However, in my first full-time social work role, there were no data collected on whether pets were part of a client's household or their relationships with animals. Recognizing this as a growth area for my agency, I was able to integrate questions regarding pets into my own intake interviews with clients. After six months, I compiled a report that demonstrated what percentage of my clients reported having pets in the household, the number of related referrals and resources I made, and qualitative feedback on any client outcomes that resulted from those referrals and resources. I presented that report alongside research from my undergraduate class on the role of the human-animal bond on human health to propose an agency-wide change to our intake forms. When reviewed by the agency's senior leadership, they felt there was significant data and compelling client narratives to make that change. While not a formal program evaluation, this small review alongside existing relevant literature review resulted in sufficient data to make an internal policy change that positively impacted our clients and will now contribute to a larger available data set for One-Health researchers and practitioners.

Policy advocacy is a core component of social work practice that works toward our professional value of social justice. This arena of practice looks at a variety of interventions and practices that social workers can make to share their with decision-makers and influence the systems that impact their client's well-being. From writing op-eds, attending city council meetings or congress committee hearings, reporting policy analyses, and publishing policy recommendations, social workers work to change policies and laws to reduce discrimination and inequities that prevent our clients from flourishing. In the field of One-Health, we've seen the power of policy advocacy in the areas of housing rights for pet owners, dual-mandate reporting of human and animal abuse, campaigns to end breed bans, and the development of grief services for pet owners and animal-care staff. These policy changes have positively shifted social workers' abilities to serve their client systems. There is still important legislative work to be done, however, to better protect the health and well-being of all in human-animal-environment interactions and relationships.

Effective policy advocacy requires several key ingredients. There are numerous great scholars and authors who have presented frameworks for policy work. For example, Kingdon's (2011) textbook helps readers identify when an idea (solution) time has come and how to bring it to actuality.

Bardach's (2012) textbook presents a concrete process for addressing social problems through policy. Pulling from the existing literature and my work in the field, I present five key areas for social work practitioners to consider in policy work;

1 Strategy: Understanding your target audience, opponents, and stakeholders
2 Evidence: Quantitative and quality data to support your position
3 Creativity: Considering the alternatives and most compelling policy approaches
4 Timing: Determining when there is a window for change and action
5 Compelling Narratives: Connection and leadership of the communities most impacted.

Advocacy Example – In my work as an ecological grief consultant, I have partnered with environmental organizations to assess how climate emotions (eco-anxiety, ecological grief, solastalgia, climate distress) impact their employees and overall workplace health. Through those assessments, we were able to build a body of data from multiple organizations on the measurable impacts of climate emotions on their workforce (absenteeism, productivity, attrition, healthcare costs, etc.), as well as collect narratives from staff, volunteers, and clients they serve. While completing workplace health assessments and listening to environmental employees, I learned that in addition to their own negative experiences with climate emotions as a result of their work, they were also having those same negative mental health experiences due to environmental and climate injustices echoed by community members in the areas they served. As such, we began exploring the potential benefits of including the mental health impacts of climate and environmental injustices in their existing environmental policy advocacy to strengthen their advocacy approaches. It was through this interdisciplinary partnership and policy advocacy that we've been able to integrate the information from my interventions to scale a new approach or prong into environmental justice policy work. Below is a breakdown of how this is connected with key policy advocacy ingredients.

1 **Strategy:** Most of my client's advocacy work is at the local and state government level. As such, they are advocating directly with decision-makers who are elected officials and live and work in close proximity to lands and communities my clients serve. According to the Centers for Disease Control and Prevention (2021), one in five Americans annually will experience a mental illness and 50% of Americans in their lifetime will be diagnosed with a mental health condition. As such, the likelihood that a decision-maker has direct or indirect experience with the impacts, costs, and realities of mental illness is high.

2. **Evidence:** As assessment tools emerge to measure climate emotions, there are opportunities to engage in community outreach and research through polling or focus groups to determine qualitative themes or capture individual stories on the prevalence and impacts. This has allowed my clients to build data sets to support the inclusion of the mental health impacts of climate or environmental injustices in their advocacy positions.
3. **Creativity:** While some decision-makers have been slow to respond to the physical health and economic costs of environmental injustices and climate change, some resonate with the data and are moved to act on the behavioral and mental health impacts of these challenges. Adding this component to advocacy approaches creates additional pathways for decision-makers to connect with the challenges their community members are facing and the comprehensive health impacts of climate inaction and environmental hazards. My clients have reviewed the backgrounds of decision-makers they are working with to see which ones have a history of speaking or acting on mental health to tailor their advocacy approaches.
4. **Timing:** In 2021, record federal funding investments in mental health prevention and treatment were made possible through the passing of the American Rescue Act. Simultaneously, there has been increased national attention to the staggering shortages of professionals in the behavioral health field. This informs my clients that decision-makers have a state of increased awareness of the true cost of mental health, as well as the barriers to treatment. As such, incorporating the mental health impacts of environmental/climate advocacy have increased potential for effectiveness at this unique time in history.
5. **Compelling Narratives:** Environmental groups and the clients they serve are often the best messengers of this advocacy approach as they are interacting with the outcomes of environmental hazards and climate inaction every day and have a greater risk to experience negative climate emotions as a result. This is a key area for partnership in which social workers can be of service in helping community members or environmental staff prepare their testimonies and offer guidance in defining climate emotions, measuring their prevalence, and connecting those with policy recommendations accordingly.

Social workers offer a unique skill set and perspective in the One-Health field, trained to attend to the human needs that arise in human-animal relationships and understand the environments those humans reside in. As such, engaging in practices like program evaluation to build and scale our knowledge base and policy advocacy to shift systemic inequities are essential to ensuring that our client's and communities' needs and voices are heard and met. Social workers work with human clients on all social determinants of health and add value to interventions with interdisciplinary partners working more directly with the environmental or animal outcomes for human interactions. Without program evaluation to guide data sets and policy advocacy to address the problems uncovered in our research, we will be unable to reduce the barriers to wellness our clients and their animal companions or neighbors face.

References

Bardach, E. (2012). *A Practical Guide for Policy Analysis: The Eightfold Path to More Effective Problem Solving*. Sage.

Centers for Disease Control and Prevention (2021, June). *About Mental Health*. https://www.cdc.gov/mentalhealth/learn/index.htm#:~:text=1%20in%205%20Americans%20will,illness%20in%20a%20given%20year.&text=1%20in%205%20children%2C%20either,a%20seriously%20debilitating%20mental%20illness.&text=1%20in%2025%20Americans%20lives,bipolar%20disorder%2C%20or%20major%20depression.

Kingdon, J. (2011). *Agenda, Alternatives, and Public Policies*. Pearson.

14

"PUFFY'S PET BOARDING"

A Second Home for Your Dog

Rachel Nallathamby

We quickly learned a great deal about fostering dogs, based on our experience with Puff. For example, while adult dogs settle into the routine and can be left alone for a few hours, for puppies, constant supervision is needed. We took in puppies who had finished the round of vaccinations only and always kept a record of eating habits and medical records in hand. With puppies, it's extremely important to pay attention to even the most minor details. Pups are curious, and so when we fostered puppies, we always kept them in a safe place where there were no harmful things to chew/bite… But either way, our first main duty was to make the dog feel happy again and know they are safe with us. So, the *first part of the day* started off with a "WALK". There is a magical bonding which happens over a walk and almost every dog I meet relaxed over a walk. Allowing them to sniff and get used to a new place is vital in making them feel comfortable. Taking the dog for a nice long walk at the start of the day not only engaged the dog in physical activity but made it a lot easier to handle the dog when they came home. For pups, we carried them along a bit and visited parks and places where they would get noticed a lot. After all, our main purpose and promise was to find them a safe and happy home. And thankfully, mostly the walks and showing off in parks paid off. The *second part of the day was* a good healthy breakfast for both the dogs and us… Evenings were reserved for play… My daughter was also young. So, games included catch and retrieve, hide and seek, and just about sniffing behind trees and enjoying the sun going down. We always prepared food for the dogs (each dog had a different meal requirement at times and so we landed up cooking a lot). Of course, the day ended (*the last part*) with another good walk before bedtime. Dogs who stayed longer had to have baths over the weekend (whenever the groomer landed up, so no particular schedule for

DOI: 10.4324/9781003335528-16

that!). Posing for pics with our dogs playing and enjoying themselves made owners/fosters happy and this activity happened all day long...

Advice for People Seeking a Similar Position/Profession

Over the years, I have learned and re-learned a lot of stuff. Nothing a book teaches you can count up as experience when you start up a new business/job. It is a great idea to go in first with the dogs which have been socialized well if you are someone who doesn't have any professional training yet. Taking care of a dog means taking full responsibility, so having a file on hand with vet contacts proved helpful to me in many situations. Also, I went through friend referrals so that helped me know the history of the dog and the owner. I found that people who come across your place on the Internet or randomly through advertisements are a bit skeptical and tend to be anxious when dropping off the dogs. The dogs can pick up on negativity or anxiousness and take time to warm up to you. After all, you will be a complete stranger to them. So, by going through referrals till I got completely comfortable handling dogs of all shapes and sizes worked for me.

Best/Most Rewarding Parts of Your Job

Having thus said, it's the most rewarding job I could have done over the years. It helped me connect with numerous people and the one thing we all had in common was our love for dogs. This helped us all support each other and network as a family and share many good conversations. This helped us create a platform for the awareness of adoption of animals and till date we are happy knowing the dogs have a good and safe home.

Challenges with Your Job

The biggest challenge is losing a dog to death. Puff passed away on 10 February 2023. She is and will be the reason why I always will advocate for animals. She was with me during the hardest part of my life, yet those days turned out to be the best with her by our side. As we mourn her loss and can't imagine our lives without her, I also know that she left us with a lasting legacy that will continue in more ways than one, connecting people and dogs across boundaries. This is my tribute to her and the celebration of her life.

Last but not the least, I encourage a lot of people to take up the job. There is a lot of need for good caregivers for dogs and cats when their owners travel. So go for it. If you are looking for a high paying job, this might be a little disappointing. But on the other hand, it will make you rich by having dog hairs on you all day long and pay you back with wagging tails, licks, and love along the way.

15

ADDRESSING THE LINK BETWEEN VIOLENCE TOWARD PEOPLE AND ANIMALS AS A GENERALIST SOCIAL WORKER

Kathryn Ford

As a result of personal and professional experiences, and driven by deeply held values, I have dedicated much of my career to supporting people who have experienced violence and victimization and improving justice system responses to these issues, including by training and consulting with practitioners nationally. However, it was my trauma therapy clients close to home, in the Bronx, who taught me an important lesson that informs my practice to this day—that violence toward people is inextricably linked to violence toward animals, meaning the well-being of people and animals are linked as well.

I began working with victims and survivors, and supporting systems changes on their behalf, as a social work intern at the Brooklyn District Attorney's Office. I became certified in Rape Crisis Counseling in college, but during this field placement, I learned much more about the needs and experiences of crime victims and witnesses and how to support their safety and healing. After graduation, I continued this work as a supervised visitation social worker. In that role, I conducted intake interviews and submitted reports to the Family Court about visits between children and their non-custodial parents, most of whom had caused harm to the children and/or their other parent.

I was then hired by a justice reform non-profit to implement a training project on children's exposure to intimate partner violence (IPV). Over the years, I worked on many projects related to these issues, but I didn't become aware of the role of animal abuse in family violence until one of my trauma therapy clients, a 12-year-old boy, told me that his mother's abusive boyfriend threw their cat out the window to its death when she tried to end the relationship. This revelation piqued my interest in this intersection and led to changes in both my clinical practice and my training and consulting.

In order to understand the impacts of animal abuse, it's essential to consider the role of animals in our lives. They are often viewed as family members, and can provide unconditional love, emotional support, companionship, and stress relief, which are especially important when experiencing the stresses and isolation of abuse. But because of the significance of pets, people who cause harm may abuse or neglect animals as a way to control, intimidate, and silence those who are being victimized. Unfortunately, these experiences are not uncommon—among women experiencing IPV who have pets, 38–72% report that their partner threatened, harmed, or killed an animal (DeGue & DiLillo 2009). In illustration, here are some stories that my clients have shared:

- A woman whose ex-boyfriend slashed her in the face denied previous violence but had realized he was dangerous when he threw her dog down the stairs.
- Another woman reported that her ex-boyfriend broke into her apartment and tried to have her dog euthanized.
- A 9-year-old boy witnessed his mother's boyfriend, who had physically and sexually abused his mother and the children, kill up to ten cats.

How does exposure to animal abuse affect children and adults? All may be traumatized and experience fear of being harmed, anger at the perpetrator, and helplessness and guilt at not being able to protect their pet. Especially when the abuse is chronic, children may become desensitized to its horrors, resulting in decreased empathy for animals and increased likelihood that they will harm animals, too. Pets are also an important variable in survivors' decision-making—18–48% of women living in a domestic violence shelter who had pets delayed leaving the relationship out of concern for their pets' safety (Volant et al. 2008). In addition, animal abuse is associated with increased risk of child abuse and neglect; use of a broader range of coercive control tactics; more severe physical violence; sexual violence; and homicide (Simmons & Lehmann 2007).

What can social workers do to address this link? One of the most important practices to implement is screening adults and children by asking whether they have pets, whether anyone has threatened or harmed the pets or failed to care for them properly, if there are any worries about the pet's safety, and whether any pet-related assistance is needed. I incorporated a question on this topic into my assessment process, and many clients answered affirmatively. Such screening normalizes survivors' experiences, enables identification of co-occurring forms of abuse, and facilitates connection with supportive services, such as veterinary care, pet-friendly housing (Giesbrecht

2021), and legal supports (Warner & Willetts 2021). Screening also strengthens risk assessment and safety planning and allows for more effective mental health intervention, since trauma, anxiety, and grief related to animal abuse can be validated and addressed. We can also utilize animal-assisted therapeutic interventions, connect clients with humane education programs, and implement specialized treatment approaches such as AniCare (Animals & Society Institute 2013).

As essential as this information is for effective practice, animal abuse is not a topic in which social workers are usually trained. Because of this gap, I conducted a literature review and developed a curriculum for practitioners which covers dynamics, prevalence, effects, screening, advocacy strategies, and therapeutic intervention, as well as civil and criminal legal responses. To date, I have trained hundreds of practitioners via 15 interdisciplinary workshops. I also participate in a local consortium, the Alliance for the Safety of Animals and People, to share resources and offer mutual support in addressing this complex and potentially traumatizing issue. It was through learning about the interconnectedness of violence toward people and animals that I was able to strengthen my clinical practice and expand my systems change efforts to more effectively support the well-being of both.

References

Animals & Society Institute (2013). *AniCare Child Handbook: The Assessment and Treatment of Children Who Abuse Animals.* Retrieved from: https://www.animalsandsociety.org/practice/anicare-child-handbook/

DeGue, S. & DiLillo, D. (2009). Is animal cruelty a "red flag" for family violence? Investigating co-occurring violence toward children, partners, and pets. *Journal of Interpersonal Violence,* 24(6), 1036–1056.

Giesbrecht, C.J. (2021). Animal safekeeping in situations of intimate partner violence: Experiences of human service and animal welfare professionals. *Journal of Interpersonal Violence,* 37, 17–18.

Simmons, C.A. & Lehmann, P. (2007). Exploring the link between pet abuse and controlling behaviors in violent relationships. *Journal of Interpersonal Violence,* 22(9), 1211–1222.

Volant, A.M., Johnson, J.A., Gullone, E. & Coleman, G.J. (2008). The relationship between domestic violence and animal abuse: An Australian study. *Journal of Interpersonal Violence,* 23(9), 1277–1295.

Warner, C. & Willetts, M.C. (2021). Protecting companion animals from domestic abuse: A comparative analysis of legal developments in the U.S. and the U.K. *Global Journal of Animal Law,* 9, 1–10.

16

CHASING IMPACT

Take That Leap of Faith

Urvashi Shobhna Kachari

The summer of 2018 was a destiny-defining year for me. It was the year I chose to align my career path with my first love – "animals". It was the year I decided to join the animal protection movement in India. Since childhood and well into my teens, I had been inspired by the likes of Dr. Doolittle, James Herriot, and Gerald Durrell. I nurtured a dream of becoming an "animal doctor"! Unfortunately, my academic capacities in school were limited to excelling at Humanities – a subject that did not support becoming a veterinarian. In my quest to get good grades in the Class XII school examinations to gain a merit-based admission into a premier college, I reluctantly let go of the dream to work with animals. Yet, as I launched forth in academic pursuits and building work experience, I found myself constantly gravitating toward animals. Looking back, it was a combination of circumstances and signs from the Universe that compelled me to explore the existential restlessness that I had been enduring. At that time, I was working for a women's empowerment organization in New Delhi. When my contract with the organization ended, I grabbed the opportunity to explore avenues for working in the animal protection movement in India. I wanted to leverage the professional experience and skill sets I had gained over the years working with various non-profit organizations to now make a difference in the lives of animals. Armed with degrees in Political Science, International Relations, and Development Studies, I set out to chase a career making an impact in animal welfare!

I started working with People For Animals/People For Animals Uttarakhand – an animal advocacy organization in Delhi that specializes in public policy and advocacy for securing better welfare for farmed animals. I contributed toward the "end battery cages" campaign that involved spreading public awareness about the issue of cruelty toward 400 million egg-laying

DOI: 10.4324/9781003335528-18

hens in India housed in inhumane battery cages. My tasks involved designing and getting billboards of battery cage cruelty displayed at prominent locations, managing a Change.org online-petition to leverage public opinion, and initiating a postal campaign wherein citizens wrote advocating for change to the Ministry of Fisheries, Animal Husbandry, and Dairying. In 2021, I took the role of Program Lead for the Ahimsa Fellowship – India's first Animal Welfare Fellowship that builds the capacities of carefully chosen young individuals from across India who have a strong motivation and commitment to protect animals. Looking back, building a Fellowship program from scratch was perhaps the most exciting part of my career as an animal advocate. From curating the curriculum and modules to customizing the learning-sessions and bringing together subject matter experts from the field together, it was a unique high to see the logo representing the Fellowship along with the signature tagline – *Compassionate Outcomes Through Advocacy* materialize!

A typical day in my work-life as an animal advocate includes managing the Ahimsa Fellowship. This includes a range of tasks, including planning mentorship sessions, documenting and reporting various aspects of the Fellowship for digital media and partner-stakeholders, and ensuring timely stewardship of the entire program. I also help raise funds as well as write policy briefs with a special focus on farmed animal protection issues.

The brightest parts of my day are when I spend time with rescued animals that have been offered a sanctuary in our office space. There is an aviary built within the premises to house rescued layer hens. It is amazing to see how respectful human-non-human-animal interactions can reveal the delightful personalities of formerly terrified and abused hens. As I step into the aviary, the boldest of the hens – *Ms. Henny Penny* comes rushing toward me, clucking with curious insistent pecks at my hand to discover the treat I have brought for them. When the hens were first rescued, they would lie huddled in a frightful heap in a corner. Yet, with time, the birds gradually came out of the shell and learned to trust. They discovered the pleasures of expressing their natural behaviors of foraging, sunbathing, and dust bathing. My advice for people seeking a similar profession would be:

i   In the vast ocean of animal advocacy, be the champion for the most abused and heavily exploited of all animals – farmed animals. Their rights are non-existent and they are often condemned to a lifetime of misery, viewed as mere commodities of food consumption.
ii Advocate most strongly for animals perceived to be the least charismatic – like fish, crustaceans, and cephalopods. Humanity is guilty of heightened cognitive dissonance when it comes to our "underwater cousins" because of the scaly otherness of these species (Balcombe, 2016). Expansion of our moral circle to include these animals under the purview of basic welfare to alleviate their suffering in law and public policy is imperative.

iii Entry-level salaries in the sector will not be financially glamorous. As your expertise grows, you can expect to be remunerated in a way that will make you comfortable but not rich. However, you will lead a life rich with purpose.
iv All skills are good skills. Eclectic education and work backgrounds foster diverse critical viewpoints which eventually serve to strengthen the movement. This is what makes the animal protection movement unique, inclusive, and progressive.

This is my story so far. I hope to encourage all of you who are ignited by an inherent compassion for animals and a desire to contribute to bettering the world for them. Take that leap of faith with an opportunity-mindset and persevere in your animal advocacy journey. It will empower you to live your life purposefully with greater meaning. As Gautam Buddha once said – in the end, only three things matter: how gently you lived, how much you loved, and how gracefully you let go of things not meant for you.

Reference

Balcombe, J. (2016). What a Fish Knows: The Inner Lives of Our Underwater Cousins. Simon & Schuster.

17

SPROUT

Companion Animal to Service Dog to Career Inspiration

Kristen Cudmore

Sprout, means to grow, spring up, shoot forth, or develop new parts. Because Sprout, my canine-companion, took on the role of my service dog guardian, recovery became about making meaning of our unwavering relationship as a team through our shared life's work.

Growing up, I yearned for a dog. Throughout my early adulthood, I volunteered as an animal shelter attendant, dog walker, foster parent, and home auditor (someone who goes to potential adopting family's homes to assess whether the home would be suitable for the dog's needs). I also volunteered for rescue organizations like the Society for the Prevention of Cruelty to Animals (SPCA) and read every training book I could and practiced with the dogs I volunteered with.

As an adult, living as a professional musician meant that I was on the road touring and I often did not know when my next paycheck would come. I worked to find opportunities to make money through teaching, writing, performing, releasing albums, and licensing my music for film/TV. An artist's lifestyle generally lacks routine and predictability, so I wanted something to help provide that stability; this led me to Sprout – a little fluffy grey terrier-mix, waiting for a home at an animal shelter.

I put everything I had into Sprout, including all the trainings I had learned from the likes of Sophia Yin, Ian Dunbar, and Karen Pryor. Sprout and I did (and do) everything together, but one particular night, a gut feeling told me to leave her at home when I biked to my soccer game. I would usually bike to the field with Sprout in a covered basket, but this one night, I did not. The last thing I remember is rolling underneath a truck and seeing the insides of the tires; I was hit by a drunk driver. My helmet did what it could, but I suffered a traumatic brain injury that left me with an invisible dis/Ability.

DOI: 10.4324/9781003335528-19

Afterwards, my behaviors changed, and Sprout picked up on this. When I started to lose my balance or feel faint, Sprout would alert me to lay down so I would not hit my head. If I lost control of my senses, she would lay on me or cause a stir to get my attention. The extensive medical team saw Spout's behaviors and found her to be a key factor in preventing me from further head injuries.

Sprout (having transitioned into my service dog) and I worked together until my symptoms began to subside. Throughout this time, I studied Gestalt psychotherapy while recording a new music album and starting a dog-caring business; but I wanted to help people the way Sprout helped me. As a result, I completed my Master of Social Work degree at Dalhousie University and started working as a clinical therapist for the Nova Scotia Health Authority – all while pursuing my service dog trainer certification.

During this time, I wrote a policy review for the Nova Scotia Service Dog Act, volunteered for a non-profit as a service dog trainer, and sat on my Community Health Board. I also conducted research around canine-assisted therapy (CAT) for those accessing our public mental health programs. I was asked to join a national technical committee to write standards for Animal-Assisted Human Services, which have been recently published by the Standards Council of Canada. Currently, I am about to submit my CAT Continuing Education curricula for accreditation by the International Society for Animal-Assisted Therapy. Additionally, I co-founded Maritime Service Dogs – a not-for-profit entity that focuses on public health research, advocacy for equitable access to service or assistance dog resources, safeguards for the wellbeing of working dogs, and educating the public on supportive etiquette around working-dog teams.

At Nova Scotia Mental Health and Addictions, I see clients who have recently been discharged from emergency psychiatric care or are in acute distress from a severe mental health diagnosis or substance use disorder. Yet, because CAT is still relatively new to government agencies, my CAT work tends to be on a consultation or advising basis. Because I believe that animals have the right to choose to (or refuse to) do this type of work, I also explore the rights and freedoms of animals that work with humans in human-serving spaces under the guidance of Dr. Cassandra Hanrahan at Dalhousie University.

Without Sprout, my life would look a lot different. She has inspired me to pursue this career by being a steadfast support during the tough times caused by post-concussion syndrome. It is my duty to honor her life by continuing to advocate for and work toward further developments in the field of human-animal interactions (HAIs). The biggest challenges I face when doing this work include: (a) getting buy-in from the public sector and decision-makers; (b) managing logistics required to deliver services with a canine co-worker; and (c) educating the public around the legitimate practice of canine-assisted interventions.

There are many pathways to canine-informed social work, but most involve some combination of an MSW, additional training in HAIs; completing a service dog training certification; and researching the field of HAIs – including ethics, animal sentience, theory, and clinical practice. It is helpful to be involved in opportunities to learn, advocate, write, speak, and participate in events where canines and humans work together. For me, this is a life-long commitment to learning.

My parting advice would be to ensure your canine co-worker loves the work as much as you do. Sprout paved the way for me to be in this fortunate position, to live out my passion – one that is built on my love for her and our indescribable connection. I best express these sentiments through (my) song and music video, "Sprout" by Language Arts ~*once I knew I found you, I would never ever be the same.*

18
ON CANINES, CONFLICTS, AND COMMUNITY

Reflections on One Health

Rajlakshmi Kanjilal

Nonhuman animals have been an integral part of my life since childhood. Canine family members played a significant role in shaping my sense of self and respect for others. My interactions with nonhumans are effortless, and the connection is almost instant. Over the years, I have observed that injustice significantly influenced my life decisions.

Human-dog conflicts are a contentious issue in Kerala, India, even today. As a 10-year-old in the early 2000s, I was shocked seeing a newspaper article about the scheduled mass culling of "*stray*" dogs. I told my mother about this. She swung to action and wrote to as many people as possible to stop the canicide. The scheduled killing was called off much like in the animated film *Isle of Dogs* (2019).

In 2010, reports of the clandestine killing of street dogs—also referred to as stray, free-ranging, or community dogs—surfaced. I was an undergraduate journalism major and an intern at a leading newspaper. I pitched the story idea to the editor who gave me three days to write an investigative report. With eye-witness accounts of killings, the article highlighted the consequences of the mass dog killings in Surat, Gujarat, in 1994 and its consequences. A plague outbreak occurred since the rat population increased, and the ecosystem was disrupted due to mass culling.

A few years later, the unprecedented Kerala floods took place in 2018, leading to loss of life, damage to infrastructure, and suffering. The disaster highlighted the lack of animal rescue and welfare preparedness and resources. As a volunteer at a rehabilitation center for dogs displaced by the floods, the categories collapsed—some were community animals, abandoned companion animals, and companion animals. The companion animals' guardians could not take them to shelters, yet to us, they were all flood-affected individuals.

DOI: 10.4324/9781003335528-20

During my interactions with activists, vets, and people interested in adopting flood-affected individuals in our care, I began to understand the process of social construction. Looking back at the history of human-dog conflicts in the region, I realized that the fear of dogs was connected to the fear of contracting rabies and dying a painful death.

Another significant factor was media framing. The media used and continue to use visual imagery of dogs frothing at the mouth or brandishing their teeth. It creates a sense of terror that remained largely unchallenged. This narrative modeled community behavior, reinforcing stereotypes and misinformation. It led to an aversion to all dogs, especially those incorrectly labeled "rabid street dogs." In part due to this fear, community dogs were often hungry, scorned, uncared for, shooed away from most spaces, and unwelcomed. The fear stemmed from an anthropocentric approach and was veiled as disgust.

The floods, and later the Covid-19 pandemic, highlighted several systemic challenges. Rapid urbanization, growing population, and crunch for space have further skewed the power dynamics between humans and animals. Community dogs were viewed as a collective responsibility of the community. In India, in the absence of government-run animal shelters, the responsibility falls on engaged communities, NGOs, and volunteers to tend to them, a minuscule percentage of the population.

A germane experience of rescuing a puppy, at age 18, who was nearly hit by a car, helped me put idealism into action. Bringing her home, and nursing her back to health, challenged my mindset about "companion" and "community dogs." While I had always expressed an interest in the canines, I began looking for ways to advocate on their behalf.

I realized the possibility of applying Animal Ethics and situating my doctoral study within Animal Studies. Working on an unconventional subject was met with skepticism and stereotypical anthropocentric assertions. I was often asked—when there is human suffering, why focus on animals? However, these experiences reinforced my resolve to work harder and bring to light the systemic oppression that harms nonhumans, humans, and the environment.

Taking an unconventional route also meant that employment remains a challenge. Some options include academic positions, alternative academic positions (alt-ac) positions, and nonprofits. As an alt academic, I work as a Project Manager and continue to explore Animal Studies and advocate for animal welfare and how it contributes to the One Health approach. Like most researchers, my interest drives research, but I have identified spaces where these ideas are heard, not summarily dismissed.

I remember being told that the only way to make a significant difference in the lives of nonhumans is to work full-time in a hands-on position. Over time, a single approach might not work and may instead require a combination of roles. While Animal Studies is at its nascent stage in India, through critical appraisal of film, I find it rewarding to highlight different animal rights issues through my work. It also indicates that Media Studies can play a role in communicating critical ideas related to One Health by leveraging popular culture.

Starting out as an activist, through my lived experience, as a person invested in animal welfare and rights, engaging at multiple levels, and forging my path has been satisfactory. To genuinely care for one's community, in the Indian context, also implies the need to nurture nonhuman communities since all our lives are interconnected. Community animals are a collective responsibility and keeping them healthy is vital to attain the goals of One Health.

19
EQUINE-ASSISTED SOCIAL WORK

A Perfect Match

Dana Spett

Horses help people connect with nature and connect with other people. The relationship between horse and human dates to 350 BCE, with evidence suggesting that a horse's skeleton has adapted to accommodate a human sitting astride (Kornei, 2020). Little did I know that growing up in the company of horses and caring for them daily would guide my life journey. I think horses are one of nature's guides and sometimes, nature's ride to connect with all living things: humans, non-human animals, and the environment.

I have had the privilege of being in the company of horses since I was five. From early childhood through middle school, horses supported my physical, emotional, and social development. This connection with horses continued through high school and university. Horses were and are an anchor that metaphorically grounds me in the universe. When social situations were marked by typical school drama, the horses in my life were always willing to show me compassion and empathy. Since horses don't use spoken language, my body language had to be measured to connect with the horses. Horses are clear communicators and strive to be balanced and safe.

My association with horses continued into my adulthood. I earned a master's in social work, married my partner, and gave birth to three incredible people. When one of my children, at the age of 2, was diagnosed with sensory integration dysfunction, she was enrolled and benefitted from traditional therapies. However, the benefits of conventional therapy stagnated, and I looked for alternative or complementary therapies to fill the gap. Research led me to therapeutic riding. I immediately worked toward my Equine-Assisted Services (EAS) certification as a Therapeutic Riding Instructor (PATH International, 2022). With background training in social work ethics, practice, and early childhood development, I put my young daughter on a horse.

DOI: 10.4324/9781003335528-21

Ultimately, my daughter's sensory diet was enriched and filled, and her needs were met. What began as a difficult time for a young mother heralded the next phase in my life journey: discovering how horses, within social work practice, can help people.

While the impetus for certification as a Therapeutic Riding Instructor was personal, I quickly saw the potential for much more and started a nonprofit center in the northern suburb of New York City. Initially, this program began with one rider, my daughter. We quickly grew from a small group of riders from the surrounding community to 40 riders. One program horse named Matt was soon joined by a second named Muffin and then a third named Panda. It was clear that horses helping people were not just of interest to my immediate family and that social work practice could be improved by including a horse in the treatment plan. It was humbling to learn that interacting with horses transcended all stages of life: as a young child, an adolescent, a teen, a parent, and older adult (I even worked with my father as his Alzheimer's advanced). What was so effective about the horse-human connection?

To begin, I recall the difference between working with clients in my early social work career, primarily children, in a traditional office setting (flat and stressful) versus working with a client outdoors, in nature, guided by horses (alive, experiential, dynamic). I remember watching children walk into my community center office. Their body language was obvious – "I don't want to be here, and I don't want to speak with this person (me)". I also vividly recall my physiological response, something like

> This poor child does not want to be sitting across a desk from me, an adult, and how am I going to get them to speak and how were they going to find the words to accurately reflect what their developing brains were experiencing?

These were stressful times for all. Being housed in a community center, I did try to complement traditional talk therapy with playing basketball, hoping words would follow. I am almost 5 feet 2 inches (on a good day) and cannot play basketball. Yet, even so, the game helped. However, I am a horse-centric person and a nature lover. Bringing my practice outdoors with a horse as a model on how to authentically connect with a client felt natural to me. This was an inflection point in my career. If I could connect with clients more naturally through moving around a court, what would treatment look and feel like out in nature, guided by horses? This simple question is my north star.

Social work is predicated on being of service. Authentic connections must ground genuine service. According to the NASW Code of Ethics (National Association of Social Workers, n.d.) and supported by international and global social work codes of ethics (International Association of Schools of Social Work, n.d.; United Nations, n.d.), being of service includes principles related to social justice; right to self-determination, dignity, and worth; and the importance of relationships – all facilitated by competent social workers with integrity. But the connection sits at the genesis and horses help humans connect.

Catharina Carlsson, a social work researcher from Sweden, explored the concept of equine-assisted practice, especially as it relates to the authentic connections that are revealed when a horse is added to treatment (Carlsson et al., 2014). Carlsson suggested that these connections between horses and humans are not based on language or spoken words. Instead, these relationships are based on non-verbal communication between living beings. For example, "are you safe; do you come in peace?" This is the core lesson from nature: "How do I secure basic needs such as food, water, shelter and live in peace?" We are all members of one large system. We must pay attention and listen to our gut or our instinct. At this intersection, there is a greater chance of authentic connection and understanding between humans, animals, and the environment.

Fast forward 20 years from earning my EAS certification and seeing the impact on the thousands who have come to our farm, I wanted to dive deeper into the empirical data around EAS and specifically explore social worker-facilitated EAS. At the age of 54, I applied and was accepted into The Doctor of Social Work (DSW) cohort of 2023 at Rutgers University, The State University of New Jersey. I wanted to supplement the anecdotal data I had been gathering and help demonstrate that horses make the best social work partners.

The overarching benefit of including horses in social work practice is the space and place where sessions occur (Moshe-Grodofsky & Allassad Alhuzail, 2022). Moving from a traditional therapy setting in an office or building, into the outdoors, in nature, guided by horses, serves as a social catalyst. Each party is stimulated by the sounds of nature, the movement, and the connection. This is known as the biophilia hypothesis, which suggests that humans have a biological imperative to relate to nature (Kellert & Wilson, 1995). In Japan, this is referred to as Shin Rin Yuki, translated to Forest Bathing to improve health and wellness (Payne & Delphinus, 2019).

I stand on the shoulders of those who have come before me. There is no secret to the innumerable benefits of human connection to nature and, more specifically, to horses. My career path is built on a solid foundation. By adding to the growing body of scholarly literature, I hope to serve as a catalyst for broader acceptance of equine-assisted social work for all interested.

References

Carlsson, C., Nilsson Ranta, D., & Traeen, B. (2014). Equine-Assisted Social Work as a Means for Authentic Relations between Clients and Staff. *Human-Animal Interaction Bulletin*. CABI International. doi: 10.1079/hai.2014.0004

International Association of Schools of Social Work. (n.d.). IASSW Home. Retrieved January 31, 2023, from https://www.iassw-aiets.org/.

Kellert, S. R., & Wilson, E. O. (Eds.). (1995). *The Biophilia Hypothesis*. Island Press.

Kornei, K. (2020, November 13). A Record of Horse Back Riding, Written in Bone and Teeth. *New York Times*.

Moshe-Grodofsky, M., & Allassad Alhuzail, N. (2022). The Significance of Space: Experiences of Arab Social Work Professionals with EAGALA Equine-Assisted Learning. *The British Journal of Social Work*, 52(3), 1492–1510.

National Association of Social Workers. (n.d.). *NASW Home*. Retrieved January 31, 2023, from https://www.socialworkers.org/.

PATH International. (2022). *Therapeutic Horsemanship: Professional Certifications: PATH Intl*. Retrieved January 31, 2023, from http://www.pathintl.org/.

Payne, M. D., & Delphinus, E. (2019). A Review of the Current Evidence for the Health Benefits Derived from Forest Bathing. *International Journal of Health, Wellness & Society*, 9(1).

United Nations. (n.d.). *The 17 Goals | Sustainable Development*. Retrieved January 31, 2023, from https://sdgs.un.org/goals.

SECTION III
Animal-Assisted Interventions

20
THE POWER OF PAWS

Working Full-Time in Animal-Assisted Interactions

Katherine Compitus

I have always felt a kinship toward animals and had the good fortune of growing up with parents who nurtured this connection. I grew up in Manhattan, the center of New York City, where interactions with the natural world are limited. However, the area in which I lived was located on hundreds of acres of green space – one of the largest parks in the city. There I was surrounded by trees, flowers, birds, and squirrels. I shared my room with my younger sister and our cats, gerbils, fish, guinea pigs, and bunny rabbits. In the summers, I would go to sleepaway camp where I enjoyed riding horses, and during the rest of the year, I would travel out of the city to visit friends who lived in more rural areas or by the beach. I found that wherever I went, I would connect with animals immediately, and although I always enjoyed my friends, I felt more comfortable in the company of the family pets and would spend hours watching and interacting (and occasionally rescuing) local fauna. As I went forward in my academic career, first obtaining a MSEd to work as an elementary school teacher, then an MSW and MA in Animal Behavior and Conservation, I noticed the similarities between behaviors, cognitions, and drives of all animals (including humans) and felt drawn to help vulnerable populations of all species.

When working on my MSW, I made sure to seek out opportunities that allowed me to study human-animal interactions. I conducted animal-assisted therapy (AAT) with pediatric patients and older adults as an intern at the Hospital for Joint Diseases in New York City and then later worked as a grief counselor for pet loss as an intern at one of the city's largest veterinary hospitals. I also became certified with several agencies as an animal trainer and I worked in force-free training with psychiatric service dogs. Around the same time, my husband and I opened a dog daycare facility in Manhattan where

DOI: 10.4324/9781003335528-23

we focused on positive animal welfare and force-free interaction between people and their pets. I completed my MSW and worked for several years as a clinical social worker – in the psychiatric emergency department at a local hospital, at a family clinic, at a school. In each position, with most of my clients, I found that everyone had something animal-related to talk about – their pets or the animals they saw in nature. I hypothesized that the human-animal bond is a universal trait, a desire to connect with the natural world. It is an affinity that all people are likely born with and it can only be erased through cultural learning or severe neglect of a person's emotional needs.

I eventually pursued and completed my doctorate in clinical social work (DSW) at NYU, focusing on the importance of the human-animal bond. I wrote often about the support and hope that we receive from our animal companions and that it is, sadly, a strength that is often ignored by mental health and physical health practitioners. I set out to change people's minds and show them that the unconditional love and lack of judgment that we receive from our pets is often what we find lacking in human relationships. As such, it is a strong bond that can improve people's mental, physical, and social well-being and can be quite disruptive when broken. I eventually founded Surrey Hills Sanctuary, a non-profit micro-farm sanctuary that is dedicated to researching the human-animal bond and how we may best enhance this bond for ourselves and for our clients.

I now work as a professor at NYU's Silver School of Social Work, where I teach about human behavior, direct psychotherapy practice, and a very popular course that I created about the human-animal bond in all its manifestations. This includes pet owners in a myriad of situations: experiencing homelessness, in an interpersonal violence situation, or having suffered a natural or man-made disaster. I discuss how to implement animal-assisted interactions (AAI) and AAT and how to counsel someone who is grieving the death of a beloved pet. Aside from my teaching responsibilities, I have a private animal-assisted psychotherapy practice and I also am the president of our farm sanctuary.

Each morning, I wake up to the sound of my roosters greeting the day. It's a beautiful and hopeful sound that always reminds me of new beginnings. I spend the first few hours of each day feeding and caring for the cows, pigs, chickens, dogs, cats, pigeons, quail, and other animals at the sanctuary. It's time intensive, but it's so important to spend time with each animal. I then return to my desk and work at my teaching duties, planning for my AAT client work, or planning my research, which currently includes a study of "cow cuddling" (the benefits of large farm animal-human interactions). My cow cuddling research involves inviting people to the sanctuary and providing them with various ways to interact with our two steers, Magnus and Callum. We then ask them to provide feedback by filling out a survey about how they felt when they interacted with the steers and how they believed the cows responded to the interaction. Animal welfare is paramount when working with AAI/AAT, so the cows are never forced into this interaction but are invited to participate. They always enjoy the company and have not yet met a person that they didn't like! As for my private practice, I used to work in person, but now primarily work via teletherapy. This means that I miss out on some of the benefits of AAI/AAT such as the tactile connection between a client and the therapy animal, but it means that I can involve more animals in my practice. My cats always seem to make an appearance during sessions, as well as my dogs and I have the opportunity to (virtually) meet my clients' pets, something that would not have been possible without teletherapy.

AAI and AAT offer a diverse range of options for social workers to incorporate into their practice. From equine-assisted psychotherapy to canine-assisted crisis response, there are many different animal species and intervention modalities that can be tailored to meet the unique needs and goals of individual clients. Social workers can work with trained animals and their handlers to provide a variety of AAI/AAT services to clients across a wide range of settings, including mental health clinics, schools, hospitals, and community organizations.

The best advice that I can give clinicians who are interested in AAI and AAT is to learn about positive training, animal welfare, and animal behavior science. We must remember that this should be a mutually beneficial and respectful relationship and the animal's needs must be considered at all times. I encourage all clinicians to take classes in force-free, science-based animal training; it is invaluable to understand the body language and needs of the therapy animal. We must remember that the therapy animals that we work with are our partners – we never "use" them, but instead we include them, and they help facilitate our work. We should always follow the "Golden Rule" when working with animals – and treat them as we would want to be treated ourselves – while still respecting their species-specific needs.

The best part of working with animals in an AAT practice is when the animals come running to greet me, or call out to me or do a "happy dance" when they see me. I also feel incredibly satisfied when an AAI benefits a human client. My clients have reported that spending time with large and yet gentle animals, such as cows, has given them the perspective to realize that sometimes they think something is huge and important and scary until they face it and then they realize that it is well within their control. My clients can practice a variety of skills when working with the animals, including distress tolerance, mindfulness (as modeled by the animals), and can even practice interpersonal skills in a nonthreatening way. I have found that people are more willing and able to talk about distressing and traumatic events when there is an animal present in the room, since a therapy animal often provides clients a relationship of unconditional care and lack of judgment – two things that we rarely find in our relationships with other humans.

The biggest challenge in working with animals is that AAI is an adaptive and adjunctive modality and, as such, can easily be adapted for any client and any situation. This means that a clinician must have solid knowledge of the ways that AAI/AAT could be implemented and must learn about best practices. I always encourage clinicians who are interested in AAI/AAT to read as much as they can about the subject and to reach out to others who are already working in the field. The more we learn about AAI/AAT, the more we can help other clinicians succeed in their own AAI/AAT practice. Another frustrating aspect of this work is the lack of knowledge of the efficacy and benefits of AAI/AAT by clinicians who are not familiar with our scope of practice. Finally, there is a dearth of internships or training opportunities for clinicians to learn in vivo how to implement AAI/AAT. We need to create more positions so that people are not running blindly into this field.

There are several ways that AAI and AAT can be incorporated into schools, volunteering, and research. One way to incorporate AAI into schools is to invite therapy animals and their handlers to visit the school to provide animal-assisted activities for students such as animal-assisted reading programs, where students can read aloud to therapy animals. This can help improve reading skills, build confidence, and promote a positive attitude toward reading or providing stress. Another way is to implement AAT programs for students who may benefit from these interventions, such as those with anxiety, depression, or behavioral issues. In addition, incorporating animal-assisted education can be a fun way to teach students about animal care, biology, and other topics.

Outside of the school system, those who are interested in AAI can volunteer with a variety of organizations that provide AAI services, such as hospitals, nursing homes, and community centers. Volunteers can help with animal care, assist with therapy sessions, or provide support for animal-assisted activities. There is also a growing body of research on the effectiveness of AAI and AAT. Those interested in this field can contribute to this research by conducting studies on the impact of AAI on various populations, such as children with autism or seniors with dementia. Researchers can also explore the mechanisms by which these interventions work and identify ways to improve their effectiveness. Overall, incorporating AAI and AAT into schools, volunteering, and research can help promote the benefits of these interventions and improve the lives of those who participate in them.

In order to find a job in this field, since there are such limited job positions that formally list AAI as an accepted and utilized treatment model, I strongly encourage clinicians to create their own paths. If they are working at a hospital, as I was, they can become involved in the therapy animal program. They could reach out to Pet Partners, Therapy Dogs International, or another therapy animal agency and become a certified therapy animal handler or team (with their therapy animal). They can help create and implement new programs when they see a gap in services or they can volunteer for an existing AAI agency, such as Puppies Behind Bars or A Fair Shake for Youth (children reading to dogs).

This is an incredibly rewarding and awe-inspiring field. I have learned as much from the animals as I have from my clients about the importance of strong, supportive relationships. The human-animal bond provides a significant number of psychological, physical, and social benefits. AAI, in all its various manifestations, allows us to explore and examine and utilize those benefits to their fullest potential. I am so very glad that I entered this field because I have seen people heal from horrible pain and suffering, just through simple interactions with another species. I love my job and I cannot imagine doing anything else. Nothing is more rewarding than to be able to help both people and animals.

21

ANIMAL-ASSISTED PSYCHOTHERAPY

Integrating "Canine Co-Therapists" into Clinical Social Work Outpatient Treatment Settings

Laurel Gray Robbins

Where I Fit into the Human Animal Interaction (HAI) Field?

I am a Clinician (Therapist) and Supervisor at Vermont Center for Resiliency. This is a trauma-informed outpatient therapy group-practice. I work collaboratively with children, adolescents, and adults to help them feel more grounded, resilient, and connected to themselves and their communities. I specialize in supporting people with anxiety/depression needs and am especially passionate about working with folks who are seeking a provider with LGBTQIA+ Lived Experience. I have three "canine co-therapists" who rotate at the office to provide animal-assisted psychotherapy/therapy with me.

My Story

I grew up with a mother who loved children and animals. I am the oldest of seven children and we are a beautiful rainbow mosaic of biological kids, adopted kids and kids of different colors. We had dogs, cats, rabbits, a horse, gerbils, chinchillas, a hedgehog, lovebirds, and a revolving door of wildlife animals we were rehabilitating (an opossum, a raccoon, and a turkey are most memorable). This is where I learned the power of caring for—and being cared for by—animals.

Based on my love for animals, everyone in my life assumed I would grow up to work in zoology or the veterinary field. As I moved into adolescence and wrestled with my own identity—I leaned on the deep, safe, and nurturing relationships I had with our pets for acceptance and support.

During this stormy period of my life, I realized I wanted to help other people to find anchors in their own storms. I started shifting my career goals from veterinary medicine toward social work. During college, I worked in a Residential Crisis Stabilization Program for adolescents. There were therapy dog-handler teams that would come to the program to visit. It was miraculous to see how these often were able to reach "defiant and explosive" kids and teens who responded enthusiastically and gently to opportunities to engage with the therapy dog. It was a light-bulb moment! This might be the way to weave together my love for animals—and strong belief in their healing powers—with my interest in clinical mental health training.

After graduating with my Master's in Social Work (MSW), I practiced as a school social worker at Pre-K–eighth grade school for five years and got my clinical licensure (LICSW). I had the opportunity to do program development and incorporate AAT/AAI into my school social work role before transitioning to working in outpatient therapy.

What Is the Work Like?

An important part of successfully incorporating therapy dogs (AAI) into my school social work role was working collaboratively with the student support school team (administrators, principals, special education, nurse, school counselors). This included conversations about liability (making sure my dog was trained, certified/registered as a therapy dog, that I had liability insurance coverage), that allergies and cultural sensitivities were considered, and agreeing to start with a small trial pilot program.

I slowly and intentionally was able to increase the scope of my AAI work at school to share the power of therapy dogs with more of the student and staff community. Within six months of starting a therapy dog pilot program, I was able to start utilizing AAI more broadly. This included individual counseling sessions with students, in anxiety social skills group counseling, and in classroom settings to support wellness and connection opportunities for all students.

Positive Aspects (Energizing, Cup Filling, Bright Spots in the Work)

I love to learn and grow and have new opportunities; I know I get bored and antsy if I do the same thing every day. In addition to the social justice values, this is a big part of why a MSW was the perfect mental health degree for me. A MSW basically says, "I work well with people"—and then you can apply that to types of work. It makes space for you to have pivots within your professional life without having to pursue (and pay) for additional schooling. So, if you are someone who knows they are passionate about helping others—and also know that they thrive when getting to flex different skills and brain and heart muscles—an MSW might be right for you too!

Challenges (Potential Hurdles and Stuck Places)

Direct social work practice is powerful, healing, and meaningful; it can also be challenging and draining at times. There is an emotional toll that comes with holding space for other people's challenges, stressors, needs, and trauma. The National Association of Social Workers has recently added Self-Care to the Professional Competencies due to the risk of compassion fatigue/burnout for Social Workers. We now have a professional and ethical obligation to find ways to take care of ourselves personally and professionally. I find self-care and Rejuvenation in nature and with Movement; so I make sure I "walk the walk" and get out in the woods to refuel and play. I also know I need to be connected to my community and that having other meaningful interactions outside my work life nourishes me.

Our therapy animals can be at risk of burnout too. An important part of the growing HAI field is being thoughtful about animal welfare. This includes making sure we are not overworking our animals and that they are enjoying the work. This is why I now have three rotating therapy dogs so they get ample breaks. This is something to think about before building your professional practice around AAI: how will you make sure the animal(s) can get the rest—and play—they need and deserve?

Thinking About This Path?

I know that when I had my light-bulb wondering-about-therapy-dogs-as-a-social-work-practice-model moment, I was desperately seeking "a Trail Map" or guide to set out on this HAI adventure. This book offers one way to gather some trail map options and decide which tools you want to add to your toolkit (or adventure pack if you prefer) in this field.

22
ANIMAL-ASSISTED THERAPY IN CLINICAL WORK WITHIN THE DISABILITY COMMUNITY

Tiffany Banks

Introduction

I knew from an early age that I wanted to be a social worker. Growing up below the poverty line in a single parent household alongside a sibling on the autism spectrum greatly impacted my decision to pursue a career in social work. When I graduated with my MSW in 2009, I had big dreams of a clinical career in which I would have opportunities to incorporate my hobbies and passions for the arts. I began my career utilizing creative art therapies such as psychodrama and drum circle facilitation to reach young autistic people and form therapeutic connections. After moving out west, my passion for creative art therapies gave way to a new passion, animal-assisted interventions (AAI). I soon found myself immersed in training and observations to become a certified AAI team with my canine companion, Abe. Abe and I have had the privilege to work together as colleagues within three different settings: schools, research, and private practice.

There are two forms of AAI that Abe and I provided in these various setting. AAI is an umbrella term that describes the use of a therapy animal team to benefit the wellness of humans. Within the field of AAI, we recognize the differences between animal-assisted therapy (AAT) and animal-assisted activities (AAA). AAT is a goal-oriented intervention that is guided by a licensed professional, which can include occupational therapy, mental health treatment, physical therapy, or speech therapy. Whereas AAA is non-goal-oriented and does not require the presence of a licensed professional. A great example of AAA in action are hospital visitation programs where the presence of animals has been shown to have benefits to recovery and emotional wellbeing.

DOI: 10.4324/9781003335528-25

AAT in Schools

When I worked in school settings, Abe and I had opportunities to support children and school staff members in different ways. I used my clinical judgment as to which children within the school could benefit from direct, one-on-one AAT. His presence in the school was well received as a form of AAA as well. From staff meetings to classroom visits, Abe was a popular addition to the special service provider team.

AAT in Research

As I transitioned from school-based social work to working in a hospital setting, my relationship with AAI changed as well. I no longer worked alongside Abe, my companion animal, but instead I had access to a team of facility animals and volunteer AAI teams through the hospital. This indirect model allowed me to focus specifically on the child, while a handler focused on their dog's safety and wellbeing. During this time, I worked in an inpatient psychiatric unit specially designed for children with neurodivergent identities. Facility canines could be requested through Child Life, and traditional AAI teams could be requested through the volunteer office. I had the experience of engaging in AAT with facility dogs and the experience of conducting research alongside volunteer teams (Germone et al., 2019).

AAT in Private Practice

I began working in private practice around the same time that I decided to return to school to pursue a doctoral education in social work. In private practice, the model returned to a triad, with me, the clinician, having responsibility over both the client and Abe again. This work requires a social worker to be able to focus on multiple streams of information at once and certainly is not a model suited for all clinicians.

Lessons Learned and Shared

One of the most important lessons I have learned on this journey is to always ask. Being the first school social worker in a rural community and the first animal-assisted therapist within that same school district taught me the importance of trying new things. I would have never had those opportunities had I not put myself in the vulnerable position of asking my supervisors about integrating Abe into my clinical work. Part of this process includes preparing yourself for these conversations with administrators and backing up your ask with information and data to support the request. Starting a new program requires not only doing your research on the efficacy and feasibility of AAI but also understanding the risks and limitations of this model. For example, in addition to the support of my administrators, I also had to do some research to ensure that I was covered appropriately by my malpractice insurance.

Another important aspect of AAI to consider is the importance of boundaries when engaging your own canine companion into your social work practice. It is essential to remember that therapy animals are pets and not as specially trained as facility dogs and service animals. On days when Abe does work, I limit time providing AAT and the rest of his day is spent passively doing AAA. It is essential to remember that this work is not for every animal. During my six-month certification process, I was taught to pay close attention to what Abe was communicating to me through his body language. This was accomplished through one-on-one coaching from my AAT trainer during three 1-hour long observation sessions. As an AAT team member, it is my job to ensure Abe's safety and wellbeing during his therapeutic experiences.

Reference

Germone, M. M., Gabriels, R. L., Guérin, N. A., Pan, Z., Banks, T., & O'Haire, M. E. (2019). Animal-Assisted Activity Improves Social Behaviors in Psychiatrically Hospitalized Youth with Autism. *Autism*, *23*(7), 1740–1751.

23
PAWS IN PLAY
The Power of Integrating Animals into Play Therapy Practice

Michelle Pliske

Introduction

"These therapy dogs can do anything!" Six-year-old Brian exclaimed as he stood next to his fellow knight, the Golden Retriever named Apollo, who valiantly held a foam sword in his mouth and prepared to defend the castle. Brian was initially referred into counseling from a local forensic interviewing agency due to suspected physical and sexual abuse. Much of Brian's work centered on creating a trauma narrative, integrating his emotions with an age-appropriate understanding of the abuse. He never spoke of his experiences to previous therapists, investigators, or helping professionals. However, he did confide in Apollo, telling his experience to a trusted friend, confidant, and protector. This trust in Apollo eventually supported and enabled Brian to tell his story to local police and child advocates. This is the power of animal-assisted interventions woven into play therapy practice activating therapeutic change.

Social work is a profession which offers the ability to work at every level of intervention from one-on-one support to community-based practice or macro-level social policy. I find children have the capacity for great insight but often need to share their stories through toys and art. A child's story often holds beautiful and agonizing truths capturing our collective humanity. My clinical practice initially fused social work counseling theories and play therapy while honoring the relationship between a social worker and client. However, my clinical practice transformed following a partnership with two therapy dogs, Apollo and Mercury. These dogs created a new responsiveness through the human-animal bond harnessing empathy as a bridge for presence and awareness to support children navigating their trauma stories.

DOI: 10.4324/9781003335528-26

Training for Partnering with Animals in Play Therapy Practice

Animal-assisted counseling utilizing play therapy practice requires a graduate degree in a counseling profession. Psychology, professional counseling, marriage and family therapy, and social work are all examples of counseling professions to prepare a mental health professional for engaging children in practice. I recommend any professional interested in animal-assisted human health first attend a program which grounds them in foundational theories for counseling psychology. Understanding the framework of theory will prepare a student for incorporating and fusing animal-assisted interventions into therapy.

Play Therapy Studies

I encourage graduate school internships, ideally within child and family therapy settings with a field instructor who has a background in play therapy studies, as a beginning foundation. Post-graduate professionals can connect with the Association for Play Therapy to begin training and clinical supervision in play therapy studies. Reputable play therapy programs will provide a rationale for their curriculum and/or be endorsed by a credentialing body. The Association for Play Therapy is a good example of a credentialing body providing clear rigor and educational oversight. Students can also find providers of play therapy who hold advanced training and credentialing in animal-assisted human health. These trainings will offer the combined art of animal-assisted play therapy.

Animal-Assisted Counseling Studies

Animal-assisted human health programs are available through universities or private institutions which support learning in animal-assisted counseling studies. Practitioners should select an animal-assisted counseling program with curriculum that supports learning in zoonotic infection control policies, the interpretation of animal behavior, cues of distress, animal welfare ethics, and methods for intervention to manage animal partners while supporting therapeutic goals for client success. Selection of the therapy animal will be dependent on the handler and the workplace setting. Practitioners learn within their training programs how to select animals for their specific roles and work setting and support the training of the animal to be successful in their career.

A Typical Therapy Day Honoring Animal Welfare and Ethics

Therapy dogs, like their human partners, can experience overwhelm, compassion fatigue, and burnout associated with this profession. I learned working with Apollo how much children trusted him and that he was greatly missed when he needed a day off. It is important to prepare children and families for ethical care of the animal who requires off days from work. However, working with two therapy dogs can support alternating the days and times when dogs are working. Staggering the dog's work schedules can provide ample days off for rest and recovery, while still providing coverage for clients and families seeking services. I consider the strengths of the animal and therapeutic relationship between the animal and the children during the week and strategically schedule my days accordingly. Every day includes scheduled breaks for rest, play, or a walk. Therapy dogs should have 'recess' time during the day for relaxation and rejuvenation.

Rewards and Challenges of Animal-Assisted Therapy

The most rewarding aspect of this work is seeing the animal and client develop a deep connection. The unconditional positive regard and authentic joy of the therapy dogs with their children creates a bright light in the day. Parents comment that the dog's presence fills them with a renewed capacity for holding onto hope. One of the more challenging aspects of this work is associated with the retirement of an animal. I deeply respect Apollo and his work, but recently retired him from therapy due to a medical need. Clients grieved the loss of his companionship and company. The handler is responsible for setting the boundary when it is not safe or ethical for the therapy animal to continue working. However, I posit the challenge of retiring a dog can be approached therapeutically. Children can learn how to say goodbye to the ones they love. Although there is therapeutic value in the process of goodbyes, that process doesn't come without sorrow.

I advise practitioners interested in working with children and animals to pay close attention to their own self-care needs for burnout and vicarious traumatization prevention. The field of child and family therapy asks mental health practitioners to bear witness to unimaginable pain and suffering in our smallest humans. The animal will undoubtedly perceive the stress and distress of their handler in addition to the client they are serving. Self-care will be required for both ends of the leash to be successful in this work.

24
"THE WORLD IS BEST VIEWED THROUGH THE EARS OF A HORSE" MY CAREER IN EQUINE-ASSISTED SERVICES

Mary Acri

As someone who has always had a deep connection with animals, I never imagined I would be able to pursue a fulfilling research career in animal-assisted therapy. I began my journey with a Master of Social Work from New York University, and three years later, started my doctorate degree in clinical social work, also at New York University. I am currently a mental health services researcher at one of two child and adolescent psychiatry departments in the United States. Over the past 15 years, I have built a research portfolio focused on reducing mental health inequities through developing and examining innovative programs that could detect, treat, and engage children and families with unmet mental health needs. Ten years ago, animal-assisted therapy was not on my radar, but through a convergence of experiences, both personal and professional, in which animals were pivotal players in human emotional health and wellbeing, my interest in this field was ignited.

In January of 2015, the U.S. Department of Justice contacted the lab I worked in (the New York University Center for Implementation-Dissemination of Evidence-based Practices Among States [The IDEAS Center]), requesting that we work with the Town of Newtown, Connecticut (the site of the tragic Sandy Hook Elementary School shooting), to assist in developing a plan to redesign and sustain the community's services for the future. It was here that I first encountered a structured and evidence-based use of emotional support canines to treat and reduce the child survivors' distress.

My fascination with the role of animals to treat emotional distress evolved to include the exploration of animals, specifically equines, in the therapeutic space. This led to being part of a group of researchers and equestrians who developed and tested Reining in Anxiety (RiA), a ten-week equine-assisted service (EAS) with cognitive behavioral therapy (CBT) elements (Acri et al.,

2021). This program has since been found to reduce anxiety and improve emotional self-efficacy in children 6–17 years of age in two pilot studies (Hoagwood et al., 2022, in press).

More recently, we have been interested in safeguarding the welfare of the animals used in mental health services research and practice by utilizing a "spit bit" to collect horses' salivary samples to detect oxytocin and cortisol levels as an indicator of stress during the intervention (Vincent et al., 2021). To be involved in this work, which is groundbreaking, is incredibly exciting. It is similar in my mind to uncovering an archeological find, uncovering the multiple facets of EAS, including mechanisms of change and impact to both human and equine.

My day-to-day work schedule consists of collaborative work with colleagues who are equally passionate about EAS and contributing to the knowledge base to assemble projects, presentations, grants, and manuscripts. Being exposed to the diverse perspectives of researchers, veterinarians, and the individuals on the ground who know the benefits of EAS first-hand is incredibly rewarding and provides me with many learning opportunities. An ongoing source of concern, however, is the lack of funding to conduct research on the benefits of EAS. Because it is such a revolutionary approach, we are repeatedly trying to disseminate knowledge about this topic but are limited in how much we can achieve given limited funding opportunities.

There is a vast future for this field and now is a very exciting time to be involved in EAS. Primarily, standardizing language and instrumentation across EAS can help streamline research and practice; universal measures have yet to be developed that can capture the relationship between the human and the animal. Another critical point of research is the mechanism of change by which the therapy works and why it works – what is occurring nonverbally during these riding services that cause a decrease in anxiety symptoms? Finally, it is incredibly important to not neglect the service animal itself. We, as human beings, exploit systems for our own need, but we need to make sure we are protecting the animals' welfare and understand how they are being impacted by service delivery.

For readers interested in this area, either as practitioners or researchers, there are multiple organizations at the national level that offer training opportunities, information, and resources. In addition to the American Psychological Association Division 17 Section on Human Animal Interaction, Research & Practice, there are several universities that have centers in human-animal interactions, including the University of Arizona's College of Veterinary Medicine and Colorado State University's Human-Animal Bond in Colorado (HABIC) within their School of Social Work. Finally, attending conferences, including the Centers for Human-Animal Bond Conference through Purdue University, can foster connections and collaborations, ensuring that the field continues to build its research base and practices.

Based on my career path, it is clear that new interests can be sparked at any point throughout one's academic and professional journey. I never predicted that animal-assisted therapy would be a direction I would pursue, but now I cannot see my career without its influences. My biggest piece of advice to those pursuing research careers within HAI is to surround yourself with people who are creative, supportive, and flexible, so that when your research interests evolve to take on new directions (because believe me, they will), your team will endorse and encourage you.

References

Acri, M., Morrissey, M., Peth-Pierce, R., Seibel, L., Seag, D., Hamovitch, E.K., Guo, F., Horwitz, S., Hoagwood, K.E. (2021). An equine-assisted therapy for youth with mild to moderate anxiety: Manual development and fidelity. *Journal of Child and Family Studies*, 30, 2461–2467.

Hoagwood, K.E., Acri, M., Morrissey, M., Peth-Pierce, R., Seibel, L., Seag, D., Guo, F., Hamovitch, E.K., & Horwitz, S. (2022). A cognitive-behavioral equine-assisted intervention for youth with anxiety: Results of an exploratory randomized controlled study. *Human Animal Interaction Bulletin: Special Issue*, 9(3), 60–78.

Hoagwood, K., Vincent, A., Acri, M., Morrissey, M., Seibel, L., Guo, F., Flores, C., Peth-Pierce, R., & Horwitz, S. (in press). Reducing anxiety and stress among youth in a CBT-based equine-assisted adaptive riding program. *Animals*, 12(19), 2491.

Vincent, A., Peth-Pierce, R.M., Morrissey, M.A., Acri, M.C., Guo, F., Seibel, L., & Hoagwood, K.E. (2021). Evaluation of a modified bit device to obtain saliva samples from horses. *Veterinary Sciences*, 8(10), 232–238.

25
PAWS FOR PLAY
Dogs in Play Therapy

Lucy Llewellyn

Growing up in rural South Wales, UK, animals were my childhood companions. I have always appreciated how the presence of animals has supported me during dark and difficult times, as well as bring so much joy to my life. After leaving school, I trained to work with children, became a social worker, then undertook a Postgraduate Diploma in Non-Directive Play Therapy (BAPT).

I knew I wanted to involve animals in my therapeutic work. After a fortuitous meeting with Dr Risë VanFleet in 2004, I discovered a fellow professional with a shared interest. Risë introduced me to the world of Animal Assisted Play Therapy™ (AAPT), a training program she had been working on for years with Tracie Faa-Thompson. This was what I had been waiting for, so I attended the first AAPT training with my dogs, Freya and Lykke. Then, I worked my way up to become a Certified Animal Assisted Play Therapist™, continuing to instructor and supervisor level. The AAPT approach can be used with a variety of species, I work with my dog, Lykke.

Lykke, a rescue lurcher, became a great asset in the playroom and joined me in child-centered play therapy sessions. She has a very sweet, playful, quirky nature and just loves being around young people. Although I occasionally took her into the Mental Health clinic (CAMHS) with me, our main work was in our home playroom where we would provide AAPT for children/young people who had experienced loss, abuse, and developmental trauma. Many of these children, without Lykke's presence, were guarded due to their previous life experiences and struggled to form healthy relationships. With Lykke's presence, they were able to engage in play with her, forming an attachment first with her which then seemed to generalize to me and others in their network. I had a 6-year-old tell me, "Lykke would never let you hurt

DOI: 10.4324/9781003335528-28

me," revealing Lykke's role in helping him feel safe and therefore more receptive to therapy.

The advantage of working within the home playroom was that Lykke could choose whether to engage in the therapy work or to leave the room. Although rare, these occasions would occur if the play became too noisy. The child could choose to change their play if they wanted her to stay, experiencing reciprocity in relationships.

I would recommend people get training before taking their animals into a work environment. Our clients can be challenging at the best of times, so facilitating a therapeutic approach with a client and animal together takes practice and skill, to ensure it is safe, mutually beneficial, and enjoyable for all. I trained with the International Institute of Animal Assisted Play Therapy® (www.iiaapt.org). I chose their program as the welfare of the animal is paramount. Activities are geared toward the dogs' personality as well as the clients' therapy goals. It is an experiential, immersive course followed by supervision. Certification is based on demonstrated competence of adhering to the principles of AAPT. I thoroughly enjoyed the training; I am continually learning and love that I get to share it with others.

Being part of facilitating and observing the developing partnerships between my dog and young people has been incredibly rewarding. Working with my dog has meant sharing a personal part of my world with my clients – a glimpse into my life that's usually withheld, making a more genuine connection and therapeutic alliance. The therapy process seems to progress much quicker with an animal present.

My greatest challenge has been some of the practicalities – I developed my home playroom so Lykke could have freedom in sessions, it was a familiar environment for her, and she was not transported or crated in a clinical environment. Short working hours and proper rest are crucial for a therapy dog's wellbeing. Lykke only had two clients a week, and when not involved, she is a family pet.

When Lykke started showing signs of sound sensitivity, I needed to retire her, as some sounds became painful for her. I'm trained to observe my animals constantly, so I could see the start of flinching behavior in the way her ears/eyes moved, and her body would stiffen very slightly and move away. Although she would tolerate this – it was not a message I wanted my clients to hear – that "you have" to tolerate unpleasant experiences and not to have a voice. By advocating for Lykke, I was validating the rights we all have to say "NO" to something that we do not enjoy.

Lykke's retirement was a huge loss for me. I continued to practice as a play therapist and social worker until the time was right to introduce a new dog. I currently have a new rescue lurcher who may join me in therapy if it's right for him.

Before setting out to train, I'd recommend thinking about how you would like to involve your animal in your work. It can help to write a job description for the animal to clarify your thinking. Who is this animal? What do they like to do? Would they be a good "fit" and is this something that they would enjoy?

One of the major frustrations is that the field of AAT in most of the world is unregulated, so can be offered by anyone, regardless of qualifications.

I know AAPT has made me a highly skilled clinician and educator, whose work may involve animals in a planned, therapeutic intervention to enable my clients to meet their treatment goals. Being part of AAPT has given me a worldwide network of supportive colleagues. It's great to connect with others as we develop and explore new ways of working.

26

FINDING YOUR HAI NICHE

April Lang

"My dog got hit by a car while out with the new dog walker and it's my fault." "I can't get the footage of the pigs at the slaughterhouse out of my mind." "Now that my cat is gone, I feel lonely and sad every day." For clients who feel connected to non-human animals, these are heartbreaking experiences. For many of them, what compounds their grief is sharing their stories with therapists who do not seem to understand the reasons for their deep despair or worse, minimize it. I, along with several of my animal-loving colleagues, do understand and thus are able to provide a safe and welcoming space for these people. Becoming such a therapist was a journey and one that has been immensely rewarding.

When I first decided to become a psychotherapist in the late 1980s, it never occurred to me that a large part of my practice would be devoted to animal bereavement or to working with vegans and animal activists – so many of whom suffer from living in a world of institutionalized animal abuse and exploitation. Once I had obtained my BA in psychology and then my MSW, my goal was to someday have my own "general" private practice. I saw myself working primarily with people who were feeling anxious and depressed as well as helping couples navigate the complexities of their romantic partnerships. And for many years that was just what I did and I found it quite gratifying.

Then, about a decade ago, I began to look more critically at the work I was doing and the populations I was serving. As an animal mom and ethical vegan, I knew firsthand the pain that comes when our non-human family members die and I was also acutely aware of the intense sorrow that can come from living in a non-vegan world. When I would speak to like-minded friends and acquaintances about how they were dealing with these issues in

DOI: 10.4324/9781003335528-29

their own therapy, a common refrain began to emerge. Their therapists were intelligent, skilled, and compassionate but when speaking to them about animal-related subjects, there was a decided disconnect. "This is just how the world is" or "We need to look for the 'real' source of pain" were not uncommon responses from these clinicians and were often perceived as invalidating by my friends. Reflecting on what I was hearing, it dawned on me that there was a need for therapists who focused on these topics – therapists who "got" it, were knowledgeable about the issues being presented, and who unabashedly marketed themselves to animal-loving clients.

To say it was a "eureka" moment would be an exaggeration, but I did feel like I found a "specialty." Over the years, many of my colleagues had developed their own areas of expertise, but I must admit I was always at a loss to figure out what mine could be. Now, of course, it's not mandatory to have a specialty or area of focus to have a rewarding and successful practice. Nevertheless, I'm grateful that I found one and that it came about so organically. I am now able to help people who help animals, something that is both exciting and immensely satisfying!

Despite my passion in this area, some friends and colleagues cautioned me that this specialty might be viewed negatively by some people. I remember when I was creating my new website and I asked a good friend, a fellow vegan and activist, to help me. Much to my surprise, he told me that he was concerned the site was too "animal-centric" and might dissuade some potential clients from reaching out. I thought long and hard about what he said but ultimately trusted my intuition and decided to take that chance. If people didn't want to come to me for therapy because of my views, then they were welcome to seek a therapist who might better serve their needs. Of course, many of the people I've seen over the years have chosen me for issues totally unrelated to animals and we have worked well together. Thankfully nowadays there are many wonderful animal-loving clinicians who are offering similar work all around the world and are comfortable and proud saying so.

There's nothing better and more rewarding than knowing that the work you're doing is making a difference in someone's life and feeling that you've found your niche. This is not to say that it is all sunshine and flowers. It is not – especially when listening to some gut-wrenching stories of animal abuse and loss. The healer in me wants to alleviate the suffering of both the human and non-human animals. I want our mindsets and our social norms to change so that every type of animal is recognized as the magnificent beings they are. The reality is that I alone won't be able to change the system – but I can do my part by supporting those working to make these changes happen.

For readers who are interested in working with this population, the best advice I can offer you is to learn as much as you can about what brings these clients into therapy, not the least of which are the many cruel ways non-human animals are treated and viewed in our world. Educate yourself about the challenges these clients face when dealing with their families, peers, and communities. You don't have to be a vegan to do this. Brushing up on grief work as well as developing a good foundation in trauma therapy can also be of value. If you care about both human and non-human animals, this is a deeply meaningful specialty to have.

27
BEAR IS MY BRIDGE

Janus Moncur

I have the privilege of working with my canine partner every day. Together, we help people who are suffering in mind, body, and spirit from adverse events. I believe it takes a certain temperament and training for both me and my partner to be successful in helping people gain relief from the misery of past experiences. It takes a great deal of courage for people to face those memories and having a canine partner creates a safe space for clients.

My journey started during a tumultuous time in my life. Being in the real estate/property management/condo conversion industry during "The Crash of 2008" with the subsequent fallout AND finding out that my significant other was facing end-stage liver disease with a year to two years to live, shook my world and changed my worldview. During the turmoil, I decided I wanted to become a therapist to be able to help other people going through a hard time. During this time, an angel in the form of a Pomeranian puppy named Jack started a whole new evolution to my existence.

As my significant other declined in health, his youngest daughter insisted she needed a Pomeranian puppy. Daddy and Daughter brought home a tiny puppy, named him Jack, and when Daughter went to bed that first night, Jack sat at Daddy's feet demanding to be picked up. Jack made his choice. I believe Jack sensed Daddy needed him more than Daughter did. Jack and I became allies when Daughter graciously allowed the puppy to move to Indiana with Daddy and I for the transplant. Jack was the only creature that could muster Daddy out of bed for the endless doctors' visits. During this time, we acquired another Pomeranian puppy that Daddy named Mack. The team was united, and the journey transformed.

I was still fumbling my way through my education. I completed a certification in coaching as well as a master's in psychology online. After returning to

DOI: 10.4324/9781003335528-30

Florida after the successful transplant, my mission to complete my education took on a greater urgency. At the same time, I discovered pet therapy. Thus, two educational training tracks transpired as Jack and Mack and I worked through the requirements, evaluation, and mentoring through CATDOGS, Inc., while I also attended Barry University for my social work degree. It wasn't until an astute professor pointed out that my work with Jack and Mack was like Play Therapy, did the idea that combining the two endeavors could become my full-time vocation. I sought additional education through Oakland University and obtained their Certificate in Human-Animal Intervention Specialist. Mack and I went on to become a certified team through NATIONAL Crisis Response Canines which opened a greater understanding of adversity and trauma which, in turn, solidified my own specialty in my social work practice.

Today, I work as an independent Licensed Clinical Social Worker (LCSW) with individuals and groups with my current canine partner who is a Keeshond named "Pandora's Peter Bear." I call our specialty therapy canine-assisted trauma therapy (CATT). I have become known for my trauma work, and Bear has become an active participant in therapeutic sessions. Bear's presence brings a calming sense of safety to the space.

Two of my most heartwarming sessions were both with First Responders who were struggling with intense intrusive past traumatic experiences. Each time, Bear instinctively knew what to do without being instructed. The first time he wedged himself next to the person who had frozen and seemed unable to continue. The man then began petting Bear and was able to recover and complete the session. More recently, Bear jumped up on the couch next to a client who seemed to be dissociating. The woman wrapped her arms around him as he snuggled his body into hers and he remained there practically motionless for the rest of the session.

The greatest challenge of my work was to create my position. As I interviewed for work as a therapist, I asked permission to bring my dog to the groups I facilitated. It took educating my associates and always obtain permission to bring my canine partner with me. Then, we had to prove our worth by showing positive results.

The best advice I have for someone who wants to incorporate a canine into their practice is to become as educated as possible. Continue both your education and that of your canine partner. Also, it is important to ensure our canine is the right dog for the job. Just because we can deal with people who are in distress does not mean our canine can. Just like not everyone can be a therapist, or a first responder, your dog may not be suited for what you want them to do. We need to be attuned to the needs of our canine partners as well. We need to learn to accurately read their low-level stress signals and respond accordingly. So, if you are considering working with a canine partner while working with clients who may express strong negative emotions, make sure your canine partner has the right temperament, additional training and exposure through crisis type training, is continually monitored for signs of stress, and given plenty of down time/play time.

I know that my greatest asset is my canine partner. It doesn't matter how much I know or how great my skills may be if I cannot connect with my client. My partner can make that happen particularly with trauma clients. According to Van der Kolk (2014), sometimes people are so hurt by other people, they cannot easily trust another human. But they may trust dogs. My canine partner is my bridge to reaching others.

Reference

Van der Kolk, B. (2014). The body keeps the score: Brain, mind, and body in the healing of trauma. Viking.

28
PANDEMIC PUPS
Research and Clinical Implications

Jessica Wriedt

In 2005, I adopted a beautiful baby boy and my life changed forever. Three years later, my son's biological half-brother was having difficulty with his adopted family, and they contacted me to see if I was open for the possibility of adopting a 10-year-old. While my family was in the process of finalizing the adoption, we had a social worker who was less than pleasant and that was the moment I decided to enter the social work field. This was supposed to be a time of joy for my family, and she made it downright miserable. I decided to go back to school and earn a degree that would allow me to assist families in similar situations and provide the care and support that was appropriate.

While I was in my bachelor's program, my oldest son started having behavioral concerns due to past traumas. On a personal level, I was receiving the best education possible by learning how to navigate the system of obtaining therapy, community services, and becoming an advocate. My son was involved in multiple therapies until he became an adult. He was in residential care at times (due to suicidal ideation), as well as wilderness, individual, and family therapy. It was at this time that I decided case management was not going to be in my future; I wanted to work with individuals with mental health concerns.

I have been working as a licensed clinical psychiatric social worker in a private practice for the last seven years, doing what I love. Working in a private practice, providing individual therapy has allowed me to expand my experience and expertise. I work with individuals of all ages, diverse backgrounds, with an array of mental health concerns. I have had the opportunity to expand my knowledge in autism and complete training that allows me to medically diagnose, with the confirmation of a medical doctor. I have also gained experience in facilitating groups focusing on social skills and parenting.

There are many benefits from working in private practice. As an independent contractor, I have control over my schedule, and I can set my working hours around my family's needs. This allows me the flexibility to maintain a work-life balance. One of the drawbacks is that most people are looking for services before or after work and school. My current schedule is Monday through Thursday from 8 am to 6 pm. This allows me the opportunity to meet the needs of my clients. Fridays are utilized to focus on self-care and to complete other life requirements.

Another benefit from working in private practice is that I can utilize multiple forms of interventions, based on my discretion, to provide services. Other agencies may adhere to brief therapy or utilize interventions set by protocol. The biggest difficulty in private practice is only being compensated when you are working directly with a client. If a client does not show up for their appointment, there is no compensation.

During my time as a therapist, I have encountered multiple clients who would bring their pets into sessions with them as a source of support. Every week, one client would bring in her dog named Charley. The client would speak on Charley's behalf and explain through Charley's viewpoint what had occurred during the previous week. In this way, the client was able to tell her story, which assisted her in building an understanding of other people's perspectives.

As a clinician, I have seen the benefits that these companions provide to their owners through the human-animal bond. Allowing clients to bring in their pets increases client engagement and decreases the number of missed sessions. I have spent countless hours working with individuals who have lost their pets and were grieving the loss of that bond. I then assisted them in processing the guilt that came when they were ready to obtain another pet and love again.

During the pandemic, I worked via telehealth, providing services to my clients. I was introduced to more pets because I was able to see people in their own environment. On multiple occasions, I saw that a client's cat or dog was curled up next to them while they were participating in a session. Working in private practice allowed me the opportunity to continue to provide services during the pandemic.

In 2020, I was enrolled in the doctoral program, working on my dissertation and experienced a great loss. My mentor in the social work field passed away due to health complications. As a coping mechanism, I decided to get a puppy to help me through the loss and the isolation of the pandemic. I was not alone in this feeling, there was a surge of individuals attempting to adopt or purchase dogs during the pandemic. I decided to focus my research on why this phenomenon was occurring. The purpose of my study was to illuminate the experiences of individuals who obtained a dog during the COVID-19 pandemic. I found that all participants obtained a dog as an underlining coping mechanism, noting that they were lonely, looking for companionship for themselves or their existing pets, and were seeking additional support.

It is important for all social workers to understand the benefits that a companion animal can have on an individual socially, physically, and mentally. It is also important to know that individuals view their companion animals as a significant attachment figure, offering support, love, and companionship. Pets are typically not included on intake forms and most social workers do not think of exploring this area with their clients. I feel that including these family members in the initial information gathering stage of therapy is critical in our quest to better understand our clients.

29
SHELTER PETS AND SHELTERED KIDS
Animal-Assisted Therapy in Juvenile Justice

Stacy L. Mendell

Animals have always been a part of my life and a source of comfort and healing. Finding my way to a career working with animals took a winding path and included careers in publishing, software, and filmmaking before I discovered animal-assisted social work. This journey began on one of the most challenging days of my life. As my daughter and I were being wheeled into the emergency room after surviving a car accident, a woman met us at the entrance and told me, "Everything is going to be okay." She was the hospital social worker, and though I never got her name, that day she inspired me to pursue a career in social work.

During my recovery from the accident, I began volunteering at a Day Shelter in downtown Austin, Texas, helping people access food and housing. On one of the hottest mornings of the year, someone left a box of four tiny puppies outside the entrance. We brought them inside, gave them food and water, and began contacting local rescue groups to arrange for their care. In the process, I watched our clients interact with the puppies and noticed how this helped them open up to me and each other. The experience changed all of us. When the rescue group arrived to take the puppies to foster care, the puppies had been named, our neighbors had created a fundraiser to support their care, and I was inspired to find a way to create a career in social work that included working with animals.

In 2011, I graduated from the University of Denver with a Master in Social Work and a certificate in animal-assisted social work. Since that time, my career in social work has included work with housing programs, veterans, hospice patients, and people whose lives have been impacted by trauma, grief, and loss. I have always been assisted and accompanied by

DOI: 10.4324/9781003335528-32

animals, dogs, cats, horses, and rats, some who lived with me, others from a local shelter.

One of the most challenging and rewarding experiences in my career was working with my therapy dog, Chazz, at a juvenile justice facility with detained and incarcerated youth.

Chazz, adopted from a prison-based training program, had earned his Canine Good Citizenship certificate, and was registered with Alliance of Therapy Dogs. He quickly became accustomed to the facility, including the noises of staff radios, alarms, and secured doors.

My goal was to create a safe place for Chazz and for the youth we worked with. This began with the introduction of a safety contract that youth were asked to sign to set clear expectations for safe behaviors around Chazz. This included any time Chazz was present in group and individual sessions, as well as when the youth were in class or in the hallway waiting to go to dinner or recreation. This initial expectation helped build rapport, trust, and respect between the youth, Chazz, and me.

Our initial sessions included teaching the youth Chazz's cues for sit, shake, and high five and allowing time for play to help the youth and Chazz build a relationship. The youth were taught to notice dog body language, and while Chazz mostly presented as happy and calm, they began to notice a yawn or paw lick that could indicate a sign of stress. Chazz was the only dog in the facility, but outside, the animal shelter was less than a block away, close enough for the youth to see and hear the shelter dogs when they were in their outside kennels. Often the youth would ask me about the animals in the shelter and if they were safe. This was an aspect of the human-animal bond I had not considered before and inspired a program to bring animals from the shelter into the juvenile facility.

The animal shelter not only had dogs in need of homes but due to "kitten season" was also struggling to keep up with the number of homeless cats and kittens. The shelter agreed to partner with the facility to help the youth learn coping skills while socializing kittens to increase their chance of finding homes.

We named the group "Kitten Kindergarten" and selected five youth who showed consistently safe behaviors and expressed interest and a willingness to participate. The group met three times a week, for two weeks. Each 45-minute session began with a mindfulness practice, followed by psychoeducation and time for the youth to train their kittens. At the final session, the youth earned a certificate from the animal shelter and the opportunity to return and volunteer at the shelter when they were released from the facility.

With the success of Kitten Kindergarten, we were able to create a group that targeted the needs of committed youth. The Humane Education group focused on psychoeducation with opportunities to practice advanced communication and social skills. Programs that allow youth who are separated from their families and community to work with animals provide opportunities for them to learn to build healthy relationships based on mutual respect and safety. Even after his retirement, the bond between Chazz and his former clients continues and I often hear from the facility staff who ask about Chazz and tell me that he is missed. While I no longer work at the facility full time, I work with youth after their release with my newest assistant, Ruby, a Golden Retriever mix who came to work with me last year. We continue to build on what Chazz helped me begin.

30
WHEN PSYCHOLOGY AND SOCIAL WORK MEET

A Clinician's Experiences in the Mental Health Field

Emily Breitenbach

My journey started the first day of tenth grade, eighth period high school psychology class. The class was taught with such passion and respect that it was hard for me not to love it. I decided to attend Slippery Rock University (SRU) in 2016 and majored in psychology. My psychology major allowed me to expand and learn about research, different areas of psychology, and how to think like a researcher. Not only did I find my love for research, but I also found my niche in psychopathology. My last semester as an undergraduate student was when I decided to step outside of my major and enroll in a social work class, animal-assisted interventions. By the end of the semester, I knew that I wanted to be a clinical social worker with a specialty in animal-assisted interventions. In 2020, I began my master's in social work at SRU.

To explore the field of social work and animal-assisted interventions, I started an internship with HOPE Animal-Assisted Crisis Response. I learned the importance of self-care for not only handlers and canines, but myself. My field instructor inspired me to continue in the field of social work and animal-assisted interventions. Over the summer of my first year, I obtained my certification in animal-assisted social work by completing three classes that included hands-on experiences. As I was going to school for my masters, I was able to gain experience with individuals who were diagnosed with a serious mental illness, helping them develop and practice life skills to maintain independence in their lives. I also completed a clinical internship which involved facilitating individual and group therapy at both a long-term structured residence and an outpatient clinic. During my internship, I was able to run animal-assisted groups, learning how to facilitate animal-assisted interventions.

Today, my role as a social worker is split amongst many jobs. I work with individuals in an outpatient program, facilitate intensive outpatient groups, complete comprehensive assessments to determine the level of care for incoming clients, and meet with individual clients to identify community resources to meet their identified needs. I work with clients with both mental health and substance use concerns. I connect with case managers, other therapists, and my supervisors to consult on cases and determine the most effective interventions for my clients. Even though I do not currently have access to therapy dogs, I am still able to connect with my clients using animal-based interventions. One example I often use with children is the Dog Game. I have the child use dog pictures to tell a story that helps me identify and understand their emotions. It is my goal to work with handlers in the community to incorporate animal-assisted therapy into my practice and, one day, be a handler myself. I currently work at an agency that fully supports the use of animal-assisted interventions and I cannot wait to introduce the interventions into my practice.

The best part of my job is seeing the changes my clients implement in their lives. In the short amount of time that I have been working in the mental health field, I have seen many clients take it upon themselves to better their lives and their mental health. I enjoy connecting with my clients and getting to know them as people. Currently, I work with a client who struggles with the loss of his pet. Taking time to effectively process his grief and managing the trauma of losing a pet is our focus. We are currently practicing ways to effectively express emotions, including writing a goodbye letter to express his feelings. Future plans are to have a therapy dog involved to provide a nonjudgmental ear to clients like him who struggle processing their feelings of loss.

The most challenging part of my job is balancing life and work. Learning healthy boundaries between work and home life can be difficult. There are some clients who do mentally come home with you, but I work hard at leaving work at the door. Self-care is a critical part of my job. I must be constantly aware of my limitations and know when to back away from a task at hand. If I am not aware of my limitations, I put myself at risk for compassion fatigue or burn out. Learning those boundaries and limitations, as well as admitting that I cannot do it all, is one of the most challenging parts of my job.

To have a job like mine, it is required to have a master's degree in counseling or social work and compete coursework in animal-assisted interventions. My advice for seeking a career like mine is to learn how to interpret and implement empirical evidence. To work in the clinical world, it is important to learn and engage in the research world. As for animal-assisted interventions, it is important to understand animal welfare and how the work impacts the dog. I highly recommend that future clinicians research canine stress, animal welfare, and self-care practices for both the handler and the dog. My last piece of advice is to learn about and practice self-care. Self-care can be the difference between a burnt-out clinician and a healthy clinician.

31

ANIMAL-ASSISTED PSYCHOTHERAPY

The Golden Standard

Elizabeth Ruegg

Background and Interest in the Field

In my early 20s, just before starting a graduate program in social work, I applied to a service dog organization for a "hearing dog" trained to support deaf and hard-of-hearing people. I was matched with Cash, a Labrador retriever who improved my situational awareness by alerting me to sounds such as alarm clocks, doorbells, and sirens.

Cash was a velvet-eared, doe-eyed wonder; she guided me flawlessly through graduate school, then accompanied me to my first professional job as a children's psychotherapist. More than once, she was my bridge to a reluctant child. "If you don't want to talk today," I'd comment, "how about brushing Cash?" A small, cautious hand reached for the brush every time. Even the most dysregulated kids were gentle with – and soothed by – her. Once the grooming started, the talking did, also. This never failed. Already a model service dog, Cash branched into her accidental career as my first therapy dog.

Preparing for the Job of a Lifetime

To become an animal-assisted psychotherapist, I earned a bachelor's degree and a social work master's degree. I completed 2,000 hours of supervised practice, then passed a national exam to obtain my clinical social work license. Next, I learned as much as possible about AAP while training my dogs (nine of them since Cash's time) to an advanced obedience standard. I spent a year earning an AAP certificate from an organization that required me to demonstrate training and handling skills, knowledge of animal behavior,

DOI: 10.4324/9781003335528-34

clinical theories supporting AAP, risk and liability management, and ethical standards for humane care and treatment of working animals.

While virtually any breed can be an excellent therapy dog, I prefer working with well-bred female golden retrievers. In general, they learn quickly and readily accept human leadership; they are eager to please and companionable – even with strangers. They are responsive but not reactive, and they don't bark excessively. Finally, their spun-gold coats and broad smiles are attractive to people who might otherwise be intimidated by large breed dogs.

Preparing dogs for readiness to work in my clinical mental health practice is a long-term, time-intensive commitment. First, we attend a year or more of group obedience lessons to earn their CGC (Canine Good Citizen) and CGCA (Canine Good Citizen-Advanced) certificates. I continually assess their temperament and appropriateness for therapy work during this time (see my blog post, *What Makes a Good Therapy Dog?*). If they seem a good fit, we participate in advanced obedience and preparation classes before attempting the challenging therapy dog test (see my blog post, *Train, Test and Register Your Therapy Dog*). Once registered as a therapy dog team, we make 50–75 volunteer visits in community settings such as hospitals, schools, and libraries. After training together for at least a year and spending another year making weekly volunteer visits to observe and proof their behavior, they are ready to join me at the office.

A Day in the Life of an Animal-Assisted Psychotherapist

My office is in a former bank and across from a town park, so we have lots of space for indoor and outdoor animal-assisted activities. While all the dogs usually come with me each day, only one is in my consultation office at any time. The former teller station behind a tall counter is their rest-and-play: a canine break room with ample space, water, toys, and snoozing mats. They each work with clients for a maximum of three 50-minute sessions per day. At midday, we take a 45-minute break to go outside, play, and relax before our afternoon sessions. We see a maximum of five patients each day.

When new clients decide to participate in AAP, I invite them to meet a couple of my registered therapy dogs. Sometimes, no clear preference emerges, but more often, I note that one or another of the dogs is particularly interested in the client, sitting beside them or making warm eye contact. Allowing the dogs to choose their clients works well. They know when "their" clients enter the office and eagerly greet them in the waiting area before leading them into the office.

Depending on the client's needs, they might groom or stroke the dog while reflecting on prior experiences; train the dog in tricks or skills to practice organizational thinking, communication, and problem-solving; or lead the dog on a walk (with me accompanying) to encourage mild physical activity that can be helpful for combatting depression. Once clients demonstrate competence in handling and leading the dog in the office and on the grounds, we may go to the park, where they can practice anxiety management or social engagement skills by speaking to other dog walkers. With practice, experience, and creative thinking, I've learned that almost any psychotherapy treatment goal can be achieved with animal-assisted intervention.

Benefits and Challenges

Inviting my goldens into psychotherapeutic practice encourages the development of the therapeutic alliance, helps clients' task persistence, and improves their motivation for behavioral and emotional change. Additionally, the dogs offer clients comforting physical contact when, for ethical reasons, I cannot. Perhaps the most significant personal benefit is that sharing my work life with my dogs is tremendously enjoyable. Given how enthusiastically they race into the office each workday, I'd have to say that they love being included, too.

A challenge of involving dogs in clinical practice is thinking quickly and managing problems efficiently. Unlike traditional therapists, who are only responsible for the care and well-being of their clients during sessions, I am responsible for both the client and the dog. I set clear boundaries at the beginning of each client's treatment to manage this. I point out the credenza in the office, explaining that the dog communicates her need for space when she lies underneath it. Similarly, if I notice stress signals such as lip-licking, I excuse the dog from the consultation room so she can relax in the rest-and-play area. These boundaries ensure that both the client and dog feel safe and comfortable during each encounter. I wouldn't have it any other way.

SECTION IV
The Inclusion of Human-Animal Interactions within Social Work Practice

32
HAI IN SOCIAL WORK PRACTICE

Janet Hoy-Gerlach and Lisa Townsend

According to the 2023–2024 APPA National Pet Owners Survey, approximately 66% of U.S. households report having at least one companion animal (CA) (American Pet Products Association, 2023); the majority of individuals with CAs in the U.S. report considering them to be a family member (Human-Animal Bond Research Institute, 2022). Given social work is a profession that explicitly encompasses people's strengths, supports, and ecosystems within a basic scope of practice, social workers are uniquely situated to recognize and respond to HAI issues related to clients. Because of the importance of people's relationships with CAs, there have been calls in social work (Risley-Curtiss, 2013) and medicine (Zinsstag et al., 2011) to explicitly include people's relationships with non-human animals (henceforth referred to as "animals") within the definition of human ecosystems in practice.

While the human client remains the primary focus of practice in most social work practice that encompasses HAI, there is increasing support internationally for including animal well-being as an ethical concern in and of itself (Bozalek & Pease, 2020; Hanrahan, 2011; Ryan, 2014). There is also increasing awareness of the need to systematically respond to the needs of both people and their animals in an integrated way to maximize well-being for both within macro practice (Hoy-Gerlach & Townsend, 2023). Integrated services that explicitly encompass the needs of *both* people and animals to support *mutual* well-being for both may be referred to as a One Health approach.

Ongoing efforts to collaborate and jointly provide services across human health and social service entities and animal welfare entities are underway in the United States and internationally (World Health Organization, 1986; Dar, Machalaba, Adisasmito, Almuhairi, Behravesh, Bilivogui, & Bukachi,

DOI: 10.4324/9781003335528-36

2022). Integrated human-animal support services (HASS) emerged during the AIDS epidemic in the 1980s and expanded as a result of the COVID-19 pandemic (Gorczyca, Fine, Venn-Watson, Nelson, Brooks, Lipp et al., 2010.) During the COVID-19 pandemic, American Pets Alive and other animal welfare non-profits mobilized resources to help affected individuals care for their animals, maintain their housing, and access food and medical care (American Pets Alive, 2023). This type of program exemplifies the positive impact HASS have on human and animal well-being as well as illustrating that such integrated interventions are possible and sustainable.

The HAB is increasingly recognized as a common, vital element of daily life for many people across the human lifespan (Bures & Gee, 2021; Fine & Beck, 2019). Relationships with CAs are often significant and CAs are seen as family members. A growing body of literature documents that animals and humans can support one another's well-being (Amio, Bastian, & Martens, 2016; Friedmann & Son, 2009; Carr, Taylor, Gee, N & Sachs-Ericsson, 2020). Given these factors, there is a range of ways that social work practice can include HAI to support humans and animals.

Grief and Loss Support Related to HAI: Social Work Responses

Pet loss can be a profoundly devastating experience for many, including both human veterinary clients and veterinary professionals. Grief and loss are unfortunately experiences associated with bonds to animals, as many species of CAs have lifespans significantly shorter than their humans. Adrian et al. (2009) found that 20% of people experienced significant grief after pet loss; of those, more than 30% struggled with grief for more than six months, with 12% reporting some functional impairment. Veterinarians experience their own complicated reactions to the deaths of clients' CAs (Fogle & Abrahamson, 1990), an aspect of their work that is not always addressed in veterinary education (Dickinson et al., 2014). Proxy measures of owner attachment to their animal demonstrate significant associations with their reported need for information from the veterinarian regarding euthanasia (Fernandez-Mehler et al., 2013). In addition, research suggests that veterinarians provide significant emotional support to owners surrounding serious illness, injury, and the decision to euthanize (Morris, 2012). Veterinary social workers support pet owners and veterinary providers during and after pet loss (Goldberg, 2019; Holcombe et al., 2016 Loue, 2022). Social workers who offer pet loss support services offer much-needed relief for people in navigating the complex emotional reactions that often emerge following the death of a beloved CA.

Supporting Animal Health in the HAB

While most CAs have considerably shorter lifespans than humans, there are ongoing veterinary medical advancements that can help prolong their health and life, benefiting both them and the people who care for them. In contrast to more traditional roles that social workers may take within the realm of HAB, some may choose to focus on research. Being involved with CA research in the hopes of extending and enhancing companion animal lives is another way to approach both human and animal well-being.

Animal-Assisted Forensic Interviews

Yet another path chosen by some social workers interested in incorporating HAB into their work involves partnering with therapy dogs to support vulnerable children during forensic interviews. Forensic interviews with children are conducted to ascertain whether maltreatment has occurred and to gather evidence in the event of adjudication (Child Welfare Information Gateway, 2023). Such conversations occur between trained interviewers and children or adolescents who may have experienced significant trauma. Complicating an already intense emotional situation, children undergoing forensic interviews must speak with a stranger about profoundly personal, frightening experiences. While these conversations are fundamental for protecting children and mobilizing services to help them recover, the experience may exacerbate their distress.

It is well-established that animals can ease children's experience connecting with a therapist in a range of settings (Melson & Fine, 2019). Involving animals in forensic interviews may relieve some of the emotional and physiological symptoms of distress in children and increase their comfort in sharing information with interviewers. In 2010, the American Humane Society embarked upon an initiative to incorporate trained therapy animals in forensic interviewing with children (American Humane Society, 2010). Initial research on therapy dog programs in child welfare contexts using randomized, controlled trial methods suggests that the presence of a facility dog during forensic interviews is associated with significant decreases in physiological stress biomarkers among children, particularly those who disclose abuse (Krause-Parello et al., 2018). Similar research with therapy dogs and handlers suggests that the presence of these teams may improve physiological homeostasis in children undergoing such interviews (Krause-Parello & Gulick, 2015). Inclusion of therapy dogs in forensic interviewing with children can be a powerful support offered by social workers who acquire the expertise to do so.

Conclusion

In sum, there is a wide range of ways in which HAI can be incorporated into social work practice. Each of the chapters in this section have integrated HAI within their social work practice to improve outcomes for their client systems (human and/or animals). Their work gives readers an inside view of how social workers are addressing needs on both sides of the HAB and provides models of HASS that can be adapted to fit the needs of local circumstances. Despite successes of model programs, more work is needed to establish and sustain these sorely needed interventions. We hope that these chapters leave you inspired to incorporate HAI and HASS in your own spheres of social work practice.

References

Adrian, J. A. L., Deliramich, A. N., & Frueh, B. C. (2009). Complicated grief and posttraumatic stress disorder in humans' response to the death of pets/animals. *Bulletin of the Menninger Clinic*, *73*(3), 176–187. https://doi.org/10.1521/bumc.2009.73.3.176.

American Humane Society. (2010). Therapy Animals Supporting Kids Program Manual. Available online: https://www.americanhumane.org/app/uploads/2016/08/therapy-animals-supporting-kids.pdf.

American Pet Products Association. (2023). Pet Industry Market Size, Trends & Ownership Statistics. Available online: https://www.americanpetproducts.org/press_industrytrends.asp#:~:text=All%20data%20was%20reviewed%20and,leading%20pet%20retailers%20and%20manufacturers.&text=According%20to%20the%202023%2D2024,equates%20to%2086.9%20million%20households (accessed 29 March 2023).

American Pets Alive. (2023). About Human-Animal Support Services. Available online: https://www.humananimalsupportservices.org/about-human-animal-support-services/#:~:text=HASS%20was%20founded%20in%20April,adapting%20operations%20during%20the%20pandemic (accessed 30 January 2023).

Amiot, C., Bastian, B., & Martens, P. (2016). People and companion animals: It takes two to tango. *BioScience*, *66*(7), 552–560.

Bozalek, V., & Pease, B. (Eds.) (2020). Bozalek, V. & Pease, B. Towards post-anthropocentric social work. In *Post-anthropocentric social work* (pp. 1–15). Routledge.

Bures, R. M., & Gee, N. R. (2021). *Well-being over the life course: Incorporating human-animal interaction* (pp. 1–9). Springer International Publishing.

Carr, D. C., Taylor, M. G., Gee, N. R., & Sachs-Ericsson, N. (2020). Psychological health benefits of companion animals following a social loss. *The Gerontologist*, *60*(3), 428–438.

Child Welfare Information Gateway. (2023). Forensic Interviewing: A Primer for Child Welfare Professionals. U.S. Department of Health and Human Services, Administration for Children and Families, Children's Bureau. Available online: https://www.childwelfare.gov/pubs/factsheets/forensicinterviewing/

Dar, O., Machalaba, C., Adisasmito, W. B., Almuhairi, S., Behravesh, C. B., Bilivogui, P., Bukachi, S. A., Casas, N., Becerra, N. C., Charron, D. F., Chaudhary, A., Ciacci Zanella, J. R., Cunningham, A. A., Debnath, N., Dungu, B., Farag, E., Gao, G. F., Hayman, D. T. S., Khaitsa, M., Koopmans, M. P. G., Mackenzie, J. S., Markotter, W., Mettenleiter, T. C., Morand, S., Smolenskiy, V., Zhou, L., & One Health High-Level Expert Panel (OHHLEP). (2022). World Health Organization: One Health

Theory of Change. Available online: https://www.who.int/groups/one-health-high-level-expert-panel/members (accessed 30 January 2023).

Dickinson, G. E., Roof, K. W., Roof, P. D., & Paul, E. S. (2014). UK veterinarians' experiences with euthanasia. *Veterinary Record*, *175*, 174.

Fernandez-Mehler, P., Gloor, P., Sager, E., Lewis, F. I., & Glaus, T. M. (2013). Veterinarians' role for pet owners facing pet loss. *Veterinary Record*, *172*(21), 555.

Fine, A. H., & Beck, A. M. (2019). Understanding our kinship with animals: Input for health care professionals interested in the human-animal bond. In *Handbook on animal-assisted therapy: Foundations and guidelines for animal-assisted interventions* (5th ed., p. 5); Fine, A. H. (Ed.). Academic Press.

Fogle, B., & Abrahamson, D. (1990). Pet loss: A survey of the attitudes and feelings of practicing veterinarians. *Anthrozoös*, *3*(3), 143–150.

Friedmann, E., & Son, H. (2009). The human–companion animal bond: How humans benefit. *Veterinary Clinics of North America: Small Animal Practice*, *39*(2), 293–326.

Goldberg, K. J. (2019). Euthanasia considerations. In *Textbook of small animal emergency medicine* (pp. 1306–1312); Drobatz, K. J., Hopper, K., Rozanski, E. A., & Silverstein, D. C. (Eds.). John Wiley & Sons. doi:10.1002/9781119028994.ch204.

Gorczyca, K., Fine, A. H., Venn-Watson, S., Nelson, L., Brooks, A., Lipp, J. L., et al. (2010). Human/animal support services: The evolution of the San Francisco model and pet-associated zoonoses education. In *Handbook on animal-assisted therapy: Theoretical foundations and guidelines for practice* (3rd ed., pp. 329–356); Fine, A. H. (Ed.). Academic Press.

Hanrahan, C. (2011). Challenging anthropocentricism in social work through ethics and spirituality: Lessons from studies in human-animal bonds. *Journal of Religion & Spirituality in Social Work: Social Thought*, *30*(3), 272–293.

Holcombe, T. M., Strand, E. B., Nugent, W. R., & Ng, Z. Y. (2016). Veterinary social work: Practice within veterinary settings. *Journal of Human Behavior in the Social Environment*, *26*(1), 69–80.

Hoy-Gerlach, J., & Townsend, L. (2023). Reimagining healthcare: Human–animal bond support as a primary, secondary, and tertiary public health intervention. *International Journal of Environmental Research and Public Health*, *20*(7), 5272.

Human-Animal Bond Research Institute. (2022). International Survey of Pet Owners & Veterinarians. Available online: https://habri.org/international-hab-survey/ (accessed 29 March 2023).

Krause-Parello, C. A., & Gulick, E. E. (2015). Forensic interviews for child sexual abuse allegations: An investigation into the effects of animal-assisted intervention on stress biomarkers. *Journal of Child Sexual Abuse*, *24*(8), 873–886. doi:10.1080/10538712.2015.1088916.

Krause-Parello, C. A., Thames, M., Ray, C. M., & Kolassa, J. (2018). Examining the effects of a service-trained facility dog on stress in children undergoing forensic interview for allegations of child sexual abuse. *Journal of Child Sexual Abuse*, *27*(3), 305–320.

Loue, S. (2022). Introduction to veterinary social work. In *The comprehensive guide to interdisciplinary veterinary social work* (pp. 3–43); Loue, S., & Linden, P. (Eds.). Springer Nature.

Melson, G. F., & Fine, A. H. (2019). Animals in the lives of children. In *Handbook on animal-assisted therapy: Foundations and guidelines for animal-assisted interventions* (5th ed., pp. 257–259); Fine, A. H. (Ed.). Academic Press.

Morris, P. (2012). Managing pet owners' guilt and grief in veterinary euthanasia encounters. *Journal of Contemporary Ethnography*, 41(3), 337–365.

Risley-Curtiss, C. (2013). Expanding the ecological lens in the child welfare practice to include other animals. *Journal of Social Work and Social Welfare*, 40, 107.

Ryan, T. (Ed.). (2014). *Animals in social work: Why and how they matter*. Springer. The Shanti Project. Pets Are Wonderful Support History. Available online: https://www.shanti.org/programs-services/pets-are-wonderful-support/history-of-paws/ (accessed 30 January 2023).

World Health Organization. (1986). The Ottawa Charter for Health Promotion. Available online: https://www.who.int/teams/health-promotion/enhanced-wellbeing/first-global-conference (accessed 30 January 2023).

Zinsstag, J., Schelling, E., Waltner-Toews, D., & Tanner, M. (2011). From "one medicine" to "one health" and systemic approaches to health and well-being. *Preventive Veterinary Medicine*, 101(3–4), 148–156. doi:10.1016/j.prevetmed.2010.07.003.

33
PURSUING A CAREER IN VETERINARY SOCIAL WORK

Angie Arora

My story of daring to dream began with profound loss. Montey, my animal companion of 18 years, passed away in my arms in 2004. The loss shook my world upside down and the grief nearly overtook me. And yet, amid such profound despair and sadness, a seed was planted that would change the trajectory of my life.

Montey was the first animal to show me what it meant to be loved and how to allow my heart to love back. There was too much meaning to his life and our bond for it to just disappear and after completing my Master of Social Work the year he died, my passion was birthed. Caring for people impacted by animal relationships was my path and I was on a mission to follow it.

I have walked alongside and honored people's grief from losing their companion animals for nearly two decades. Through facilitating community-based support groups, providing professional grief counseling, and supporting clients with end-of-life decision making and support after loss, I continue to learn and be inspired by the powerful layers of human-animal relationships.

Throughout my journey, numerous opportunities unfolded. But these opportunities did not just avail themselves to me. Many times, I had to create them. Before knowing that veterinary social work existed, I worked with an animal hospital and created my own role. I dared to intentionally dream and follow what I knew to be true; as a social worker, I belonged in an interdisciplinary veterinary team. As a result, I helped build a hospital pet loss program where I supported clients as they navigated their pets' end-of-life journey and grief after loss.

DOI: 10.4324/9781003335528-37

As a relatively new social worker with little experience in veterinary medicine, I didn't grasp the complexities of what it meant to work in a veterinary hospital setting. With their own exposure to primary and secondary trauma, working in highly stressful environments with little attention to wellness, I witnessed veterinary professionals in all roles suppressing their emotions and thoughts, leading to individual and team burnout and compassion fatigue.

Despite my desire to support both clients and the staff, not having fully dealt with the loss of Montey and having no clinical supervision led to my own experience of compassion fatigue. The cumulative residue took such a toll on my emotional, cognitive, and physical health that I made the decision to leave the hospital.

As I worked on my own personal healing, I felt a deep pull to learn more so I could one day go back and support the veterinary professionals who held a special place in my heart. I became certified as a Compassion Fatigue Specialist and explored how veterinary medicine was rampant with unresolved trauma at micro, mezzo, and macro levels. I have now spent more than a decade working with veterinary professionals – medical staff, support staff, and leadership – building knowledge and skills to address burnout, secondary traumatic stress, and compassion fatigue.

I provide trauma-informed coaching for veterinary professionals and psychoeducational wellbeing training for veterinary teams. I work with animal hospitals, animal welfare organizations, and zoos to provide embedded wellbeing services to their teams. I support veterinary initiatives across North America advocating for the importance of equity and inclusion in all well being initiatives.

As one of the few racialized veterinary social workers in North America, I understand the importance of addressing the lack of racial diversity, equity, and inclusion within veterinary medicine and its allied professions, including social work. While visible representation is only one part of inclusion, I want other racialized social workers to know they belong in this profession. I deeply understand how experiencing oppression impacts wellbeing and create space for veterinary professionals who have experienced discrimination and systemic marginalization to process the impacts of such trauma.

What I've learned from my experience as a social worker addressing human-animal relationships is that those who desire to work in this space must be ready to forge their own path. Social workers need to seek and pursue opportunities to demonstrate their value and impact.

I believe we are on the cusp of a transformation. As the awareness of the importance of social work grows, we must be ready to seize the opportunities. Hold your vision so clearly in your hands that the actions you take are intentional, meaningful, and aligned. Seek out others paving the path and build mentorship opportunities. Shadow and observe their work so you can see what is possible. Reflect on the value your social work training and experience has as it relates to human-animal relationships and create new opportunities. Network with organizations that can benefit from your expertise and build relationships. Some opportunities take time to build while others can happen on the drop of a dime. Be clear enough in your skills, knowledge, and value that you can pivot quickly. Working at the cross-section of human-animal relationships requires us to be adaptive, reflective, creative, and mission driven.

As I reflect on my experience, I am eternally grateful to the animals that have shaped my life in powerful ways. Montey, Pouncer, Enzo, and Daytona have left forever prints not just on my heart, but on my life's purpose. Experiencing their love fuels my passion to help the many professionals who allow for human-animal relationships to flourish in such powerful ways.

Once you find your mission and passion, you've created your north star. We are only beginning to scratch the surface of how social workers can impact human-animal relationships. This is an exciting time to join the movement and dream big.

34
THE INTEGRATED APPROACH

One Social Worker's Roundabout Career Journey Incorporating Veterinary Social Work and One Health

Christina Carr

Background

As a child living in Alaska, animals, wildlife, and nature were a part of my every day. As a teenager in Tennessee, I worked as a dog walker and pet sitter and made a reputation in my neighborhood for being the one to call. I started my academic journey in college with course work in nursing, early childhood education, sociology, psychology, and then environmental science, as well as initially pursuing music performance. These courses as an undergraduate led me to pursue my bachelors in environmental studies where I focused on sociology and the ways that societal structures shape the lives of individuals and communities – humans and non-human animals. I enjoyed learning about issues such as co-housing with companion animals for those currently unhoused and the interconnected social history of human and animal welfare. I started seeing the One Health thread more clearly, all of my interests were intertwined. After a series of opportunities in community development and mental health communication, I pursued my master's in social work and simultaneously the veterinary social work (VSW) certificate at the University of Tennessee. Social work for me always included animals, and the VSW philosophy is to uphold the dignity and respect of all species within a strengths-based and evidence-based approach. During this time, I sought diverse field placements in equine-facilitated groups and school social work that integrated animal-assisted interventions, as well as integrated trauma-informed grounding and mindfulness-based work. My graduate assistantship with the VSW department introduced me to the macro and micro VSW implications with organizational development and interpersonal infrastructure.

Current Career Snapshot

Throughout my career, any given day in my work life may look slightly different from the last. I have worked with a variety of ages and communities, in schools, courts, advocacy agencies, therapy offices, and grief centers. At some times, I have focused on animal-assisted therapy and program creation, and other times, my focus was on clinical work.

Currently, I practice social work at a grief center, where I serve as a grief counselor. The grief center is part of a non-profit hospice, which includes palliative care, residential and at-home hospice services, community outreach, and training. The hospice organization incorporates volunteer therapy animal teams to visit patients, families, and staff. Through grief work, I have partnered with these teams in workshops, groups, and children's programming.

Clinically, I see clients one on one, in groups, and in workshops or experiential settings. I support nursing and medical staff in weekly interdisciplinary meetings and staff trainings. I utilize supportive grief counseling techniques, Trauma-Focused Cognitive Behavioral Therapy (TF-CBT), strength-based approaches, and the companioning model to normalize and validate each client's unique experience. Core concepts from VSW that I use daily include grief and loss, compassion fatigue, and animal-assisted interventions. I have also led a pet loss support group for several years which seeks to create a safe and open space to name and acknowledge the important losses of significant animals in our participants' lives.

The Best, Most Rewarding Part of My Job

You may be starting to see how my career path has unfolded. It required a certain comfort level with openness and uncertainty. My career advice is to explore the systems, ideologies, and practices that you are passionate about. For me, it was VSW, with animals and loss just naturally integrating. That word – integration – is what I would share with you today.

Integration is the most rewarding part of the work I do. Integration is the moment that a traumatic event is addressed and becomes part of a client's broader history. Integration is a powerful tool in strengthening systems and in seeing broader connections. Integration requires balance in practice. At this time, working as a grief counselor, I have found balance with my client work by reading literature and providing peer reviews for manuscripts in human-animal bond literature. Integration is how I am able to do this meaningful work I do sustainably.

Challenges and Additional Advice

Challenges in integrating social work and human-animal interactions in a career often come from the fact that these career paths can be quite diverse and not immediately clear. It requires adjustment and working within structures, agencies, and timelines. Working in this field of social work is about the building of a career and is often an ongoing journey of expanding and exploring. I recommend finding agencies or platforms to gain experience that meet your values and standards.

Over the years, I am so grateful I have gotten to work with emerging professionals and interns who have asked me for advice. My go-to tip is to join professional organizations that align with your passions and values. Find community in journals, local chapters of professional groups, and cohort organizations. Doing this early on in your career provides incentives – with introductory rates and opportunities for growth and leadership. The organizations I connected with are CABI's Human-Animal Interactions Journal, the National Association of Social Workers, and the American Psychological Association's Human-Animal Interaction Section. I began involvement with these groups while in graduate school or soon after and have greatly appreciated the opportunities, continuing education, and access to literature and research. A career path is the journey that we go on – and those we connect with on the way are what shape our future.

35
CAREERS IN ONE HEALTH

Social Workers' Roles in Caring for Humans and Their Companion Animals

Lizett Justa Gutierrez

I came to understand the HAB while working at a holistic veterinary practice. The experience led me to complete my studies as a registered veterinary nurse. Over the course of 18 years, I worked in intensive care, emergency triage, internal medicine, and finally in comparative animal research in the field of respiratory science. Ultimately, compassion fatigue and moral stress caught up to me and I decided to pursue a career focused on enhancing the HAB. I spent two years teaching in a Title 1 trilingual (Dine, Spanish, and English) school where my students learned about humane education, basic husbandry, and care of our classroom pets. My next progression in the field came by way of the Animal-Assisted Social Work (AASW) certificate at the University of Denver where I completed my Masters of Social Work degree. More recently, I completed an academic certificate in veterinary social work (VSW) through the University of Tennessee Knoxville.

Today, I proudly practice as a bilingual home-based therapist in a community mental health agency and hold dual licensure as a clinical social worker and as an addictions counselor. Virtually all of my clients receive Medicaid and live below the poverty guidelines. A large percentage of the families I serve are undocumented. My training is steeped in trauma-informed interventions such as eye movement desensitization and reprocessing (EMDR), cognitive behavior therapy (CBT), and dialectical behavior therapy (DBT). I modify each of these interventions in a culturally responsive manner. Themes for therapeutic support are trauma, attachment rupture, and acculturative stress. If the family, youth, and pet are amenable, interventions can include the family pet, utilizing the Triangle model (Jones, Rice, & Cotton, 2019). Animal-assisted interventions can guide families slowly into more intensive

DOI: 10.4324/9781003335528-39

clinical interventions. Providing interventions which are respectful and flexible to the needs of my clients and families are a priority.

I work with Latinx families who straddle the cultural differences between their method of pet husbandry versus the dominant U.S. acceptance of the HAB. I use the word versus because in my experience, Latinx families generally have a different approach to veterinary care, behavior training, and husbandry. A general theme I have noticed in my clinical work with Latinx families is that many parents use empty threats to "rehome" or "abandon" the pet as a disciplinary and/or consequence tool in response to the behaviors of youth. This creates a considerable amount of emotional stress and can backfire on parents. For parents who were not raised to see pets as extended family, it takes psychoeducation with an awareness of acculturative stress for the family system to understand the impact of welfare or attachment threats toward the family pet.

I understand these challenges because of my own background. I was brought to the U.S. at the age of two from Lima, Peru. My parents are indigenous to the Amazonas and Andean region. In these regions, animals are viewed for their function and not for the companionship that non-agrarian cultures have fostered. I grew up acculturated to dominant American norms such as the human-animal bond. In contrast with our parents' experience, my sister and I created an attachment to our pets that was based on companionship and not utility.

Best/Most Rewarding Parts of My Job

There are several rewarding parts to my job. An example is when I get to create a bond with the family pet and can engage in play with the pet and the youth. Many times, the youth I work with are not accustomed to adults showing genuine interest in their pet, let alone teach them about basic husbandry, preventative healthcare, and therapeutic play. Additionally, I enjoy connecting families to free or low-cost veterinary care, including spay/neuter services to help prevent pets from being relinquished to the shelter or abandoned.

Challenges within My Job

While the biggest challenge to my work is that I do not have a trained therapy animal, I find creative solutions. I use stories, videos, and stuffed animals (depending on the age of the youth) to assist with psychoeducation, attachment exercises, and building empathy. Another challenge I have is when parents give away the family pet. This takes an emotional toll on the youth and is a challenge for everyone.

As I have navigated through a variety of career positions, the HAB has been a consistent theme. I feel that the steps I took to get to where I am today honors the lives of all the animals I provided care for and the many pets who have shared my home and life.

Reference

Jones, M. G., Rice, S. M., & Cotton, S. M. (2019). Incorporating animal-assisted therapy in mental health treatments for adolescents: A systematic review of canine assisted psychotherapy. *PLoS One*, *14*(1), e0210761. doi:10.1371/journal.pone.0210761.

36
ANIMALS ARE MY TEACHERS

Maureen MacNamara

Social work was not my first career; in fact, my education and experience focused on biological sciences and animal behavior. My first jobs included veterinary assistant, dog trainer, riding coach, and horse trainer – in fact, I was one of the first women in the US to be licensed as a racehorse trainer. When a friend suggested I apply for a job as an instructor for a high school vocational horse program, I jumped at the chance. I imagined the students would be similar to my riding students: dedicated to improving their skills, drawn to horses, and willing to learn. I was surprised when, on the first day of classes, I found the majority of students to be angry, uninterested, and confrontational. At a time before "alternative high schools" and special education programs, the district had "dumped" these challenging students in the horse program with the rationale – "anyone can shovel horse s**t." Because working with horses can obviously be quite dangerous, I was extremely troubled by this situation. In a panic I called a friend of mine, who was a therapist working with extremely troubled youth. We strategized the best approach to help keep both the kids and horses safe. From this conversation and subsequent mentoring, I began to match kids and horses with similar behaviors. Thus, more defiant students I placed with pushy colts and more nervous kids were assigned to older, more settled horses.

The results were very encouraging. Chronically truant students came to school, and a number of students improved their grades and applied and were accepted to community college programs or obtained well-paying jobs. Even more exciting were the behavior changes I witnessed. Students demonstrated improved negotiation and cooperation skills (with horses and people) and a reduction in angry outbursts. I was so inspired by these results that I decided to figure out a way to be involved in and develop this type of program.

DOI: 10.4324/9781003335528-40

My path diverged from the animal training world to exploring, through networking, attending conferences, and talking to professors, how I could develop animal-assisted therapy (AAT) programs. Passion drove me and I made appointments and spoke to strangers, some of whom have become close friends and colleagues. Through this exploration, I discovered social work. In particular, I discovered that part of social work that focused on administration, programs, and policy.

My MSW program prepared me to think critically, manage change, and work from an interprofessional focus. I analyzed the trends related to the emerging field of human-animal interactions and made a career plan to work in the field. After lots of volunteering and positions as directors in increasingly complex social service organizations, I joined the staff of an emerging HAI organization. As the vice-president of Programs for Delta Society, I worked with therapists from across the nation and co-created a number of AAT program protocols and development strategies. Several of these programs served as the foundation for AAT programs in the US and across the world.

I have learned from this career, first, to become an excellent social worker separate from animal interventions or inclusion. Hone your skills in engagement, assessment, and evaluation. Even if you see yourself as a clinical social worker, learn how to think about systems and the intersection of culture, community, and environmental forces. As one therapist told me, "Animals are like rocket fuel, once you add them to the therapeutic environment lots of things happen, very fast. You need to be good at managing and working in the therapeutic environment first, then add animals." This applies to director or development positions as well. Understanding how these systems work without animals will help you better understand the impact of including animals.

It is also important to develop strong interprofessional practice skills, move beyond working collaboratively with other health care providers to those outside human health and well-being. Learn from attorneys, financial experts, people in labor and different vocational professions. You never know where networks will take you and who you know will be more important than what you know. In these arenas, do not be afraid to let people know that you do not know something. Some amazing insights will come from people who have a totally different focus on life and its challenges.

And finally, I feel it is extremely important to work with animals *other than your personal or family pets*. I learned a great deal from both horses and dogs who were with me for training or performance. The relationship, levels of trust, and communication requirements are very different when the animals are not our "most beloved." It is similar to the differences between relationships with family members as compared to colleagues or staff. Understanding and appreciating this difference will improve your observational skills and your capacity to see the animals as distinct individuals.

I feel strongly about this issue as I have observed many therapists override or ignore stress-related behaviors in their animals because they "just know he loves this work." It is my perspective that animals are not here to heal us, they are here for their own purposes. That some choose to help people is a gift not to be taken lightly.

37
A SOCIAL WORK PATH TO TEACHING IN HIGHER EDUCATION

Kristie Abbs

Working in the field of social work over the past 20 years has taught me how important the journey becomes when carving our path to serve others. Social work is a dynamic field allowing us to serve those with many different needs. Like many, I chose an initial area of work based on what I felt strongly about and where I wanted to make an impact. My career path started in the medical field. I wanted to help those with medical needs, focusing on individuals residing in nursing homes and hospitals. These positions allowed me to use social work practices to ensure care for patients, develop new programs to foster healthy lifestyles, and provide support to the patient and their families, as well as the staff, and the greater community.

While in these healthcare settings, I began to conduct therapy in a private practice setting. One of the psychiatric doctors had a private practice that allowed me to begin serving clients' mental health needs. Learning how to combine mental and physical health support assisted me in bridging the gap between the two and learning how they work together to impact those we serve. The ability to work in the psychiatric unit of the hospital gave me the opportunity to learn about severe mental illness and hone in on treatment modalities to ensure effective treatment for my clients.

As an avid learner, I returned to school to earn my Master's in Education in a small rural school in Pennsylvania. During one course, I learned from a guest speaker about the high need for behavioral health. I was interested in combining the behavioral aspect of treatment into my already established practices of health and mental health realms. As a result, I spent a good part of my career in behavioral settings. As a result, I understand how behaviors impact people's actions and ultimately impact their functioning.

As I continued to work in the social work field, I became interested in an academic position. I began teaching at a community college and found a new passion. At this point in my career, I wanted to share my experiences in social work and teach upcoming social workers how to serve those in need. After teaching in this setting, I discovered I wanted to teach full-time. When looking for positions at different universities, I found out that I needed my doctorate in social work to obtain one of these positions. While the master's in social work can serve as a terminal degree for this profession, teaching is different. Therefore, I enrolled in an online program at Capella University to earn my doctorate. I continued to work as a full-time social worker in behavioral health, taught as an adjunct professor, and raised a family. While the workload was immense, I found it exhilarating to learn more about social work and work toward what I hoped would be my final destination in my social work career.

After earning my doctorate, I began applying for an Assistant Professor position. The process took longer due to the COVID-19 pandemic. As we all know, everything shut down, and the world took some time to convert back to prior functioning. The pandemic made us look at the impact on people within society, and the effects still impact all of us now. After the first year, I accepted a temporary one-year position and then took a full-time tenure track position as an assistant professor and the Director of MSW Field Experience. My hard work, experiences, and determination helped me reach my goal.

I enjoy teaching and bringing my years of practice into the classroom. I was fortunate to have many experiences with different populations and practice areas to broaden my scope of social work, and I highly suggest going this route before becoming a professor. The students love hearing real social work stories and the impact social workers play on society. I believe that the goal of teaching is to help the students learn essential areas of social work identified by CSWE. I work to do this by making learning fun through the use of different learning modes.

In the Director Position, I work with Master's level students in finding placements in the community, oversee their tasks leading to meeting their competencies, handle problems that arise, meet with students and supervisors, train supervisors, oversee recruitment, conduct research, and work with community partners all to help develop competent social workers in the field.

The best reward of teaching at the college level is the excitement of the students as they learn about social work and think about how they want to go out into the world and make a difference. The contagious enthusiasm helps me remember the importance of social work and all of the great things we do to help those in need. The students are eager to learn and, after leaving the program or after a class is over, often come back or email with sentiments like, "I learned so much in your course," "You were right," or "I will never forget this activity." This feedback lets me know that I have made a difference in the life of the student who will make a difference in the life of someone else.

38
PROVIDING EFFECTIVE SUPERVISION FOR VETERINARY SOCIAL WORKERS IN PRACTICE

Rebecca Stephens and Tracey Harris

Beginning the journey in social work over 30 years ago in Australia, our career focus has been supporting social workers in practice through the provision of quality supervision and training. The memories we hold of our supervisory experiences throughout our career have influenced and shaped the direction of our supervisory practice and leadership. Recalling our experiences evoke emotions that are both pleasing and disappointing. As supervisees, we have both felt supported and encouraged to thrive within our professional roles, whilst at other times, left wondering if there was more to supervision. Such discrepancies in these experiences ignited a mutual passion and commitment to contribute positively to the role of supervision. We made a commitment to support supervisors and help ensure social workers receive quality supervision by designing evidence-informed models, tools, and frameworks to support the supervisory process.

Tracey founded Amovita International in 2007, and with Rebecca joining the following year, our quest to positively influence the practice of supervision began. Fifteen years later, as leaders in supervision, we provide a range of supervision options for hundreds of professionals across many disciplines globally. Social work is diverse and interesting when supervision is at the core of our practice. We feel strongly that supervision is the cornerstone of social work practice and when provided well, it enables social workers to feel supported, valued, and appreciated. Whilst much is written about many aspects of social work supervision, to date, there is little research on the characteristics that enhance effective supervision in social work practice. Developing our evidence-informed supervision models, each one tailored for professionals in different fields of practice and stage of career, has enabled us to provide and promote quality supervision that supports practice capability and professional excellence.

Our respective roles with Amovita International, Tracey as CEO and Rebecca as the International Consultant, enable us to diversify and expand how we deliver and promote best practice in supervision. Regularly travelling across Australia, a typical day in Tracey's working life is providing supervision to social work students, practitioners, senior managers, and CEOs. She also offers training on many aspects of supervision, including how to use our evidence-based supervision models.

Based in the United Kingdom, Rebecca's focus is on researching and developing innovative approaches in supervision to enhance practitioner capability using the PETS® supervision model. Having connections to professionals whose work involves human-animal practice, including veterinary social workers, enables us to provide supervision and training that is specialised and tailored to meet the needs of social workers and maintain endurance and practice excellence in the complex work that is undertaken.

We know from research that the vicarious impact of practice, particularly amongst professionals interacting with humans and animals, is significant. We also know that using an evidence-based model as well as attending supervision training increases supervision effectiveness. With emerging and growing fields of practice involving human-animal interactions such as veterinary social work, using the PETS® supervision model enables supervisors to focus discussions in an integrative manner. The PETS® model considers the relationship between key areas within the supervisee's role such as human-animal practices, meeting organisational requirements, providing support, and engaging in ongoing growth and development. As the components of the model inter-relate in supervision discussions, supervision becomes a dynamic supervisory ecosystem that enables it to remain effective over time.

Providing effective supervision can be a transformative experience for supervisees, both personally and professionally. However, supervisees often express concerns about supervision being cancelled given the lack of time to provide it, or when it is predominantly focused on the tasks and processes in their role rather than reflection on their work. It is, therefore, a crucial part of our work to promote supervision as an essential part of practice and ensure supervisors are also well supervised. We have found that having an evidence-informed supervision model such as PETS® directly influences the practice of supervision. It enables the supervision environment to remain dynamic and focus on the supervisees' needs. It assists to build and maintain supervisor capability and ultimately a positive and engaging supervisory relationship.

Supervision ought to be an integral part of practice throughout a social worker's career. Your role is important, and engaging in supervision using a supervision model assists to reduce the risk of professional fatigue and burnout. Using a supervision model to focus discussions enables you to set an effective agenda and achieve key outcomes. We would encourage new and experienced supervisors and social workers to attend training that includes how to provide and receive effective supervision and use a supervision model to set the agenda and guide supervision discussions. Training should also include a range of professional tools and resources used in supervision that enables it to be dynamic and focused.

Training and supervising professionals who work with humans and animals about the PETS® model is immensely rewarding. It can at times feel challenging shifting the mindset of supervisor's who place greater value on more task and process supervision. But when they appreciate how using an evidence-informed supervision model can be to structure and focus reflective discussions, supervision becomes a transformative experience. We hope sharing our career journey and the work we do to promote and provide effective supervision inspires you to achieve practice excellence in your career through engagement in effective and dynamic supervision.

39
SOCIAL WORK OUTSIDE THE BOX

Emilie Evans

My route to the human-animal interaction field, as it is for so many others, has been circuitous, yet extremely valuable. My first inklings of interest in the HAI field occurred during my undergraduate studies when I chose to major in biology on a pre-med track and minor in sociology to combine my interests in the natural and social sciences. After graduation, I was adrift and ended up working as a receptionist at a veterinary clinic exclusively for cats. Working with the cats at this clinic, I witnessed firsthand the power of the human-animal bond, as well as the effects when that bond is broken or never fostered in the first place. I became fascinated, which brought me to enroll in the Master of Social Work program at the Graduate School of Social Work at the University of Denver (DU). I spent my second-year internship working with DU's Institute for Human-Animal Connection and a sanctuary known as the Zoology Foundation, where I conducted research on the state of humane education in the United States and led educational camps. These internships helped me gain hands-on experience with fostering the human-animal bond, conducting HAI research and engaging in humane education practices.

When I graduated in 2020, finding work, let alone work in the HAI field, seemed an insurmountable obstacle. I applied to job after job, finding the most relevant ones on the job boards of the Colorado Nonprofit Association and Association of Professional Humane Educators. Both boards post diverse job offerings that are often relevant to HAI. Eventually, I came across an open role at Morris Animal Foundation (MAF) – Veterinary Research Assistant.

This role involved communicating with participants of the Golden Retriever Lifetime Study (GRLS) to ensure accurate and complete data collection. GRLS is a longitudinal cohort study following 3,044 golden retrievers

DOI: 10.4324/9781003335528-43

throughout their lifetime to collect data on malignancies and lifestyle. While it was a role that involved fostering the human-animal bond to support research efforts, it was not quite where I wanted to be. I wanted to be involved in study design, managing research efforts, and writing manuscripts related to HAI. I came to my supervisor with what I wanted to do, and we worked out a plan for how I could get there. It wouldn't happen immediately but with patience and effort, I worked my way up to the Veterinary Research Manager role. What got me there was highlighting my talents and skills and how they could be better utilized. I took on projects that interested me and volunteered where I was needed. This demonstrated that I was capable and eager to do more, and I am lucky enough that MAF is the type of employer that recognizes and rewards that.

My new role as Veterinary Research Manager involves managing the operations and day-to-day proceedings of the GRLS. I ensure our relationship with participants and veterinarians is maintained, that data integrity is upheld, and crises are managed when and if they arise. Additionally, I conduct research projects utilizing GRLS data. I absolutely love working at MAF and am happy to continue working here for a long time!

Of course, that does not mean that everything is perfect. As with any job, there are obstacles and challenges. The main challenge I face is that MAF is an organization focused primarily on veterinary medicine and animal health. Since it isn't an organization that primarily hires social workers, at times it can be tricky to highlight the importance of social work in what we do. It might not always seem apparent to my coworkers. I find that the most effective approach is to emphasize that we aren't collecting the data from the dogs directly but from the human participants. In addition, humans are the donors that keep MAF afloat, choose to participate in future research efforts, and who read our manuscripts and make decisions that affect animal health. If we cannot connect with humans, we cannot help the non-human animals our organization is dedicated to.

Despite any roadblocks that may come up, I love the work that I do and enjoy working for MAF. I would highly recommend a similar position to anyone interested in HAI research. My recommendations to find a role such as mine are to be open to unusual opportunities. Look at roles in organizations that aren't purely social work based and don't be afraid to stretch outside of your comfort zone. Social workers have a unique skill set that equips them for a plethora of roles. Be creative in how you market your social work degree. Job applications and interviews are an opportunity to sell yourself, do not be afraid to sing your praises!

During your interview and once you receive your job offer, keep an eye out for any red flags that might indicate the organization isn't supportive: if they are unwilling to answer your questions, unwilling to discuss benefits, or lack clarity or consistency. Strive to find a place that encourages your growth and values you as a person by examining benefits; benefits are a great way to see if their actions back up what they say. Try to connect with people in the organization to see if their experience matches up with what you learned during interviews and from browsing the organization's website. Don't be afraid to trust your gut and run the other way if needed. Job searches can feel daunting, especially within niche fields. Just remember that there are many unique roles that social workers trained in HAI are perfectly equipped for!

40

ADVOCACY AND PAWPRINTS

How a Dog Changed My Career

Amber Depuydt-Goodlock

Background

I have been working in victim services for almost 25 years. I graduated with a bachelor's in science, with a double major in Psychology and Gender Studies. During my college years, I volunteered with a community sexual assault services program as a victim advocate. Following graduation, the organization hired me to coordinate the victim advocacy program. I absolutely loved supervising our 25+ volunteers. Eventually, my passion for the work encouraged me to return to college to purse a Master's in Social Work so I could expand my work with survivors in a therapeutic setting.

My Why

One afternoon, I was sitting in the courtroom supporting a young child testifying. She could barely see over the wall of the large witness box. The defense attorney kept telling her to "SPEAK UP" and "We can't hear you." I watched this terrified child become more withdrawn with every demand. I did my best to reassure her from the gallery but could not overcome the intimidating presence of her abuser. She shut down. The judge ordered a brief recess. As we rushed out of the courtroom, the prosecutor pled with me to find a way to get her back on the stand to finish her testimony. If she could not, the case would be dismissed. I was not new to this, but for some reason, this broke me. I felt honored to advocate on behalf of survivors but felt defeated by the way the criminal justice system seemed to re-traumatize victims, especially children. It was this night my partner met me at the door with an early birthday present – a picture of a German Shepherd puppy and a training magazine. I opened the magazine to a centerfold story about a child sexual abuse survivor who was able to get through testimony against her abuser with the help of a police K9. I will never forget the chills that ran up and down my arms. Research on the positive impact of the human-animal bond was in its infancy, but intuitively, I knew that a well-trained dog could provide comfort to a trauma survivor in a way that even a skilled therapist could not. This was the start of my journey incorporating trained dogs into my work with survivors of sexual violence.

Facility dogs are professionally trained dogs placed with a professional working in an educational, mental health, healthcare, or criminal justice setting. Facility dogs must pass the same public access test used to ensure service dogs are safe in public and must be annually evaluated to ensure maintenance of these standards. Following an extensive application and interview process, a facility dog is matched to a handler in a professional setting. These high standards are critical when working with vulnerable crime victims, especially children.

To date, I have had the pleasure to work with two facility dogs, both trained by Canine Companions (https://canine.org/service-dogs/our-dogs/facility-dogs/ for more information). I had Matty from August 2013–2021 and now Chewy from October 2021 to present. On an average day, Chewy greets and sits with children as they wait to be forensically interviewed at our Child Advocacy Center. Chewy's calm demeanor puts children at ease. In many instances, children and caregivers start sharing stories of their own dog – an instant icebreaker. When it is time for the forensic interview, children feel empowered by walking Chewy to the interview room where he curls up at their feet or next to their lap. This is where he stays, unobtrusive, for the entirety of the interview. Since a forensic interview is part of a criminal investigation, it is critical Chewy remains unobtrusive and does not attempt to engage a child in play. At post-interview, Chewy gets to have a little more fun demonstrating his skills, including his ability to fetch! The goal is to encourage movement and bring the child to a more neutral, playful state. I want children to leave our Child Advocacy Center laughing, smiling, and remembering the center as a safe place.

When Chewy is not participating in forensic interviews, he may participate in counseling interventions focused on emotion regulation. Chewy's training in 40 task-based commands provide the foundation to incorporate him in different activities while also providing space for safe touch and physical comfort. Chewy may also attend court hearings with children and adult survivors. His skilled training allows him to curl up behind a witness stand, next to a child witness, without an observer ever knowing he is there. This is important because criminal justice professionals, primarily defense attorneys, have objected to the use of a dog to assist a vulnerable witness since dogs are often well liked by people, potentially causing a juror to have more empathy for the witness holding the leash. Therefore, it is critical that any dog stepping into a criminal justice setting has a high level of training, consistency in behavior, and a calm, unobtrusive demeanor.

The Benefits

The smiles. So many smiles! Team members and clients of all ages look forward to seeing Chewy. Children get excited for counseling appointments and group sessions where they get to spend time with Chewy. When walking down a hallway, people smile when they see Chewy and stop to talk, usually to him, and me as an afterthought. The joy Chewy brings to clients, multidisciplinary team members, and staff, brings me a great deal of joy in my work.

The Challenges

Honestly, the challenges are minimal. The two challenges most impactful in my work as a handler are time, or lack of, and the grief that comes from losing a working dog. Incorporating time to care for a facility dog during a busy day can be challenging. They have to be a priority and you have to be flexible. Secondly, there is grief and loss. The grief of losing a working dog is different than losing a pet. The personal grief may be similar, but with a working dog, you are also honoring the grief of so many others – clients, team members, and staff. Yet, the benefits and rewards clearly outweigh the challenges.

41

TRUE JOY

Animal-Assisted Play Therapy

Jacqueline George

> Enter into children's play and you will find the place where their minds, hearts and souls meet.
>
> (Axline, 1964)

Once upon a time, many years ago, a young lady showed up for her first day on the job. She had been told the job would be to go to daycare centers in the city to consult with staff regarding children who were demonstrating problem behaviors. However, on that first day, her supervisor told her, "By the way, you'll be doing play therapy with the preschoolers at the daycare centers." "Umm, great!" the young lady replied. "And what exactly is play therapy?"

Thus began my lifelong journey of working with children using play therapy, helping them heal from trauma and resolve problems. That supervisor sent me to national training programs regarding Child Centered Play Therapy (CCPT) and I fell in love with this therapeutic approach of working with children and their families. Play is the language that children speak, and toys are the words of that language. Through the years, I attended many trainings, learning to speak the language of play as effectively as possible, and in 2001, I attained the credential of Registered Play Therapist–Supervisor. Anyone interested in exploring the field of play therapy will find information at www.a4pt.org, including the requirements to become a Registered Play Therapist.

Throughout my years as a LCSW, I have maintained a schedule consisting of seeing six people per day (three in the morning and three in the afternoon). Certainly, some play therapists work longer days in order to have a shorter week. Personally, I find that I give each client my best when I balance my

DOI: 10.4324/9781003335528-45

time between home and work. Additionally, life balance requires self-care to avoid vicarious trauma and/or burnout. What that self-care looks like is different for each therapist, but it is an important piece that cannot be slighted if one hopes to thrive as a therapist for many years. A critical component is to figure out what helps you leave work at work, rather than carry your clients' problems around with you.

The field of play therapy has a lot of relevant quotes and some of them indirectly address self-care. My favorite comes from George Bernard Shaw, who said, "We don't stop playing because we grow old; we grow old because we stop playing" (Wynner and Goldring, 1967). I feel that the best therapists have fur and four legs, which brings me to the next major step in this story – Animal Assisted Play Therapy™ (AAPT).

After being a Registered Play Therapist-Supervisor for almost 12 years, I began working at an agency that had equine therapy services as well as play therapy services for clients. I felt like I had died and gone to heaven, as this job combined the career I loved with the opportunity to work alongside my favorite animal. The agency sent me to two four-day intensive AAPT trainings and I began involving horses in my play therapy work with children. Unfortunately, that agency turned out to be an unhealthy work environment and I found myself opening my own private practice. No matter how I looked at my own space, however, there simply was *not* room for a horse, even a tiny horse! That is when cats entered my life.

I have had dogs and cats (and other animals) as pets throughout my life, so cats were not entirely new. What was new was AAPT's approach toward animals. The relationship with the animal is of primary importance and it involves truly *listening* to what your therapy partner is communicating. Respect and honor toward the animal are equally as important as the respect and honor one shows toward a client. Further, in AAPT, the goal is for the animal to really enjoy their "job" while you, their human, are constantly alert for stress vs happy signals and making sure they have the ability to remove themselves from a session if they feel inclined to do so.

In AAPT, all animals bring their natural selves to the therapy sessions. We are not looking for overly trained animals or for them to behave in a manner that is outside their normal manner of behaving. For example, I have two therapy cats working with me, Deyanna (a beautiful Ragdoll) and Skippy (a gregarious orange tabby). Neither of them typically enjoy sitting on a person's lap for a given period of time (although Deyanna sometimes will). Due to that, they would "fail" the test of a national organization that certifies cats in animal-assisted work. However, both cats bring a host of positive qualities and experiences to my therapy sessions with children, adults, and families. Deyanna is a laid back, affectionate cat with a quiet and calm demeanor. Skippy is an active cat that intensely loves interacting with people. Both cats have been clicker trained by child clients to do a variety of things, including being able to complete an obstacle course. My play therapy work is enhanced as the interactions the cats have with clients help with everything from improving emotional regulation and decreasing stress and anxiety, to improving self-concept. Further, the length of time a client is with me is frequently shortened due to the cats' impact on therapy sessions.

Anyone wanting to learn more about the field of AAPT can read the award-winning book *Animal Assisted Play Therapy* by VanFleet and Faa-Thompson (2017). Additionally, the website www.iiaapt.org has information about trainings.

Perhaps the biggest challenge of AAPT is the split attention required on the part of the therapist. Although I was a highly skilled play therapist before beginning AAPT work, I found it temporarily felt like I lost my skills as I learned how to split my attention between the communication of the client and the communication of the animal. However, the effort has more than paid off by working with animals I love. I invite you to join the AAPT journey. You will be forever happy you did so!

References

Axline, V. M. (1964). Dibs: In Search of Self (p. 33). Ballantine Books.
VanFleet, R., & Faa-Thompson, T. (2017). Animal Assisted Play Therapy. Professional Resource Press.
Wynner, E., & Goldring, E. (1967). Never Too Late: A Study of Mature Students (p. 96). Pitman Publishing.

42

A ONE HEALTH PATH TO SUPPORT HEALTH AND WELLBEING

Debbie Stoewen

Of all the things close to my heart, it was the love of animals that first shaped the course of my life. In a defining moment, when I was 13 years old, I knew that I would become a veterinarian. This knowing drove me to study hard, attend a university, apply to veterinary school, and graduate five years later. Despite the odds, this vet-by-heart became a vet for real.

Upon graduation (*Ontario Veterinary College* 1983), I spent the first years of my career in general and emergency practice, upon which I founded the *Pioneer Pet Clinic*, a family-centered companion animal hospital. With room in my heart for helping children as well as animals, I began fostering with *Family and Children's Services* (1995–1999). Introduced to, and inspired by, an alternate helping profession, I returned to school in 2000 to take undergraduate coursework in social development studies at the *University of Waterloo* (2000–2003), completing a Master of Social Work at *Wilfrid Laurier University* (2005). As the first person in North America to be a veterinarian and social worker, I then merged my background with a PhD in Epidemiology at the *University of Guelph* (2008–2012), specializing in veterinary decision-making and veterinary-client-patient communication.

I had imagined that I would work at a university, but the universe had something else in mind. As an interdisciplinarian, I became the Care & Empathy Officer (CEO) and Director of Veterinary Services for *Pets Plus Us*, a highly innovative pet health insurance startup, from 2013 to 2020. With this company, I had the privilege to create a fully accredited veterinary continuing education program called "The Social Side of Practice" for veterinarians and their teams across Canada. I've given hundreds of presentations on veterinary wellness, veterinary-client-patient communication, teamwork, organizational culture, and leadership, becoming a renowned veterinary health and wellbeing speaker and educator. I also provided a nationwide pet loss counseling service for pet owners and a communication skills training program for my coworkers. Each day was different, requiring self-discipline and long hours (admittedly) to keep the balance, as I was responsible for each of the initiatives every step of the way. Outside of *Pets Plus Us*, I served as the Director of Veterinary Affairs at *LifeLearn Animal Health*, where I developed educational offerings to help veterinary professionals address the challenges of practice.

I've volunteered with, and am a member of, several veterinary and social work associations, provincially, nationally, and internationally, including the *Canadian Veterinary Medical Association* as the *CVJ's* wellness columnist and the *World Small Animal Veterinary Association* as a member of the Professional Wellness Group. I've published two book chapters as well as a variety of articles in veterinary and social work journals and newsmagazines.

The most rewarding part of my work has been making a difference in the lives of others; as a veterinary practitioner, caring for my patients and families; and then as a social worker/educator, supporting the wellbeing of veterinary professionals, and in this, the wellbeing of their patients and families too. Knowing my work had an increasingly broader reach, that I was helping more people and animals than ever before, mattered. What also mattered was being part of something bigger than myself: the company, a community that I believed in and was proud of, and likewise, believed in and was proud of me. Belonging, mattering, and 'doing what matters' has been fulfilling.

My biggest challenge was managing the unknown. There were times when I knew things, from the deepest part of myself, and times when I didn't. It can be hard to push forward when you don't know where you will go or what you will do, especially when you pursue an unconventional education or career path. I have had to remain trusting and hopeful in the face of uncertainty.

This year, the 40th since my graduation, I was honored with the *2023 OVMA Outstanding Veterinarian* award for outstanding contributions to the veterinary profession. As veterinarians – and social workers – we are caregivers, helpers, healers, facilitators, guides, connectors, and advocates. Each of us makes differences that stretch infinitely around us, the difference in one making a difference in another, and so on. We can't know where any one difference necessarily begins or ends. The beauty in this is that *we all count* – you, me, *every* one of us. And *our journeys count*. As you continue yours, I mine, and us ours, I offer a few insights to ease the way:

- Within the questioning, there is a knowing. Follow your heart.
- Believe in yourself. What's real on the inside can become real on the outside.
- Don't be afraid to take the unconventional path. Trust in the unfolding.

- One thing can lead to another so do the thing before.
- We can show up and stand out in so many ways.
- The greatest reward is making a difference in the lives of others.
- Be part of something bigger than yourself. It nurtures the spirit.
- Be somewhere where you belong. It sustains the heart.
- Do things that matter to you. And matter in the doing.
- Live into the unknown. Trust. Hope. Every day.

43
WEAVING HUMANE EDUCATION INTO SOCIAL WORK

Maggie Lantzy and Sarah M. Bexell

From systematic oppression and a myriad of "isms," pandemics, mass extinction, violence, climate change, and more, the need for humane education has never been greater. With a systems approach grounded in social-ecological justice, humane educators embrace the ideals of kindness, compassion, and respect for humans, other species, and the natural environment to ensure understanding of the interconnectedness of the world. Humane education addresses societal issues through the encouragement of empathy and compassion to empower students to take action to strengthen communities and all Earth systems.

To address intersectional oppressions, authors Maggie Lantzy and Sarah Bexell have separately and together implemented humane education with non-formal education sites and within formal school systems.

Maggie received a B.S. in psychology and a master's in social work with a certificate in animal-assisted social work. She is also a Certified Humane Educational Specialist. With a background in animal training and applied behavioral analysis (ABA) therapy for children with autism, Maggie knew she wanted to combine her passions of working with people and animals. While earning her MSW, she learned about humane education and knew that this field would be central in her life. Following graduate school, Maggie was hired at the Zoology Foundation, an animal sanctuary in Colorado. As the program director, Maggie created and implemented humane education camps, field trips, group tours, and more for sanctuary visitors of all ages. Through these programs, she continually witnessed what she had always known and believed in – our innate connection to the natural world. At the Zoology Foundation, she also began collaborating with Sarah on humane education research, curriculum development, and the creation of the Humane

Education Practitioner Certificate (CHEP) at the Institute for Human-Animal Connection (IHAC).

Sarah earned a B.A. in biology and minor in environmental studies. She went on to get a M.A. in biological anthropology and specialized in primate behavior where she conducted thesis research on the behavior of three endangered species. It was through this degree that she learned that humans were driving mass extinction of the animals that she loved. She decided to take an action-oriented approach. She pursued an M.Ed. in science education and PhD in early childhood education. Sarah felt strongly that if humans understood how their behavior was harming others, they may alter their behaviors to protect species that also need a thriving Earth. She discovered humane education while doing doctoral intervention design, a conservation education intervention for students in China that shared the minds, social behaviors, and emotions of other species to promote empathy and protection.

Humane Education Careers

Depending on your setting, the day-to-day of a humane educator could look very different. Previously, Sarah and Maggie had positions at organizations where they created and taught humane education programming. During Maggie's time at the Zoology Foundation and Sarah's time at the Chengdu Research Base for Giant Pandas, they were responsible for curriculum development, scheduling, marketing, registration, and of course, teaching. Currently, Maggie and Sarah focus on humane education for adult learners in a university setting. On any given day that could include teaching graduate courses, guest lecturing, designing new courses or educational interventions, or research into whether humane education interventions are effective. Through the CHEP certificate, Maggie and Sarah have seen various professionals implement humane education into their current or ideal setting.

Humane education can be integrated into any field. Because of this, there is not always a clear career path for a job in humane education. Often, this means forging your own path and convincing others that what you are doing matters. Find what you are passionate about and what you are good at. Any field of study can be applied to the protection of human health, species protection, and environmental preservation. The field of humane education is truly inter- and transdisciplinary. Choose what suits you best and specialize in what you feel will make the most impact.

Seeing the impact you have on an individual and the lightbulb moments when someone makes connections makes the work worthwhile. Sarah and Maggie love seeing how an interaction with an individual animal or nature can make this type of connection. Humane education gives someone a way to validate feelings they may naturally have about other humans, other species, or Earth, and provides direction for making a positive impact.

Alternatively, this work is hard, sad, and frustrating. Humane education works to solve what we call "wicked problems." There are no quick fixes, and if solved too quickly, we could create more harm. Change takes time.

We live in a polarized, anthropocentric society and people don't always agree with what we do, including others in social work. We've had people in our field challenge humane education because they don't see value in including other species and Earth when we haven't solved human problems. Humane education helps learners to understand, accept, and then live by the fact that human well-being and survival is utterly dependent on the health and well-being of Earth and biodiversity. This is one of the most important goals of integrating humane education into social work. Finally, it can be difficult balancing your opinions and biases with meeting students where they're at in a world where people, especially youth, are facing incomprehensible challenges. But it can be done, as the root of humane education is compassion.

Humane education is challenging and rewarding. Study hard and don't give up. Find your people, build community, and fight like hell.

SECTION V
Human-Animal Interactions Focus within Human and Animal Organizations

44

EMERGING PRACTICES IN ANIMAL WELFARE

Doug Plant

Having a social work background, I never expected to find myself leading an animal welfare organization. How and why would a social worker (MSW '81) find a role in a traditional humane society where the focus was clearly on saving animals? My career at Michigan Humane started just over five years ago, at a time when there were no such roles in this field. But the good news is, due to the growing field of veterinary social work (VSW) and community social work outreach roles, my path is rare but no longer unique.

As a graduate student, I found my calling in working with individuals struggling with psychological disorders. As most of us come to understand, working with individuals often requires focusing on family needs. We must be willing to address environmental factors such as systemic racism, cultural and economic influences, as well as challenges of the human condition, to assist families navigating the complex world around them. You might be surprised that these client issues are commonly experienced by veterinarians and technicians as they serve pet owners and their families. Most veterinary practices and sheltering organizations provide animal care to a wide array of families, including those who are struggling with financial limitations, health problems, transportation, access to resources such as veterinary care and adoption, and the many complex issues associated with living at or near poverty. But therein lies the problem; our current veterinary medical and sheltering fields are often times not equipped to deal with the complexity of problems some families face.

It is an often-stated belief that most folks going into animal welfare do so to work with animals and prefer to not deal with humans. Early in my tenure at Michigan Humane, I heard this repeatedly, especially when I would bring up the idea of how we can be more human-centric in our work. I observed

DOI: 10.4324/9781003335528-49

staff struggle with managing concerns of clients who had little or no money to pay for care; clients who clearly had emotional issues; or being available to those who had to make the difficult decision to have their pet humanely euthanized. I saw these challenges and learned that they were common in most animal humane organizations around the country. So, I took the step of asking many of the veterinarians and staff what was behind the belief that animal welfare people don't like to work with other people. And not surprisingly, I learned that it was not about disliking humans. In fact, many of these folks were socially conscious and quite comfortable in conversations. The primary reason for this belief, I learned, was that they feared having to address the human condition – because they were never provided with the tools and techniques to be helpful. Coupling this with the limited time available to provide support in a busy veterinary practice or sheltering facility made it clear to me, that although this was a big problem, it was a solvable one.

As I scanned the environment for solutions, I came across two key facts. First, the field of VSW was starting to make gains through the University of Tennessee – Knoxville leadership. This was a game-changing development in both the animal welfare and social work fields. Embedding MSWs in the veterinary practice to support the medical team, while being available to directly assist the individual or family facing their own challenges, created a significant solution to so many of the issues. The second fact was the reality that the field of VSW was new and finding and hiring certified staff was not only a quantity issue but one of expense. At one time, most animal welfare organizations struggled with resourcing the animal side of their business and therefore rarely could afford to add a new but necessary role. Here is the good news: I have seen this dramatically change at many of the more progressive organizations around the country. They have begun building these positions into their budgets and have been taking on social work interns to understand how to best deploy them. While in its infancy, this progress opens opportunities for social workers who have a desire to work within the sheltering environment.

The VSW path is one that fills a unique need in the field. With the demand on veterinary services nationally, there is intense pressure to manage the influx of clients. Support staff are overwhelmed and historically underpaid in comparison to the human healthcare field. The VSW is being seen as an important part of the interdisciplinary team bringing both solutions and capacity. Private and non-profit veterinary clinics are seriously looking at the VSW role in their business model.

There are several more ways in which a social worker can bring their skills and experience while serving the mission of an animal welfare organization. Presently, there is a paradigm shift, well into its third year of progression, from a reactive/intervention approach to one of prevention. Almost every large animal welfare organization and many mid-size ones are making this shift. Not only is the prevention model less expensive (at Michigan Humane, animals cared for in shelter cost about $600/animal while those cared for in the community cost just under $300/animal) but, more importantly, this model has a positive impact on upstream efforts – it helps keep pets in their homes and out of shelters.

Community outreach programs are growing throughout the field and focusing on more than just animal needs. For years, Michigan Humane has operated a pet food pantry in Detroit, providing pet food and supplies to anyone in need. Interviews with our pantry clients have consistently told us that families who struggle with pet food insecurity are just as likely to struggle with human food insecurity, housing challenges, transportation issues, and many other basic needs. This is the reason that our Manager of Community Solutions is an MSW. This role oversees our pet food pantry and most of our outreach efforts in the community. This approach brings animal resources (food, supplies, dog houses, etc.) to families in neighborhoods where poverty is a serious factor in their ability to have companion animals. Since it is our belief that companion animals play a key role in healthy, engaged families, we do everything we can to ensure that resources are provided to assist in keeping families together. But here is what we found that makes this even more exciting: families inherently trust animal welfare organizations once they learn we are there to help them keep their pet. With that trust comes an open door to the family and their conditions – both human and animal alike. Due to that level of openness, I firmly believe we have an obligation to identify and help solve both human and animal needs where we can.

Michigan Humane along with many animal welfare organizations are now designated field placement agencies for students at the BSW and MSW levels. We provide internships for macro and micro students deployed in several areas of our organization where we interface with the public. The interest in the recruitment of social work interns within animal welfare organizations is gaining great steam across the country. This is further evidence that administrators and program leadership recognize the value of social workers in this environment. For the student, this plays a vital role in understanding how their passion for helping humans and animals can be nurtured.

Another opportunity where we are deploying social workers and students is with our Field Services team. This team provides outreach in the neighborhoods throughout the city of Detroit, answering calls about stray or injured animals. The social worker supports the interactions with residents by ensuring they have resources for their animals but also assists human needs through information and referrals. Follow-up is provided to make sure the resident finds the assistance they need. Our newest program provides high-quality veterinary care to individuals who cannot access care at a veterinary clinic. Disabled adults, older at-risk adults, and those lacking reliable transportation are the most likely to be unable to receive the animal care they need. This outreach team includes a veterinarian, veterinary assistant, and social worker (staff or student) to care for the animal in the client's home. In that setting, the social worker plays a key role in helping to identify resources to encourage a healthy environment for the pets and the humans. As we often say, the pet is only as healthy as the family who loves and cares for it.

All these examples of animal welfare organization programs illustrate what an exciting time this is for the intersection of social work and animal welfare. Fostering the passion of helping others through the lens of the family's companion animal creates a dynamic and positive arena for social workers. The prevention mindset of working within communities to keep families together has resulted in saving many lives, both human and animal. The need for veterinary and community outreach social workers is emerging and finding great enthusiasm and support in the field. Through this work, we can positively impact families and stabilize neighborhoods – leading to more humane communities and better lives for both humans and the animals they care for.

45
LESSONS FROM HORSES LED MY CAREER

Aviva Vincent

I came across the term veterinary social work sitting alone in the research center at my university, one-semester into my doctoral program shortly after a conversation where it was suggested that I consider transferring because HAI in social work was "not research". That was when I knew I was on the right path.

Though linear in reflection, my path to my current career took an incredibly iterative path. And through it all, animals have always been present. Though there were many dogs at home – along with chickens and bees – horses have been an ever-present fixture. I grew up in a lesson stable where no one used the term "therapy", but my experience was very much therapeutic. I found safety and leaned to feel and express empathy, courage, and perseverance from equine educators. I carried their teachings from the age of four with me through adulthood.

In my senior year of high school, my mentor took me to a photoshoot at High Hopes Therapeutic Riding Center in Old Lyme, Connecticut. From that first experience, I was enamored. In college, I pursued a liberal arts degree while I continued to ride, teach riding lessons, and train young horses. After graduation, my plan was to pour my experience and love of horses into a business – a small stable that was intended to be a family-run therapeutic riding center. During the purchase of the property, the town rezoned the property as wetlands. Within eight months, the business was gone, and the land was residential. At a loss of what to do next, I stepped away from horses and turned to a variety of short careers. With the support of loved ones and sage advice, I found my way to the School of Social Work at University of Connecticut. This was the first experience where I fell in love with learning,

DOI: 10.4324/9781003335528-50

I excelled in the classroom, and saw the connection between education and a future career.

After working post-MSW for United Way, Community Investment, I had the opportunity to relocate and reinvest in my education. My wife and I relocated to Cleveland, Ohio, for advanced degrees and training. In this doctoral social work program, I proposed researching the human-animal bond, and specifically, how animal-assisted interventions may support youth mental health. At first, I was met with resistance – it was suggested that I transfer to another program as "HAI is not an area for social work research". Yet, with the support of profound mentorship, I stayed in my program. This is important to share because, as I learned from peers, students often feel the need to conform to the expectations they are presented. This is an invitation to challenge the process while exceeding the outcome.

Once I knew I was supported in this professional endeavor, doors continued to open! I was supported by Dr. Elizabeth Strand to complete the Veterinary Social Work Certificate program to supplement my doctoral education (I then taught the AAI module for five years). I was accepted to an inaugural fellowship with Animals & Society, and student in Spit Camp at the Institute for Salivary Bioscience Research. With this training, I created a new partnership between the school of dental medicine and social work for my research which looked at physiological indicators (e.g. oxytocin, cortisol, and alpha-amylase) of children with a known anxiety, pre-and-post intervention (Vincent et al., 2020). In short, kids who were known to be afraid of the dentist played with dogs before their appointment for ten minutes and then brought the dogs with them into their appointment. What we found was that all children in the study were able to complete their dental work without pharmacological intervention, even though they had needed sedation in prior appointments. While this study was with dogs, it was the precursor for my current work, using the same methodology but with children and horses.

While in my doctoral program, I started working as the program director at Fieldstone Farm Therapeutic Riding Center. This is the point where prior experience, education, research, and passion for horses began to converge. In this capacity, I was responsible for ensuring high-quality programs in adaptive riding, hippotherapy, carriage driving, and ground lessons for community participants. Currently, I maintain my certification for therapeutic riding instruction and facilitate groups for veterans while focusing on research and education.

I joined the faculty at Cleveland State University in social work with a dedication to continuing research and teaching veterinary social work. My wonderful colleague and friend Lisa Wibog, LISW-S, and I founded Healing Paws LLC, a small business dedicated to training and consultation for veterinary social work and practices of animal-assisted interventions.

No longer is the consideration of animals in social work relegated to hobbies and niceties. Human-animal interaction is an interdisciplinary field for education, research, and practice. If you find yourself considering any work in this field, I welcome you with open arms and a cup of tea. More specifically, a question I often get asked is, "Should you get a doctorate"? My oversimplified answer is this: if you want to be a researcher or teach at a university (full-time) – yes, especially if you have a topic or question that you *really* want to think about and research for about five years – yes! If you want more credentials – no.

In hindsight, I can see how I was on a path from my childhood experiences with horses to where I am today. Social work careers in One Health continue to expand and evolve as social work as a field expands its recognition of the importance of animals in the lives of humans. As long as animals are in our lives, there will be an infinite number of teaching, research, and community work opportunities.

Reference

Vincent, A., Heima, M., & Farkas, K. J. (2020). Therapy dog support in pediatric dentistry: a social welfare intervention for reducing anticipatory anxiety and situational fear in children. *Child and Adolescent Social Work Journal*, 37, 615–629.

46
A SOCIAL WORKER'S LEARNINGS FROM THE HUMAN-ANIMAL BOND

Animals as Family, Healers, and Colleagues

Dillon Dodson

Background, History, and Interest in the Field – My Story

My first friend was my neighbors' dog, Corky. At the age of 3, without having the words to describe what I have since come to understand, animals brought me a sense of contentment, belonging, and of course, unbridled joy. My second friend was Corky's human sister "Marielle", who has remained my very best friend 35 years later. And so, this became my first learning – how animals can foster connection, and how together humans and people can make indelible marks on our hearts and souls.

I am blessed that my life has been surrounded by animals. Whether wild, livestock, or domesticated, my dad made sure we always had a menagerie of animals waiting to be fed and admired. My dad was my first foray into what it meant to be animal obsessed. There was never a dog that crossed his path that didn't receive a pat on the head, a kiss or bone from his pocket. Coming by it naturally, he also grew up in a household that cherished the human-animal bond (HAB); adoration for animals is in my DNA.

While my kindergarten dream was to be a veterinarian, my desire transferred to caring about people as I grew older. I became a registered social worker and settled in the youth homelessness sector, specifically supporting survivors of human trafficking. It is in this work and in engaging equine partners in therapy that I saw first-hand that animal healing was not just my own lived experience but rather universal. My passion grew, leading me to enroll in a Veterinary Social Work (VSW) postgraduate program and was elected board member of the International Association of Veterinary Social Workers. In this way, I honored my second learning – follow what brings contentment, belonging, and joy.

A Day in the Life

My current position is hybrid in nature. When onsite, a workday typically involves wandering through the halls of the Toronto Humane Society (THS), creating relationship with colleagues and the four-legged friends who currently call our shelter "home". Other activities include attending program development meetings and/or meeting with pet families experiencing crisis and in need of our services.

When I work from home, my aims often remain the same but with increased time on the computer and more sporadic puppy cuddles from my Pyrenees mix, Murphy. I spend the day speaking with referring agencies, pet families, or solidifying partnerships with human and animal services. Work often involves project or program establishment or management, whether preparing for presentations, supervising social work student practicums, developing staff wellness initiatives to foster compassion satisfaction, vicarious resilience and moral alignment, or exploring gaps in our community for pet owners experiencing marginalization.

Advice for Others Seeking a Similar Position/Profession

The best advice I can offer is to invest in yourself. Make time for continued education even if it is unclear if/when that training or certification might be of benefit. Appreciate that your path may not be entirely clear, but, over time, will unfold in a manner which you could have never imagined. If animals and a belief in the HAB is a passion for you, remain committed, find ways to transfer, and/or bring your skills together.

The other major element to prioritize is taking care of oneself. As a clinician who experienced vicarious trauma firsthand, getting to know yourself and paying steady attention is paramount to ensuring your ability to practice. Careful evaluation of one's willingness and ability to analyze what our work gives us, as well as what it may take from us, is invaluable and only you know what is most suitable.

Most Rewarding Parts of the Job

Drawing on lived experience as well as direct clinical application, it is a truly unique experience to elevate the HAB in a professional capacity. Working in a field where the recognition of the mutually beneficial relationship and the influence this has for holistic wellness is profound. VSW illuminates and advocates for wellness through meeting the needs of both people and their pets, and the most rewarding part of this is to be able to witness the beauty in the bond. The most rewarding part of my job is witnessing love actualized. Love for the animals, love for each other, and love for our community. To walk with others who are so passionate and so dedicated to their craft and to other souls is powerfully emotional and a gift that knows no bounds.

Challenges with Your Job

The primary challenge related to the VSW field is its infancy state in Ontario, Canada. With any emerging field, there remains an innate degree of uncertainty. Being comfortable with "grey" is imperative. That said, undetermined roles, responsibilities, and pathways bring opportunity for development. In line with the infancy of VSW, there is a need for continued growth in terms of equity, diversity, and associated power analysis and dynamics. Animal welfare is a space of intense values, morals, and subsequent emotions. Having a strong sense of oneself as a practitioner, including our influence and spaces for advocacy, is paramount.

An additional challenge relates to the propensity for isolation. Finding ways to build community is critical. Establishing multidisciplinary teams and external connections with others doing similar work is important to ensure continued wellness and maintenance of ethical practice.

How to Get a Job Like Yours

If you are working with humans, there are animals that could benefit. Consider the best manner to do this work. This might be micro, mezzo, or macro – based on your organization and community. In what ways can you interject the HAB into your current work? What skills do you have that may be transferrable? What proposals might you put forth to foster this relationship? Awareness of your passion as well as the importance of the human-animal bond are critical first steps.

47
ELEVATING THE LIVES OF ANIMALS AND OUR RELATIONSHIPS WITH THEM

Molly Jenkins

For as long as I can remember, non-human animals have been my friends and often the ones I seek out above all others. As a child raised in a single-parent home with few family members to keep me company, animals provided me with a sense of belonging, companionship, and the space to be wholly myself. I can still feel the joy of seeing my dog, Riley, long gone now, bouncing from the ground when seeing my face after a day apart. Or the solace of knowing we could always trust, uplift, and care for one another. It was perhaps my early relationship with him, combined with my love for other pets and all living beings, that first made me dream of a career focused on animals.

I started as many others have – with the goal of becoming a veterinarian. At the age of 10, I would ride the public bus across town to volunteer after school at my local humane society. By the time I entered college, my days were filled with studying biology, walking dogs, and scrubbing kennels, eventually working my way up to veterinary assistant in a clinic close to home. However, following graduation, I started questioning whether veterinary medicine was truly the path for me or simply one I had never thought to stray from. Although I wanted animals to remain at the forefront of my career, I was becoming increasingly interested in issues of social justice and helping people in need. That's when social work and the study of human-animal relationships entered my life.

I'm fortunate to live in beautiful Colorado, home to the University of Denver's Graduate School of Social Work. When I enrolled in 2006, the school offered, what was then, the only social work certificate program in the country focused on the healing effects of the human-animal bond. I knew I had struck gold, and for the next two years, I was a sponge for all things related to this emerging area of practice. Over time, the program has grown by leaps and bounds, educating students from around the world, leading innovative research, and promoting the interconnections between people, other animals, and the environment. In fact, I have been privileged to return to my alma mater as an adjunct faculty member, teaching MSW students for the past five years through the university's Institute for Human-Animal Connection.

Six months after receiving my MSW in 2008, I became a program assistant for American Humane Association, a national nonprofit which, at the time, was committed to both animal and child welfare. My initial responsibilities focused on assisting with efforts to strengthen the child welfare system, but I was always looking to collaborate with the organization's animal welfare and human-animal interaction (HAI) teams in the hopes of moving in that direction.

That perseverance paid off two years later when I had the opportunity to study the well-being effects of human-canine interactions for children with cancer, their families, and participating therapy dogs. This was a pivotal career moment, allowing me to connect with others, build my confidence and writing skills, and contribute to the growing HAI knowledge base. I often look back on these experiences with gratitude, knowing much of them were a matter of being in the right place at the right time. But, I also made the most of these opportunities by learning, listening, and keeping an open heart to what might come next.

Around this time, I reconnected with a fellow social worker, my DU mentor Philip Tedeschi, to co-edit a multi-author book called *Transforming Trauma: Resilience and Healing Through Our Connections With Animals*, published in 2019. While this project was a genuine cloud nine experience, I still found myself struggling to find a job focused on animals when I left American Humane after the grant-funded study ended in 2018.

The challenging truth is the HAI field remains small and often requires great patience and creativity for those who wish to devote their lives to the profession. For three years, I worked largely outside the field, finding ways to stay involved through teaching and serving on boards and committees. Then, in 2021, I saw a senior writing position open at the Dumb Friends League, one of the largest community-based animal welfare organizations in the U.S. Having never worked in animal sheltering or marketing before, I wondered if I had the creative chops to do the job. But, I viewed this as an exciting chance to grow and leverage my experience to advocate for animals and the people who love them most.

In this position, I've been inspired by the myriad ways animal welfare is evolving to meet the needs of people and animals, especially those who have been historically marginalized and underserved. Each day, I have the privilege of contributing to these initiatives, sharing their impact, and using the written word to build community and promote animal well-being.

These responsibilities, plus learning from my devoted colleagues and the animals in our care, are so rewarding.

I've always felt one of the best things about social work is the ability to make a difference through a variety of means. And with an ever-increasing appreciation for animals and the roles they play in our lives, there has never been a better time for social workers to find their place in this field. Dream jobs may not immediately arrive on our doorsteps, and it is often up to us to create them, but being a part of this professional community is wondrous. My advice is to approach the process with humility and patience, connect with others and seek understanding, take care of yourself along the way, and remember the ones, both human and non-human animal, who help you get there.

48

THE BEST WAY TO HELP PETS IS TO HELP PEOPLE

Elina Alterman

My path to being an animal shelter social worker was far from linear. As an immigrant child whose parents gave up the world they knew best so that my opportunities would never be limited, I felt pressure to Succeed with a capital "S." I always loved animals and had wanted to be a veterinarian when I was a child, but as so many other young girls, I believed that science wasn't for me. It never occurred to me that there might be other careers that involve animals. I was passionate about helping people, even more than the traditional ideas of "success." Coming from a family in which too many relatives perished in Hitler's concentration camps, Stalin's work camps, and through the forced relocation of the Koryo-saram, I have always been acutely aware of the privilege of being alive and wanted to use the myriad of opportunities that I had been granted to somehow help others. I just didn't know how.

My resume is a reflection of the various attempts I made at finding the right career and finding Success. I was a community organizer in Boston while receiving a bachelor's degree in Sociology and Latin American Studies. I worked as a foster care social worker and a maternity care coordinator in rural North Carolina while receiving dual master's degrees in Social Work and Public Health, with a concentration in Maternal and Child Health. After direct practice, I tried my hand at federal-level policy work, doing a postgraduate fellowship on Capitol Hill and working for a Congresswoman from California on healthcare and women's and children's legislative priorities. After my fellowship ended, I made the decision to leave the Hill, but stay nearby and use the skills that I had developed. I spent the next two years engaged in government relations for a well-known Washington DC nonprofit, focusing on equity issues in healthcare. The work left me depleted and the commute in DC left me exhausted. What restored me over and over was the connection

DOI: 10.4324/9781003335528-53

with my dog, and I spent my weekends hiking with him in the West Virginia mountains. I began to look for any jobs revolving around healthcare, equity, advocacy, and policy in the Midwest, still not thinking about a career in animal welfare.

I ended up moving to Wichita, Kansas, and working as a program officer at the largest health foundation in the state. My job was to build advocacy capacity across the state, funding nonprofits that worked on various social determinants of health. I loved my job. Finally, I found a space in which I could work on all of the many things I cared about – voting rights, immigration, healthcare, housing, criminal and juvenile justice reform, and more. But there was always one thing missing – animal welfare, which connects to mental health, housing, and so many of the other issues we were trying to address. However, my arguments as to why the foundation should provide funding for animal welfare as it related to human welfare fell on deaf ears.

After five years as a funder, I left and took intentional time to figure out what I wanted to do with my life. During that time, three life-changing things happened: (1) My partner and I moved to my hometown of Lawrence, Kansas; (2) I met the new Executive Director (ED) of the Lawrence Humane Society (LHS); and (3) the COVID pandemic hit. People were losing their jobs and their homes, and on top of it all, having to surrender their pets – layering trauma on top of trauma. The new humane society ED and I shared the same understanding of how animal and human welfare are interconnected and so a new position was created for me – Senior Manager of Social Work at the LHS.

In this position, I was responsible for conceptualizing and building our Crisis Pet Retention (CPR) program. Through the CPR program, we seek to help pets and people stay together through poverty, houselessness, job loss, domestic violence, and other systemic inequities. In addition to low-cost and subsidized veterinary care, we distribute pet food, provide temporary animal boarding, and provide low-income pet owners with the cost of pet deposits and pet rent so that pet ownership is not a barrier to accessing safe, affordable housing. In the two and a half years since CPR's inception, we have seen the number of pets surrendered by owners go down by as much as 25% in one year.

Through my transition from a more traditional social justice career path to my current career as a social worker in the animal welfare field, I've discovered a dichotomy I can't seem to understand – it seems that many people believe that you're either someone who cares about animals *or* someone who cares about people, but you can't be both. The fault is on both sides. I've found this kind of black-and-white thinking within the animal welfare field, where pet owners are immediately distrusted, and within the social work field, where caring about the welfare of animals is considered to be frivolous. I hope that new generations of social workers realize that they do not have to choose – they can be both. I use the skills and knowledge that I accumulated during my human-focused social work career every day within an animal shelter. Animals don't pay rent, buy groceries, or pay for healthcare, the humans do. The best way to help animals is to help humans. And if we, as social workers, don't value pet ownership and the role that an animal plays in their owner's life, we will never be able to truly and fully serve the client as they deserve – as a whole human.

49
CENTERING RACIALIZED LIVED EXPERIENCES FOR HUMAN AND ANIMAL WELL-BEING

Mueni Rudd

I am a liberation-focused community champion dedicated to creating brave space wherever I contribute. I believe in ownership and unlearning dominant society's exhausted approaches to healing and growth from perspectives of whiteness. As a Black woman and Kenyan American in this movement, I value being in the right relationship with historically oppressed communities. My mother is a Black woman, my grandma was a Black woman, my great grandmama was a Black woman, and her mama was too. No matter where or who I work with, I center Black and other historically oppressed folks. I am a street scholar formally educated as a social worker and sociologist. The current role I serve at CARE (Companions and Animals for Reform and Equity) affords me the ability to support racially minoritized people by centering them, creating safe spaces to engage them, and very often paying them. Our collective work at CARE divests from dominant society's approaches to supporting racially diverse humans and their companion animals all over the country.

My interdisciplinary behavioral science background and liberatory perspectives are an asset to any professional role I hold. As a social work graduate student and now professional I focus on engaging in audience-specific authentic and healthy multicultural dialogue to lead community-centered work. I levitated to mezzo- and macro-level roles mostly supporting nonprofit, government, or university programs or initiatives. Every social work class and field placement were opportunities to expand where I created a space to discuss and reflect on the state of race relations in America from multicultural points of view. The two Council on Social Work Education (CSWE) competencies I aligned with as a graduate student were Engage Diversity and Difference in Practice and Engage in Practice-informed Research and Research-informed Practice. I actualized this in part by practicing ethical citation. This entailed pulling from contributors of color who go against the often EuroAmerican, male, white, Christian, heterosexual, English-speaking, and middle or upper class perspectives available in the literature and mental health curriculum. Research tells us that this current dominance of perspective is most harmful to people of color, sexual minorities, and women. Therefore, scholar advocate pursuits to champion these groups is research informed and community centered. This type of alignment to the movement prescribes ongoing advocacy that prioritizes racial lived experiences while addressing cross-cultural communication, awareness, and healing. I intentionally pull mindful facilitation and conflict mediation techniques directly from social work practice as instruments to confront the shame and lack of conversation between racial or ethnic opposites. I role model this level of race mindfulness in my contributions in an effort to cultivate racial consciousness and unlearn the Western alternatives that avoid issues of racial diversity and cultural differences.

I am here to support and be in constant conversation with Black and other historically marginalized communities. I consider myself new to human and animal well-being work, but I am rooted in my values and am willing to make important recommendations for meaningful change in this field. I have awareness of and knowledge about the important nuances of intersectionality in equity work, as well as a willingness to share knowledge with community.

Much of our society, let alone the One Health industry, unfortunately, lack racial consciousness and contributes to colonial harm against Black and other people of color. I challenge white and other historically privileged social workers serving human and animal well-being to take ownership of their positionality first. To achieve improved racial progressiveness, white and other historically privileged people or institutions must understand their identity as white in addition to sharing power and resources. Additionally, a social work identity does not qualify for allyship or integrity to the movement. Social workers of color must alternatively consider striving to divest from capitalistic notions of work and worthiness. We have to prioritize our own humanity and role model that to our collaborators and supporters. Black and other people of color belong in One Health work. Our ancestors have a long history of harmonious relationships with animals and the environment. That knowledge and practice of connectedness is ancestral.

The community-centered work I support at CARE relies heavily on my liberatory practice of existing and past methods. This includes but is not limited to racializing the diversity we invest in. In the spring of 2022, my division proudly funded CARE's first research with Historically Black Colleges and Universities (HBCUs). Both campuses are in Texas, one at Huston-Tillotson University (HT) and the other at Prairie View A&M University (PVAMU). Undergraduate research assistants of color supported these pilot studies under the guidance of diverse university faculty. HT's sociology and business department explored the effectiveness of research strategies to use in cities across central Texas to determine race or ethnicity-based ownership and utilization patterns of companion animal-oriented businesses. Public health professors at PVAMU examined the relationship between communities of color living in South Texas and their companion animals. Both studies focused on human and animal well-being utilizing their unique academic disciplines and centering on pet families of color.

My division and I continued the trust-building relationship with HT the following semester by funding an undergraduate course titled Animals & Society. I had the honor of joining another professor of color at HT to coteach their first human and animal well-being course. The course examines the practices and values in American society holds for animals and human relationships and expectations, with an emphasis on the perspectives of people in marginalized communities. In the Winter of 2022, I began coordinating a library donation from CARE consisting of human and animal well-being material. Aside from research, CARE has also funded scholarships for veterinary students of color at Tuskegee University.

HBCUs are the ideal academic environments where racial empathy is promoted and role modeled. HBCUs' community-centered beginnings can still be found on campuses today, challenging white colonial patriarchal norms of individualism. Funded or quantifiable commitments with HBCUs creates stronger interactions, experiences, and relationships with Black and other people of color we want conspiring for the future of One Health solutions.

50
UNEXPECTED IMPLEMENTATION OF AAI IN CRISIS WORK

Denna Hays

Throughout my child welfare career, I learned many social workers face their workday with nothing more than their passion, a name badge, and a manila folder. Those who stayed in the field would often reference an invisible toolbox of interventions and skills they developed throughout their career. These toolboxes brought normalcy to ever-changing regulations and treatment modalities that become the reality of a social work career. Yet, animal-assisted interventions (AAIs) were rarely an option available to those I served. My own childhood experiences led me to learn more and add AAIs to my own toolbox.

In May 1991, I met a puppy that would become my best friend, and change the trajectory of my life plan. During our 15 years together, we figured out life, dating, marriage, parenthood, etc. You name it, we experienced it. On June 1, 2006, I said goodbye to my best friend and faced a void I was not sure how to fill. Fast forward to August 2017, while sitting at a local business, I realized I had been mourning my four-legged friend for 11 years. I told my husband I was ready to get my own dog and he told me to get a goldfish. On September 9, 2007, a 3-pound Toy Australian Shepherd chose me to be his owner. He was the runt of a large litter and was very quiet and semi-withdrawn. As we walked out the door, this shy little dog, named Ziggy, instantly took his place by my side and in my toolbox. I am not sure either of us expected the journey we were about to embark upon. As the Founding Executive Director of a Children's Advocacy Center (Center), I was aware of research-supported AAIs when working with individuals who had experienced trauma. But what about the professionals who worked with these individuals?

Being able to take Ziggy to work with me was incredible. Having spent years sitting at a desk for 12–14 hours per day, having Ziggy with me required me to take breaks. Bathroom breaks provided fresh air, laughter, and silly conversations. As our confidence grew, our breaks began to include others. Our building landlord and his staff would greet us on the sidewalk or wave from the windows. Others asked where we worked, which provided the opportunity to share information about those we served. Some days, Ziggy would even convince me to leave work early, or on time, so we could attend events to support the socialization skills he would need to demonstrate during the therapy dog testing he would be required to pass. As Ziggy's confidence continued to grow, so did mine. I began to see changes in those directly around us. Our landlord began to bring his dog to work and would share the positive impact his dog was having on himself and his staff. Ziggy and I began attending professional meetings together, and soon enough, the professionals were arriving at meetings with treats and toys and their chosen seat was on the floor next to Ziggy. Many shared the impact Ziggy was personally having on them.

When Ziggy was approximately 15 weeks old, our community was struck with tragedy when we experienced a horrendous child death. I remember asking Ziggy, "how can we help?" I quickly learned our help did not need to be elaborate. Others did not need for Ziggy to do tricks. What they needed for this small puppy to sit quietly next to them, as tears ran down their faces and they ran their fingers through his fur. This experience led to many others where Ziggy's interactions with children, families, and professionals involved moments of silent petting, quick kisses, or a quick game with Ziggy's favorite work toy, Flat Christmas Raccoon.

In 2019, a co-worker's dog, Deuce, joined us at the Center. Deuce and Ziggy spent their days interacting with children, families, professionals, and staff. Those visiting the Center would often express their gratitude for being able to interact with the dogs. Children were often overheard telling Ziggy, they were afraid when they first arrived at the Center, but he had made them feel safe and brave. The morale of my staff improved, as they attended meetings with a dog on their lap or close to their side. Staff took breaks with the dogs, taking quick walks or playing a favorite game. The atmosphere of our building filled with laughter and smiles, all associated with the presence of Ziggy and Deuce. In January 2022, I changed jobs and became an assistant professor at a local university. I wondered how Ziggy and I would integrate into our new setting. Would we have the same impact? To my delight, we are having the same, if not more impact within the university culture.

On campus, we teach AAI courses. We also engage students and faculty while walking on campus or attending campus events. Ziggy is often greeted by name as students share their struggles with classes, friends, and integrating into college life with my now 15-pound dog. When friends are having a tough day, students will bring them to my office to sit and pet Ziggy, often with minimal interaction with myself. It is difficult to estimate the impact Ziggy has on others. But, it is clear that the crises faced by members of our community, both professionally and personally, can be overwhelming. Ziggy is a great remind that even a brief interaction with someone can make a difference in the life of another.

51
LAW ENFORCEMENT, SOCIAL WORK, AND THERAPY DOGS

Angela Kenbok

Who I Am and What I Do

I am a Police Social Worker embedded within a police department in Pennsylvania. Police social work (PSW), like law enforcement, focuses on maintaining the welfare of residents by monitoring the community. Police officers and social workers collaborate together to prevent and intervene against issues for the safety of the community.

Being a first responder is both exhausting and rewarding. I can experience empathy and compassion firsthand while watching individuals go through some of the most challenging experiences. Advocating for those individuals allows me to be a voice that was not heard before. The goal is to provide them with any therapeutic or social services needed for long-term enhancement.

My Background

I obtained my Master of Social Work from Slippery Rock University where I spent time focusing on forensic social work, animal-assisted therapy (AAT) and human-animal interaction (HAI). Prior to my PSW career, I spent several years working in dual diagnosis facilities, providing services to individuals struggling with both addiction and mental health.

What Drove Me to the Field

I always wanted to be the person to help end the suffering that individuals were going through and to improve lives and communities. Social workers can provide more control over individual's lives and help them fulfill their

DOI: 10.4324/9781003335528-56

potential as humans. Those struggling are capable of being and doing better. However, they seldom realize it or lack the knowledge to know a better way; to know that better existed.

Every Sunday evening, a volunteer would bring his dog to the facility I worked at to interact and build relationships with the clients. Over time, I observed these individuals gain the hope, courage, and strength they needed to begin their recovery. Having the opportunity to witness the benefits this dog provided pulled me to learn more about animal-assisted intervention (AAI).

An Average Day

Each day at the department is such a unique experience. I have to be prepared to take on whatever situation arises. My day may start with a pile of police referrals on my desk or a dispatch call where my services are needed. I provide follow-ups, case management, short-term counseling, host community events, or spend time building ongoing collaborations. My services help build rapport and work through crisis interventions until long-term services are available.

How I Incorporate AAI

A big part of my job involves AAI. I can include HAIs in short-term counseling and events by collaborating with animal-assisted crisis response volunteers and their dogs. They participate in counseling sessions, youth events, and community events. I've also been able to work with a service dog agency that has participated in events specifically structured for veterans.

Dogs' ability to connect with people seems limitless. There has yet to be a population I have encountered who has not been assisted by the inclusion of therapy dogs. During short-term counseling, clients of all ages and backgrounds appear more relaxed and confident. During library events, children light up at seeing a dog. They engage and read to the dog. During the Veteran's events, with dogs present, veteran's opened up and shared more about their traumatic experiences. I witnessed many of them reaching out to pet a dog before speaking of a traumatic experience. The smiles I witness from both the individuals and the volunteers during these interventions are truly amazing.

Best/Most Rewarding Parts of My Job

Being a social worker is one of the most meaningful occupations as we are constantly striving to make positive impacts. Helping people find hope provides me with a strong sense of accomplishment. Sometimes, I am referred a client and I think "How am I going to possibly help this person?" After advocating and researching for the best possible treatment, I can sit back and acknowledge the satisfaction of being in a position where I am able to make a difference. Social workers are given the privilege to work closely with some of the most vulnerable individuals and give them the courage to work on their strengths, helping them make positive improvements in their lives.

Challenges with My Job

Along with the rewards comes the challenges. Burnout is a challenge all social workers risk. Often, I need a reminder of why I am a social worker and why I chose this career, and that comes back to my compassion and empathy – things that shine best when I make my self-care a priority.

We witness a lot of disappointment and failure and want to fix everything, but sometimes our clients will relapse or reoffend. They may not follow through with services or agree with our suggestions and sometimes not ready to accept help. However, our job is to be there for them when they are ready. One of the best ways to overcome challenges in the field of social work is to remind myself why I chose this career; to help people. Yes, it takes patience, and sometimes, a loud voice, but it is always rewarding to know that I can help those in need.

Advice/Words of Wisdom

For those thinking about entering the field of social work (or law enforcement in my case), or those already in the field, I encourage you to prioritize your self-care. If you don't take care of yourself, how can you possibly address the needs of your clients? We need to be strong, motivating, and encouraging. In order to maintain self-care and continue feeling compassion, boundaries need to be in place. Turn your phone off after hours, be direct and to the point, say no when you need to say no. Boundaries are healthy and needed.

Continue to look for areas to improve or broaden your education too. There is never "too much" research or education when it comes to a career in social work. Attend as many trainings or webinars as possible to learn new ways to interact with and serve your clients the best way possible. Above all, maintain your heart. Stay positive. And take care of you.

52

POLICE SOCIAL WORK

Partnering with Animals to Help Heal Communities

Alyssa Peters

If you were to come into my office at the police department, you might notice Stewart, my all-white mouse, who resides in a little pen in my office. This mouse was affectionately named by clients after the mouse in the movie Stewart Little. Stewart enjoys an important role in my office. Children and youth particularly enjoy the benefit from his presence. He provides a listening ear and never spills a secret or judges. Youth light up when they come to my office and notice the cage with a little white creature inside, curiously sniffing at the newcomer. Several of my shyer clients sit in front of his pen, listen to my questions, and tell Stewart the answer. Stewart also teaches about consent and the importance of being gentle with animals. If he doesn't want to be held that day, for example, he doesn't get held that day.

On some days, clients are lucky and come in on a day where a loveable chihuahua/pug mix is at my side. Cookie, an adorable little bug-eyed dog that accompanies me to work and provides emotional aid to several of my clients. She is 14 years old, but you wouldn't know it if you looked at her; she is spry, energetic, and sassy. Yet, Cookie overcame a significant loss. Cookie lived with her same owner for 12 years. Unfortunately, her owner became ill and was no longer able to care for her. She made the difficult choice to give Cookie up to Senior Heart Rescue and Renewal, a program that specializes in taking in senior dogs and placing them in foster homes instead of shelters.

My husband and I agreed to be a foster family for this program and were presented with Cookie. She had a tremendously hard time adjusting. She would cry for her past owner and search the home. Cookie was also rather… plump. She was a round little thing at this time and my husband affectionately referred to her as the 'sausage'. We began working with and training her to eat dog food again and getting her back to a healthy weight. She was

DOI: 10.4324/9781003335528-57

very loved and spoiled in her previous home and would only eat human food. Cookie grieved for her previous owner for a long time while going through this transition and entering a new phase in her life. But, eventually, she adjusted and is now quite happy with us in her new permanent home. Cookie's story is one that I often use when I have clients struggling with grief and loss or adjusting to a new situation. Seeing Cookie as happy as she is, laying contentedly in their lap, seems to help them realize that they might eventually be happy again too.

My job as a Police and Community Social Worker mandates that I am flexible and can quickly adapt to diverse settings with a wide variety of people and circumstances. Social workers embedded in police departments are relatively new, but these types of positions are growing as communities see the positive impact. To be effective at my job, I find it important to keep up with current research, as well as recognize when I do not know something. I must be willing to seek help or advice.

My job is to assist members of the community. Mainly, I accompany police officers responding to a crisis or emergency. I also assist community members without police involvement. I help with immediate crisis situations as well as help people find the resources they need to prevent recidivism or further victimization. This job has many facets. I handle referrals from the police, fire department, emergency medical services, the local magistrate, the local school district, the community, and individuals within the community who reach out to me directly with a need for assistance. I help people find affordable housing, financial support, adequate food and clothing, shelter, therapy, programs, etc. I act as their advocate and often provide general case management until that individual or family no longer needs me.

I was not always interested in police social work. In fact, social work wasn't even on my radar when I first started my academic path. I started my undergraduate degree in 2016 at Westminster College. I majored in Child and Family Studies with a minor in Psychology. During most of this time, I knew I wanted to work with people, but I didn't know quite what or how. It was at this time that I took a social work elective course and I fell head over heels in love. After graduating Westminster College, I began my Master of Social Work (MSW) through Slippery Rock University (SRU). During my time at SRU, I became certified in cognitive behavioral therapy (CBT) and animal-assisted therapy (AAT). It was also at this time I was provided the opportunity to intern at a police department as a social worker.

From my internship experience, I felt I found my home and was fortunate to land a full-time job as an embedded social worker within a police department. My workdays are always different and many are intense and busy. One day, I may go with police officers on a suicide call or an overdose case. Some days are filled with client meetings – for a follow up, a check in, or short-term counseling until a therapist can see them. Other days are spent running community programs and events. And yet, other days are spent writing notes, making phone calls, networking, and conducting research.

If you think you might like to be a police social worker, you first need to obtain an MSW. But even more importantly, you need to be a resilient individual with a strong self-care routine. Both social work and law enforcement have high rates of burnout, compassion fatigue, and secondary and vicarious trauma. When you put the two together, it can compound these issues. An ability to set boundaries and effectively network and communicate are needed skills. This job (and social work in general) can be tough, so a thick skin is a must, but so is the ability to be gentle and kind. Balance is the key.

While my job is tough and challenging, it is also incredibly rewarding. It is exhilarating to see people go from struggling to thriving. I enjoy helping people navigate through their healing journey; nothing is more rewarding than seeing people move past their challenges and embrace a new, healthier way of life.

53
SERVING PEOPLE AND ANIMALS
A Worthy Career

Christine Kim

I recently received a phone call from one of my MSW professors – an accomplished man I respect immensely and someone who was formative to my understanding of social justice in social policy and practice. I was flattered that he called me and eager to reconnect. But as we began to catch up, I began to feel a familiar sense of shame creep over me. I most certainly have accomplished a lot by anyone's standards. I graduated from the University of Pennsylvania with my Master of Social Work to then learn in the trenches what I could not learn in the ivory tower. I took entry-level case management positions in housing first programs for the most vulnerable residents experiencing homelessness in Philadelphia and Los Angeles.

After that, I joined the social work continuing education and training operations at a large social work educational institution, giving me exposure and opportunity to develop and manage some of New York City's biggest social work professional development programs. The experience in workforce development helped me move to another nonprofit environment, supporting immigrant women job seekers in New York City. And while I loved my time at the nonprofit, an opportunity came calling from the New York City Mayor's Office that I could not refuse. I worked for Mayor Bill de Blasio for three years, half of which was overtaken by the scramble to respond to COVID-19 in the epicenter of the pandemic.

Looking back on my work history, I'm relatively satisfied. So then why the feelings of shame? At the time of the call, I had just left my three-year tenure at the Mayor's Office. When my old mentor asked what I did there, I told him that I was the director of the Mayor's Office of Animal Welfare. He grew silent. Only when he heard the words "COVID-19 pandemic" did he perk up and said, "Oh, I bet you used your social work degree for that."

I agreed. But internally, I knew that I had actually used my social work degree for everything that I did at the Office.

My old mentor's reaction to my work was familiar. As an undergraduate social work student, I was assigned the task of finding a cause to volunteer which would serve as a writing topic for the semester. I distinctly remember typing into a search engine, "veterinarian and social work + NYC." I was delighted to have Hope Animal Hospital turn up in my search engine results. I remember meeting with Juliet, a social worker and co-founder of the veterinary practice.

She was incredibly generous with her time. She explained to me that the convergence of animals and social work was not limited to veterinary hospitals; there was an emerging field of social welfare and justice issues that intersect with animal welfare issues. With excitement, I went back to my class to report my findings. My instructor was dismissive. This was the common reaction among most of my instructors throughout my social work education. They did not see the connection. I was dismayed but not discouraged. My natural interest remained even if it wasn't being nurtured by my formal social work education.

Several years later and out of school, while working in Los Angeles, CA on Skid Row, a 52-block area known for having the country's highest concentration of people experiencing street homelessness, My Dog Is My Home was born. Today, My Dog Is My Home is a national nonprofit organization dedicated to increasing access to shelter and housing for people experiencing homelessness and their animals. It was born out of my experience as a case manager assisting people who had experienced chronic homelessness get off the streets and into their own supportive housing units. Several clients had animals and were having difficulty navigating the system with their furry companions.

The work at My Dog Is My Home was the first time I officially learned about the concept of One Health. It was introduced to me as a framework for thinking about the relationships between ecology, zoonotic disease, and human public health. I applied it to My Dog Is My Home on a more domestic scale – the person, their companion animals, and the home in which they inhabit (or in our case, don't have access to inhabit). My experiences with My Dog Is My Home led me to every corner of the US and eventually to the NYC Mayor's Office. I became the first Director of the Mayor's Office of Animal Welfare, the first office of its kind in the country.

During my tenure at the Office, I focused on animal issues but also the human dimensions of animal welfare. This was a category of work not about the animals themselves but about the people who cared for them – our veterinarians, animal shelter staff, companion animal guardians, and animal advocates. The area was rich with programs and policies to develop, including ones that addressed the impact of COVID-19 on animal caregivers.

In retrospect, I am proud of what I have accomplished and how much the field has grown. Slowly, I find myself needing to explain less frequently that human-animal bond issues have a place in social work and they *do* matter. This work is important, and it is a great time to be exploring this field. My advice to you is that you do not have to choose a career that focuses on either animals or people. If you are open to seeing it and willing to go out on a limb, you'll find the connection points everywhere. Animals are a part of our lives, there is no divorcing animals from our daily experiences despite our traditionally siloed educational systems and career paths. Let your curiosity guide you and pursue what compels you. If your passion is animals and social work, there is a path forward even if you're among the first to walk it.

54
SOCIAL WORKERS' ROLES IN CARING FOR HUMANS AND THEIR COMPANION ANIMALS

Adeline Wong

I am a certified animal-assisted psychotherapist and certified substance abuse counsellor. I am also the founder of Human-animal bond In Ministry (HIM), a social enterprise in Singapore with a vision to build a supportive loving community with animals that brings hope and healing to those affected by crime and marginalisation. At HIM, I merge my skills to provide animal-assisted therapy, training, and services to inmates, ex-offenders, their families, youth at risk, those with mental health problems, and other marginalised groups.

I have been serving clients in the prison ministry for the past 12 years, but my personal experience with the prison system goes back to my infancy. I have no memory of my father, who was arrested for drug trafficking before I was born. As an infant, I was carried into prison to visit him, until he was sentenced to death when I was two years old (in Singapore, drug trafficking is a capital offence and carries the death penalty). Because of the shame and stigma surrounding his incarceration and death, my family kept the details from me. I grew up without an identity, facing shame, rejection, and loneliness. During those years, animals were my most faithful companions, who were always there for me and who accepted me without judgement.

It was only in my twenties that I found a new faith and in the process, gaining a new identity and a new community that loved and accepted me. When I came to know the truth about my father's incarceration, I wanted to help other inmates' families, those who were facing the same struggles that I once did. I wanted them to experience the same comfort and love from animals and from a supportive community that had helped and healed me. I also wanted to help inmates break out of the cycle of crime and drug abuse, to build a new life for themselves and their families.

DOI: 10.4324/9781003335528-59

That was how I decided to pursue training in animal-assisted psychotherapy as well as substance abuse counselling and then to create HIM. As founder and director of HIM, my job is never boring. Every day holds new activities and challenges. We run animal-assisted activities for other social service agencies and non-profit organisations with client groups ranging from youth at risk, mental health patients, elderly with dementia, etc. Our volunteers who help run our activities include ex-offenders, and the interaction between them and the beneficiaries helps to increase awareness and reduce stigma about ex-offenders. I also conduct one-on-one animal-assisted psychotherapy and substance abuse counselling sessions with individual clients, including drug addicts and traumatised youths. I also partner with a psychotherapist to conduct group sessions (process groups coupled with animal-assisted activities) for recovering addicts. In addition, HIM provides training and employment opportunities for our clients. As a result, some of my days involve training clients in pet grooming, pet transport, pet photography, baking, or gardening. Sometimes, I go into prisons to conduct training or counselling for inmates. I also travel to different churches and organisations to give talks about our work to raise support and awareness for our beneficiaries. And every single day, I have my own 'personal therapy' time with my team of eight beloved animal co-therapists (one dog, three cats, two guinea pigs, and two rabbits) – I cherish the seemingly mundane tasks of caring, feeding, and grooming, during which I can unwind from my day and just enjoy being with them.

The best and most rewarding part of my work is being able to help people who are struggling and hurting – to see our animals bring comfort to a client during a therapy session, to see addicts break free from their prison of drug addiction, to see ex-offenders gain meaningful employment through animal-related services and training to regain dignity and rebuild their lives. I know my work is impacting lives, relieving suffering, increasing awareness, and decreasing stigma, and that brings so much joy and fulfilment to what I do.

There are challenges, too – sadness and disappointment when a client goes back to drugs despite our best efforts and anxiety when an animal is unwell. There is also the daily pressure of managing a social enterprise where, by definition, most of the clients are struggling financially and unable to pay for services. This means that much of my time is also spent raising funds and keeping a careful budget. It also means that my pay is much less than others who are similarly qualified and holding a 'regular job'.

Do I have any regrets? Definitely not! It means a lot to me that my work is helping others who are facing the same struggles that my family and I once did, and that keeps me going. My advice for others who are seeking a similar career is – Find out where your passion meets the world's needs, then seek training and like-minded volunteers and supporters who will journey with you. It will be worth it.

55
ANIMAL-ASSISTED THERAPY IN AN ISRAELI PSYCHIATRIC HOSPITAL

Patricia Tiram

My Background

Our family always had several pets, and as a teenager, our cat helped me cope with a serious illness and surgery. Animals, however, were put aside during my college years. I graduated in 1970 from Central Washington State University with a BA in Anthropology and in 1975 with an MSW from the University of Washington. Between colleges, I worked at a Seattle hospital and as a social work student, worked at two inner-city agencies and at a suburban mental health center.

After graduation, I enrolled in a program for American social workers in Israel. With only rudimentary Hebrew, I flew to Israel. On arrival, my culture shock was profound: I rode buses with live chickens, goats sometimes trimmed lawns, and home phones were a rarity.

Though I met Israeli social workers with BAs, I also met "social workers" without credentials. Finally, a social work law, delineating the roles and required training of social workers, was passed in the late 1970s. Working initially in social welfare and rehabilitation, I married an Israeli of Yemenite descent and had two children.

From 1987, I worked as a social worker at the largest psychiatric hospital in Israel. In 1998, the hospital opened a 100-bed hostel for Holocaust survivors with long-term hospitalization needs and I became the first social worker. Because of their traumatic backgrounds and histories, communication with our residents was often difficult and I became interested in animal-assisted therapy as a way to connect with my patients. I completed a course in animal-assisted therapy through Hebrew University and Koret School of Veterinary Medicine in 2007. Working with adults at the hospital and children

DOI: 10.4324/9781003335528-60

in my community, my primary animal partners were my two dogs, Casey (a Keeshond) and Sky (a Samoyed). After retiring at age 62, I was asked by the hospital administration to continue working at the hospital, so I opened my own business as an animal-assisted therapist.

My Schedule

My schedule was part time, usually six to seven hours a week, working two consecutive days and orchestrated around meals, medications, and cigarette breaks. Sickness, renovations, or lockdown (forensic ward) could cancel a session. All but two wards were closed (danger to self or others). Although much of my work was done in groups, I also worked with patients individually – both inside and outside in a courtyard. One patient Sky and I worked with at the hostel, was an 88-year-old Holocaust survivor with apparent mutism. After working together several times, one day he reached out and began petting Sky. Several sessions later, he started to say a few words and eventually talked to me about his mother. Another Holocaust survivor, during group therapy with Sky and I, spoke about the two dogs he'd loved as a boy in Italy but were killed by the Nazis because they were "Jewish dogs". In later groups, he was able to talk about his family.

In another ward, my cockatiel, Lindo, and I worked with a very withdrawn Ethiopian young man who, with Lindo on his head, would look at himself in mirrors on the ward. As a result, he became noticed more by patients and staff and was later released. On the same ward, I allowed a young woman to snuggle with my cat, Lucky, in her bed, which led to a breakthrough in her condition.

Challenges

Social work can be challenging enough, but adding an animal to the mix can take much more concentration. Animals need to be cared for and some animals may fear certain people or situations. Clients may need to learn how to approach an animal without harming it and the client should be protected also. Accidents do happen, but prevention is foremost.

Both patients and staff can be difficult at times and some may openly show animosity toward you or your animals. This may be hard to change, but ingenuity, creativity, and humor can overcome many obstacles.

My Advice for Those Wanting to Incorporate AAI Work

- Take a human-animal intervention course, become knowledgeable about AAI.
- Enlist your director/boss to support an AAI program. Enlist the help of staff when working with withdrawn or difficult clients.

- Work with animals you and your clients are comfortable with (for instance, most devout Muslims won't touch a dog).
- Your health and that of your clients and your animal partners must always be a priority.
- Pay is important. A formal agreement/contract is essential and should include, when possible, travel expenses.
- Give lectures on HAI to promote your work and the field in general.

Animal-assisted therapy can be fun and exciting, heartwarming, and memorable and can enrich your professional career. If you are a social worker willing to embark on a true adventure for you and your clientele, this may be for you.

SECTION VI
Human-Animal Interactions Focus within Academia

56
FINDING PROFESSIONAL AND PERSONAL MEANING THROUGH HUMAN-ANIMAL INTERACTION ACADEMIC RESEARCH

Jen Currin-McCulloch

My Personal and Professional Formative Years

Growing up, my father was a veterinarian and a big fan of bringing my brother and me to work. I had the opportunity to be by my dad's side in the operating room, welcome clients into their clinic rooms, and interact with all of the pets staying overnight at the animal hospital. While drawn by the connection that I shared with the animals, I struggled seeing animals in distress and not being able to converse with them about their pain. When deciding on my field of study in college, I knew that veterinary medicine wasn't the perfect fit for me; however, these early lessons from the veterinary world spurred my interest in the field of psychology and supporting people through grief and loss. My last semester as an undergraduate I took an introductory social work course and fell in love with the profession's focus on the person in their environment. I went straight into a social work master's program and chose a field internship in a hospice setting. My social work practice spanned over 20 years and took place in oncology, palliative care, and hospice settings. In my final years in practice, I had the opportunity to serve as principal and co-investigator on research studies investigating ways to reduce physical and psychosocial distress among cancer survivors. These research projects fueled my passion to enter a social work doctoral program to (a) gather the training to explore how people cope with existential health crisis, and (b) to develop interventions to reduce survivors' distress.

Following my graduation, I was hired as an Assistant Professor at Colorado State University's School of Social Work (CSU). Different than most social work programs, CSU has an affiliated research, education, and outreach program, Human-Animal Bond in Colorado (HABIC), that aims to explore and advance the benefits of the human-animal bond. I introduced myself to Helen Holmquist-Johnson, PhD, the Director of HABIC, and shared about my work with animal-assisted therapy while working in a hospital setting and my interest in connecting to researchers in this field. Helen introduced me to Lori Kogan, PhD, a Professor of Clinical Sciences for the College of Veterinary Medicine and Biomedical Sciences at Colorado State University. Lori graciously introduced me to her team of researchers, Cori Bussolari, PsyD; Wendy Packman, PhD, JD; and Phyllis Erdman, PhD. Each brings practice and research expertise in grief, loss, and/or human-animal interactions. The team graciously welcomed me into the fold and we have been a dream research team, both supportive and productive.

From our initial research project together, I felt right at home and eager to share my qualitative research and social work practice expertise. A grant from HABIC funded our first project exploring the grief experiences of disabled individuals who have lost a service dog through retirement or death. While working on this project, COVID-19 emerged and altered almost every aspect of our daily lives, including a shift in our work and social activities to the confines of our own homes. As a team, we wanted to understand how pets potentially served as an emotional and social buffer for dog and cat guardians or created additional strains during this time. Our other projects include studying the guilt experiences of pet parents, how pets serve as social supports for those diagnosed with cancer, and how people memorialize their companion, service, and therapy dogs.

An Inside Look into My Daily Life As a Social Work Academic and Leader

My role in academia requires that I wear many different hats and hone my expertise in three main areas: teaching, research, and service/leadership. At this point in my career, I teach two social work direct practice courses each week and find creative ways to teach students how to integrate research into practice and practice into research, the Council on Social Work Education's (2022) Educational Policy and Accreditation Standard #4. For example, I share how I use social work interview skills within research interviews, how I transfer research findings into the development of an intervention, and how to find opportunities to integrate research into daily practice.

To peek inside what my research weekly activities entail, I have focused on my activities from the past week. Building on grant writing experiences from my oncology social work practice, I was able to partner with our team to write a grant to a human-animal interaction non-profit organization to seek funding for a project studying how cancer treatment impacts companion animal guardians' relationships with their pets. I also spent several hours analyzing breast cancer survivors' narratives of how their pet dog and/or cat served as an aid or hindrance in their coping during cancer treatment and recovery. I then met with student research assistants to review common themes we found in the survivor's narratives and developed initial ideas for educational resources to support survivors in reducing distress encountered in navigating financial and behavioral strains in caring for their pet. Lastly, our research team met to write the results section of a study that explores how service, therapy, and companion animal guardians memorialize their pets in online memorial platforms.

In my remaining time, I perform service and leadership activities in which I am able to share research findings and knowledge to enhance the quality of life among individuals experiencing grief, loss, or health-related existential distress. For instance, our research team is partnering with cancer treatment and support organizations, as well as companion animal service providers, to create practical resources that cancer survivors can utilize to build an individualized pet support care team. With the help of our student research assistants, we have created an interactive resource where Colorado cancer survivors can pinpoint their region on our interactive map and choose services such as pet sitters, transporters, mobile groomers, or low-cost vaccination clinics. We also created an animated short video for service animal organizations to aid them in building infrastructure to prepare for and support handlers when their service dogs retire or die. Our research findings have received recognition by animal service organizations and veterinary medicine providers which has led to presentations for VetVine, International Society for Anthrozoology, the International Association of Assistance Dog Partners, and a university-based diversity research forum. Utilizing research outcomes to inform assessments, clinical protocols, and resource tools for those experiencing a loss or health crisis truly warms my social work heart.

How to Secure Roles in Social Work Academia and Research

If you are positioned in an academic setting and are interested in pursuing research in human-animal interactions, you can attend conferences and webinars offered by organizations like the International Society for Anthrozoology, the American Psychological Association's Human-Animal Interaction Section, and Animal-Assisted Intervention International. As an interested student, you may want to seek out social work programs that have an affiliated veterinary medical school and inquire about research assistant roles that would provide opportunities to garner human-animal interaction research mentoring. Applying for post docs can be another route to build skills and research networks. You could also partner with clinicians working in animal-assisted therapy, service dog organizations, or companion animal organizations to evaluate their client's unmet needs or the positive impacts of their services on human-animal relationships.

If you are pondering a transition into academia from social work practice, you will find that your clinical skills apply well to academic and research settings. The same skills that you use for interviewing and assessing clients' needs will transfer well to designing and leading qualitative research interviews. The ability to network and broker resources will be instrumental in forming research-community partnerships and creating resources that will be useful in developing psychosocial interventions. Your communication skills will be essential in writing professional manuscripts and leading presentations where you can offer practical suggestions for enhancing human-animal bonds.

Finding Meaning in My Work

Transitioning into academia, I feared losing the sense of meaning that I felt in supporting those going through a health crisis and their caregivers. However, being able to participate in research interviews, analyzing participants' narratives about their experiences, and building resources to support people in coping with adaptations to their relationships with their service and companion animals has fostered my existential wellbeing. I always felt that at the bedside I was able to have many small wins, while in academia as a researcher, instructor, and leader, I feel like my daily activities can have more extensive, lasting impacts.

Recently, I experienced the pleasure of integrating my social work practice and research in a full circle moment. While in practice, I encountered many individuals trying to plan their cancer treatment around their pet's care; yet, we had no formal infrastructure to assess and support their needs in caring for their companion animals. Now, with the budding national awareness about One Health frameworks that acknowledge the value of human-animal bonds in personal wellbeing, there are more organizations focused on enhancing these bonds. CancerCare, an organization that I frequently turned to for financial grants for my patients, has recently developed the Pet Assistance & Wellness Program (PAWS) to support companion animal guardians in helping them to keep their pets at home. When I called them to learn about their services and share about our team's research, they asked me to join their PAWS professional advisory board to build infrastructure and resources to enhance survivors' bonds with their pets. This full circle opportunity will enable me to utilize my training to give back to the organization which was invaluable to me in being able to care for my clients.

I find immense joy and meaning in mentoring students in the classroom and with research activities. I have the opportunity to mentor social work students across the BSW, MSW, and PhD programs and occupational therapy and exercise physiology students for whom I serve as the chair or committee member of their dissertation or thesis committee. Seeing their research outcomes and joy in their work makes me excited for the future.

On a personal note, in my first year at CSU, my dad's cancer became terminal and he died right after classes ended that May. Being involved with this line of research and leadership has allowed me to carry on his life work of fostering human-animal bonds. Each professional milestone feels like a continued bond to my dad.

Challenges with Working in Human-Animal Interaction Research

As a new field of social work practice, we have limited assessment tools or practice protocols to support individuals in caring for their companion, service, or therapy animals. Even more limited are funding mechanisms for human-animal research initiatives. I am hopeful that with the publication of this book and the impact that social workers, psychologists, and other human-animal interaction specialists increasingly have on One Health initiatives that we will be able to raise awareness about the needs of humans and animals in their dyadic relationships. Additionally, I am hopeful that increased exposure will also lead to more funding mechanisms to support One Health research initiatives.

Last Words of Advice

As someone who went back for her PhD in her mid-40s, I want to encourage you by saying that it is never too late to follow your research dreams. As social worker researchers, we are ideally positioned to bring our unique perspective to One Health initiatives. My final words of advice would be to take a risk and seek out collaborators who can nurture you on your journey. I would not be doing this tremendously fulfilling personal and professional work without the support of my mentors, colleagues, and research team.

Reference

Council on Social Work Education. (2022). *Educational policy and accreditation standards for Baccalaureate and Mater's social work programs.* https://www.cswe.org/getmedia/94471c42-13b8-493b-9041-b30f48533d64/2022-EPAS.pdf

57
THE PROFESSOR AND "THE PIT BULL LADY"

Yvonne Smith

I am an associate professor of social work at Syracuse University. That identity was hard won. But I am, and have long been other(ed) things, too: a horseman, pit bull rescuer, and mourner for the lost farms of my Ohio hometown. Becoming a social worker and researcher seemed to require me to hide my deep connections to the non-human. I sensed what ecofeminists have argued for decades: work with animals or animal-related issues would lead people to associate me with a devalued "feminine" sentimentality. The work, seen as the opposite of "serious" science, would make me a soft body, not a sharp mind, an object, not an actor. I knew how I wanted to be known. I'm embarrassed to admit how long it took me to find the courage to unite these seemingly incompatible interests.

In 2004, when I began working toward my M.A. at the University of Chicago, I got some messages loud and clear. First, social work was concerned with increasing social justice. Our primary focus ought to be changing the systemic forms of oppression that so cruelly shape people's lives. Second, social work was "hard core," a profession based on science and devoted to the toughest human challenges. This appealed to me in spite of, or maybe because of, its stereotypically masculine tone, and in spite of the fact that most of us were not men. We learned the "ecological perspective," but when we talked about the environment, we meant the social (read: human) one. My fascination with theory and ethnographic research kept me in Chicago for seven more years as I worked toward a PhD in Social Service Administration. I had absorbed the idea that if I wanted to make it in academia, I should keep my connection to non-human animals to myself.

But when I left campus each day, I passed through a run-down but still very beautiful city park just west of the UChicago campus to my place on Martin

DOI: 10.4324/9781003335528-63

Luther King Jr. Drive. I lived across an invisible line (a literal "redline" on the old lending maps). I was one of few White people in my neighborhood, which was home to many working- and middle-class Black Chicagoans as well as many who were very poor. My place looked out over Washington Park where people fished, picnicked, hit golf balls, raced motorcycles, rode their horses(!), walked dogs, showed off their sound systems, partied, and bought and sold all manner of things—snow cones, tee shirts, drugs, sex, and litters of pit bull puppies.

In the eight years I lived in the Washington Park neighborhood, I stopped counting how many abandoned, maltreated, or otherwise wayward animals I brought home. I delivered pet food to homeless dog owners and got a reputation as the person to call about a desperate animal. When a stranger asked me to meet him to rescue a pit bull puppy with a horrifically broken jaw, I went. How could I live with knowing suffering like that continued when I had the capacity to help? I worked with two animal rescue groups in Chicago—one for cats and one for pit bulls. Their financial support and connections helped me and my partner feed, vet, train, and rehome many animals. I had become a crisis interventionist for our neighborhood's pets— "Hey, are you The Pit Bull Lady?" This work, which I kept separate from my academic work, filled my heart.

When I interviewed for my job at Syracuse, my presentation had nothing to do with animals. But I met a colleague, Paul Caldwell, who was teaching a new course on equine-assisted therapies. Encouraged, I admitted that I was a "hard core animal person," and that I shared his interest in the ways human and non-human animals are interdependent. I was interested, not just in how animals can help our clients heal, but in how we might address the ways our interactions with animals (and the animals themselves) are impacted by systems of privilege and oppression.

To my surprise, my colleagues supported the development of a course we called "Social Work and the Human-Animal Bond." This consistently popular course begins with a simple question and a couple of difficult answers. *Why study animals in social work school?* The answers, which we discuss over the next 14 weeks, go something like this: *Because non-human animals matter deeply to humans and our relationships with them are shaped by the same social forces that create and sustain social inequality.* We talk about animal-assisted therapies, the racism People of Color experience in adopting pets, and about the systemic inequalities—from housing discrimination to mass incarceration—that challenge access to mutually positive human-animal relationships. We talk about the social *and* natural environment and the interlocking oppressions that make human-animal studies (HAS), feminism, and anti-racism inseparable.

As it turns out, social work *does* have room for animals. The One Health Perspective has given us a compelling new frame for this still-radical project.

My hesitation to work in HAS reflected misogynistic associations between women and animals and the idea that "real" science views animals as biological objects, not social subjects. But as I continue to work in this area, I feel more whole as a scholar. The years caring for the maltreated bodies and spirits of animals, writing grants, collecting data—it can all be here. For that I am indebted to the trailblazing work of pioneers in HAS—like Carol Adams, Donna Haraway, Barbara Noske, and Christina Risley-Curtiss—and all the social workers who have taught, written, and researched in the "wilds" of HAS. They left us a good trail.

58
HOW I BECAME THE "DOG PERSON" AT WORK

Ashley O'Connor

I have always loved animals, but as a young child realized that I did not want to become a veterinarian due to the stress of that type of work. I obtained my MSW degree in Boston in 2010, passionate about working with veterans. I moved to California to be a research assistant at the Veterans Association (VA) in San Francisco and adopted my first dog from a local shelter when I was 28 years old. I named him Link and I quickly understood the power of the bond between us, especially living in a new place. He helped me get out and explore nature, which I had always wanted to do, but never before had the drive. At the same time, I met a veteran at work who was partnered with a service dog. I saw how they helped each other and also how their relationship benefited the people around them. I quickly decided that I was going to learn everything I could about service dogs for veterans experiencing mental health concerns. I still have the banner from my first presentation in 2012 on the topic hanging in my office.

In 2013, I entered a PhD program for social work, and upon completing coursework, I reached out to the lead VA researcher involved with exploring the impact of service dogs on veterans with PTSD. The research was being conducted out of state, but I told her I did not care where I had to move, as long as I was able to be involved. One month later, I received a call from an Iowa number and soon moved there to coordinate a VA study where my work included traveling around the Midwest checking in on veterans and their emotional support and service dogs they had been paired with through the VA study. Through this experience, I became aware of a seeming disconnect between individuals who were focused on human services and "dog people". I knew that I was both, and that if I was going to work in this world, I needed to make sure I understood the animal side.

I went back to school to get a second master's degree in humane studies and moved to Alaska, of course with Link by my side, taking a job at the University of Alaska Anchorage as an associate professor. This was 2019, so a few months later, the pandemic hit and all my planned research was out the door. During this lonely time, I began fostering for Alaska Animal Rescue Foundation (AARF). My first foster pup was a beautiful husky I named Loki. This experience reinforced to me the power of the human-animal bond.

As a result of my foster work and seeing how hard the volunteers worked to help humans and dogs in very rural areas in Alaska, I decided to study how this work impacted both the involved dogs and humans. I had a terrific research assistant and student in our social work department, Jastice Medel, and the findings we uncovered were fascinating. Our participants shared that there are both positive and challenging aspects to dog fostering in Alaska. They discussed building community within the city and traditional communities and shared stories of rescued dogs that created positive changes in the dogs and the volunteers. They noted how difficult it can be to not put the dogs' needs ahead of their own. Finally, they shared the social awareness and cultural humility they gained from the fostering experience. These outcomes highlight the complex relationship between animals, the environment, and humans.

While I loved my research, the Alaska VA was calling me back. They became one of five VAs to conduct a five-year pilot program to provide canine training to eligible veterans diagnosed with posttraumatic stress disorder as an element of a complementary and integrative health program. I am now acting as the coordinator for the PAWS pilot in Alaska, as well as the service dog champion providing education to veterans and colleagues on partnering with dogs for various health concerns. In these roles, I get to talk to veterans who love dogs and help them get connected to service dog organizations and with service puppies in training.

If I had not taken risks, or failed to reach out for new opportunities, I would not be in my dream job right now. So, my advice to those who want to work in the field is to network, not be afraid, and to believe that you have what it takes to explore a new world. Make sure that you stay on top of the literature and knowledgeable about new animal-related policies. It is so rewarding to know that I am able to combine my passion of dogs with my desire to work with veterans. You can too!

59
SOCIAL WORKERS' ROLES IN CREATING INCLUSIVE COMMUNITIES FOR ALL ANIMALS

Human and Non-Human

Jedediah Bragg

Social work is an interdisciplinary field with a diverse cadre of professionals. My past is varied, from serving in the Air Force to working in healthcare and community social work. Originally, I am from a rural community where education isn't a high priority. Stemming from a childhood that included poverty and discrimination, I wanted to become a social worker so future generations would not have to go through the same challenges. My journey included completing my bachelor's in social science, master's of social work, and a Ph.D. in social justice and research methodologies. My educational achievements led me to community social work within the LGBTQ community and various local human rights groups. I am a researcher who focuses on positive social supports and a faculty member in an MSW program who teaches macro social work and research methodologies.

Being raised in a rural community, animals, especially dogs, were central to my life. I experienced only brief periods when I did not live with a furry companion. Typically, those times ended with a loss, but everything would change for the better when a new four-legged companion moved in. Slowly, I shifted my work and personal focus to human-canine interaction (HCI). I started with actively training a new puppy, while simultaneously taking formalized courses in HCI, animal behavior, and animal-assisted interventions.

I currently live with my four-legged co-worker, Koa, a small Jack Russell Terrier. Through the shift in my career toward HCI, I began to partner with my university's Occupational Therapy Department and their Professor Paws Project. This project was designed to educate the community and future allied health professionals about service dogs' roles, abilities, and benefits. Following the founder of Professor Paws, I became the first faculty member to partner with the project, and immediately began training Koa as a therapy dog. Additionally, I sought out every HCI learning opportunity I could, including post-graduate certificates and training certifications, eventually becoming a Certified Animal-Assisted Intervention Specialist. Even today, my HCI educational journey continues. As my role (and Koa's) grew, more and more social work students began to ask questions about HCI and social work, including their role in aiding clients who depend upon a canine for support, how they could partner with a dog to aid clients, what needed to be done within the community to improve the lives of both humans and animals, and where could they gain more education about human-animal interaction and animal-assisted interventions.

These questions led us to produce fundamental changes to the Professor Paws Project. With Dr. Isaacson (the founder of the project), I began to implement an expansion of the program to include information about emotional support animals (ESAs), therapy dogs, and animal-assisted therapy. This education was available to all students, faculty, and staff on our campus, and even community members. Our effort produced a concentration year practicum for MSW students where they could focus on canine-assisted interventions, community engagement, and related research. All of this was done within the framework of a critical aspect of the Council on Social Work Education's definition of Environmental Justice, "*Environmental justice affirms the ecological unity and the **interdependence of all species, respect for cultural and biological diversity**, and the right to be free from ecological destruction*" (Council on Social Work Education, 2015). As such, I focus on the benefits of the human-animal bond. However, we must also consider how this bond can impact the animal, both positively and negatively.

On an average day, when not conducting research (with Koa asleep in the office), I complete a wide array of tasks. We live in communities designed for people – less so for animals. Yet, our communities also include those who depend on canines to help navigate their daily lives. I work with non-profits, students, and community members to help them consider accessibility issues with service animals. I encourage them to think about the Americans with Disabilities Act and the Fair Housing Act concerning service dogs and, to some degree, ESAs. We focus on policies, accessibility, housing, homelessness and pet ownership, and even green spaces for working canines. All of these are macro social work issues within the lens of environmental justice. Unfortunately, currently, the state of Oklahoma lacks legislators, organizations, and communities that have thoroughly considered the rights and roles of canines that work alongside humans.

Working in the realm of animal-assisted interventions and human-animal interaction is both extremely rewarding and endlessly frustrating. As social workers, we give voice to the voiceless. Advocating for our co-workers and their four-legged partners fits in that area. Nothing is more rewarding than explaining the various roles canines play in our lives and the ways humans are positively impacted by canines – and seeing that moment when an individual, executive board member, or local official "gets" it. Most people have experienced a childhood puppy or lifelong companion, including the benefits of the relationship as well as the feeling of loss when it ends. When they connect our goals with their companion animal experiences, they often become our greatest champions. Meanwhile, our work can also be frustrating due to the ever-expanding potential roles of canines, coupled with the lack of education and misinformation – including fraudulent canine "certifications". Yet, we mustn't give up on working to change systems for the better.

There is a great deal of need for macro social workers. Pick up any newspaper, and this becomes apparent. This is also true in work related to improving communities for canines and their humans. There are two key things to consider when looking for this policy, research, and community-level work revolving around human-animal interactions. One is to look for jobs using terms such as animal welfare, animal education, or anything animal/social justice related, rather than social work. There are many jobs out there, but if you cannot find one, you can also work to create one by educating others on the need in this area. The second suggestion involves education. While some of you are finishing (or have completed) your BSW or MSW and are perhaps thinking, "I'm done with school", I suggest that it might be helpful to acquire more education – it can enhance your power to create lasting systemic changes for both humans and other animals.

Reference

Council on Social Work Education. (2015). 2015 educational policy and accreditation standards for baccalaureate and master's social work programs.

60
DESIGNING A DIVERSE SOCIAL WORK CAREER

Meghan Morrissey

I wake up to a breathtaking view of the Rocky Mountains from the farm where I live. As I put on the kettle, the sound of my neighbor taking her dogs out and the horses whinnying is the perfect soundtrack to my sanctuary. Depending on which job I'm working that day, I head to my computer, the barn, or the mountains. If I'm off to the barn, I'll arrive early to warm up the horse I'll be working with or take a little ride myself. I set up the arena, always prepared to move if needed as the space is not dedicated specifically to my clients. I often work with adolescents, so I consult briefly with the caregiver when they arrive. Sessions typically begin with body and mind warmups, before moving into containing the crisis of the week, skill development, and processing. I close sessions with a cool down, for both the horse and client, a mindfulness exercise, and a recap which includes homework. I consider myself in the business of putting myself out of business, prioritizing empowering clients and their community to practice skills outside the session to ameliorate mental wellness. Life ebbs and flows, so the amount of support and type of intervention needed changes throughout time.

Though animal-assisted interventions are not always a part of my treatment plans, I often find ways to integrate nature and sentient beings toward helping clients feel connected to their environments. For example, when I'm working as a co-responder in rural Colorado, taking in the enormity of the mountains helps ground me, as I receive change-of-shift report from the night before. Then, the wait-wait-wait and rush-rush-rush of crisis work, which could include providing case management, evaluating an incarcerated individual, attending the hospital for a placement evaluation, participating in a SWAT call, or following up in a client's home. Even though my crisis work doesn't involve animals directly, I often recommend including family

DOI: 10.4324/9781003335528-66

companion animals in the safety plans I facilitate. I "prescribe" 50 dog cuddles per day or encourage decorating the safety plan with the latest Instagram-famous kitten.

On those days when I commute to my computer, I hear the neighs of horses as I meet with my research team, Dr. Kimberly Hoagwood, Dr. Mary Acri, and Dr. Aviva Vincent. We discuss ways to move the field of equine-assisted interventions forward. A protocol developed by our team at New York University, Reining in Anxiety, combines cognitive behavioral therapy elements into arena games that can be taught by adaptive/therapeutic riding instructors. We are excited to "meet the client where they are at" physically and enhance human-equine interactions with evidence-based practice. Within the research study, I train and provide supervision to riding instructors, design learning aids for the research protocol, and publish results.

I love the flexibility that social work offers, a thread that aligns my current income streams, allowing me to have a diverse career. I am a social worker, therapist, yogi, horse enthusiast, herbalist, researcher and above all, a lifelong learner. I have my B.S. in Psychology from Fordham University and M.S.W. from New York University. I earned my Post-Masters certificate in Equine Assisted Mental Health from Denver University. I am an independently licensed social worker, a licensed addictions counselor and an AcuDetox Specialist in the State of Colorado. I am also a PATH (Professional Association of Therapeutic Horsemanship) Certified Therapeutic Riding Instructor.

When I graduated from Fordham University with a Bachelor's of Science in Psychology, I wasn't sure where to go next. So, I began a temporary job at New York University Child Study Center, which turned into a full-time role in education administration. While working full-time, I started a Master's research program, but then transferred to a Master's in social work. I completed my coursework in three years due to working full-time, volunteering as a sexual assault crisis counselor, and completing PATH Certified Riding Instructor certification concurrently. I was able to create a first-year internship for myself at my job location, conducting research and clinical evaluations for children and adolescents with autism spectrum disorders. My second year internship was at New York University Langone Health Hospital, where I was able to rotate through many units, including surgery, emergency, pediatrics, epilepsy, and transplants. My experience in school offered diversity, flexibility, and excitement.

Now, in practice, I am a social worker everywhere and anywhere, which can be great and sometimes inconvenient. These skills can be hard to turn off. I can be talking to a friend and thinking about how to encourage change talk, or I could be traveling abroad on vacation and helping a stranger through a panic attack. Sure, social work training helps me personally, but I've found that reflecting on what you have to give and being intentional about where to give it can provide balance and sustainability.

While many experiences contributed to my pursuit of a social work degree, I credit my final decision to a woman in Argentina living on a small farm. She showed the therapeutic potential of the human-horse connection, propelling me to design a diverse career path in One Health that nurtures my curiosity and empowers me to do good in the world.

I wish I could protect my clients from this inherently unsafe world. Social work is an *insatiable* profession, as outlined by the Ten Grand Challenges that we are charged to solve when we graduate. But instead of feeling overwhelmed by broken systems, injustice, or the daily grind, I remember that I am impacting the world – on a macro level by publishing research, on a mezzo level by supervising clinicians, and on a micro level by reflecting something to a client that they didn't see the day before. My heart feels full and I am satisfied.

61
HUMAN-ANIMAL-ENVIRONMENT INTERACTIONS IN SOCIAL WORK AT THE UNIVERSITY OF DENVER

Jaci Gandenberger and Nina Ekholm Fry

The Graduate School of Social Work at the University of Denver in Denver, Colorado, has offered courses in human-animal interaction since 1996. Today, graduate students can pursue a three-course certificate in Human-Animal-Environment Interactions in Social Work (HAEI-SW) within their MSW degree. When I (Nina Ekholm Fry) took over the coordinator role for these courses in 2021, my first task was to implement changes to the curriculum and certificate title that emerged from a two-year long process involving multiple stakeholder groups. The new certificate content drives current and future states of social work and human-animal-environment interactions, especially in clinical and community practice settings. The title change from *animal-assisted social work* to *human-animal-environment interactions in social work* reflects how the certificate prepares social workers to understand the importance and impact of interactions with animals and with the environment that are aligned with the core values of social work and the identity of the profession. Social workers trained in HAEI-SW center social work actions within intersecting systems of health, wellness, oppression, and violence between humans, animals, and the environment, in settings such as mental health agencies, community programs, schools, animal shelters, and veterinary clinics. Students are required to apply critical and culturally humble approaches anchored in social work ethics when considering these complex relationships under the guidance of expert faculty. The content of the HAEI-SW certificate is informed by the work taking place at the Institute for Human-Animal Connection (IHAC), a research and professional education institute at the University of Denver.

I (Jaci Gandenberger) am one of the instructors in the HAEI-SW certificate and a research associate at IHAC. Due to the many professional options possible for social workers, my career path has not been linear, but I could not be happier about where it has taken me. I originally pursued an MSW at the University of Denver with a goal of providing clinical services to refugees, but during my graduate studies realized the high risk of burnout for me, personally, were I to choose this direction. This was an important and necessary realization. Going into my graduate studies, I also wanted to use my time as a student to pursue something novel to me. While I had always loved animals and have had them in my life since I was a child, I had not thought about human-animal-environment interactions in a professional sense. As a graduate student research assistant at IHAC, I quickly realized that the work here goes deeply into the relationships between people, other species, and the environment to improve the health and wellbeing for all. Further, the research is deeply rooted in core social work values. To give you a sense: my first project as a student examined a person-centric approach to access to veterinary care in under-resourced communities and my second project explored how prison inmates were affected by participating in prison-based dog training programs. By graduation, I knew I had found my career home. Since then, as a post-MSW fellow at the institute, and later a research associate, I have delved into the impacts of animal and nature interactions on students in a residential treatment facility and studied whether a culturally competent approach to client interactions could impact their participation in low-cost veterinary care services.

One of the best parts of my job is teaching students in our HAEI-SW certificate program. We start the first day of the first of three courses by exploring why understanding human-animal-environment interactions may be important in social work and coming up with examples of applications in professional practice. Without fail, students imagine scenarios and services that fill entire white boards. In the foundation course, topics include improving policies around petkeeping in affordable housing, recognizing how concepts such as One Health are derived from traditional ecological knowledge, supporting the mental health of veterinarian staff, and learning about healthcare-aligned ways to include interactions with animals in psychotherapy. And those are just a few examples! One of my favorite parts of the course meetings is discussing current topics in human and animal health and how social workers trained in this area can contribute to change through a justice-focused systems perspective. I also love being able to share our latest research with my students, and they in turn enrich my thinking about the topics we study. My work is, however, not without challenges. Social workers work with populations that are vulnerable within the systems that they exist in and navigate – the experience of animals within these systems is like this as well. It can feel heavy to work with people who may lose some of their most important relationships, those with their pets, for financial or other reasons outside of their control, or to hear the stories of animal suffering that often arise in our work.

As with any social work area, self-care is essential. In my case, self-care involves spending quality time with my dogs and immersing myself in the natural beauty of Colorado.

If you are interested in a career in HAEI-SW, especially in research and academic teaching, we have some advice to share. Firstly, do not be afraid to put yourself out there! Ask your professors to connect you to colleagues knowledgeable about human-animal interactions and seek out your own experiences. Secondly, as academic study of human-animal-environment interactions is still considered specialized, you have to be tenacious and persistent in finding opportunities to learn and to be part of professional groups. Thirdly, when you have the opportunity to learn and work in human-animal-environment settings, truly show up. If this is your interest, it should be reflected in the amount of time you spend on it during any given day or week. Say yes to opportunities and notice connections between common social work issues and human-animal-environment interactions. We hope that you will be excited by HAEI-SW and create your own opportunities in service of a more just future for all.

62
SUPREME DOGS, DREAM JOBS

Yvonne Eaton-Stull

Background

I always knew I wanted to work in a helping profession. I have a BA in Psychology, an MSW in Clinical Social Work with a concentration in Forensic Social Work, and a DSW in Social Work. Many years ago, when I was working as an Outpatient Therapist, I had a supervisor challenge me saying "We need more clients in groups". I responded, "What about having groups with therapy dogs?" I had to write up a proposal and present it to the Board of Directors – and they approved it! That began my career in animal-assisted social work. I knew this is what I wanted to do, and I have been fortunate to be able to work providing animal-assisted intervention in a Community Mental Health Center, a College Counseling Center, and now teaching animal-assisted social work at Slippery Rock University in Pennsylvania.

An Average Day

In the Community Mental Health Center, I provided individual and group therapy to adults and children/adolescents with mental health needs and was able to include one of my yellow Labrador Retrievers once a week. Kids groups were also a fun part of my day, and I offered animal-assisted anger management, self-esteem, and other topics.

In the College Counseling Center, I brought one of my labs weekly to campus. We hosted "Mondays with Maggie" where students could just come and visit Maggie. This was a great way for students to become familiar with the Counseling Center should they need services in the future. I was able to create other fun events to enhance participation and increase knowledge of counseling services. Therapy dogs were also part of our interventions following tragedies, such as suicides.

Today, I am fortunate to share my knowledge and experience at Slippery Rock University (SRU) in Pennsylvania where I teach both undergraduate courses and graduate courses in animal-assisted social work. SRU offers an undergraduate minor in animal-assisted intervention and a graduate or postgraduate certificate in animal-assisted social work. In this role, I work with many local therapy dog teams who volunteer their time and assist my students in applying their knowledge providing animal-assisted activities and therapy to various groups in the community.

Most Rewarding Parts

There are so many rewarding aspects of my career. Being able to share my dogs to make difficult life circumstances just a little more tolerable for individuals is so worthwhile. I loved creating ideas for individual therapy or developing animal-assisted group activities, but seeing the amazing interactions was always the highlight of this work. Unbelievable interactions, such as a preschooler with autism who was non-verbal talking to my dog Maggie and bringing his teacher to tears; my lab, Zeus, unexpectedly pulling me down a hall in a nursing home where a man had fallen; my dog, Maggie, suddenly sitting on the lap of a student brought to my office in the midst of a panic attack; or my dog, Chevy, pulling determinedly through a crowd to get to a distraught young girl at a funeral. These experiences would make anyone a believer in the power of the human-animal bond.

Challenging Parts

One of the saddest situations is when an organization denies the offer to bring therapy dogs into the facility to provide support. In my experience though, once an organization sees the dogs in action they become believers. I think it is important for all of us to work with these individuals and organizations to slowly bring them onboard. Offering to give a presentation, providing letters of support from others, or bringing a single dog in to meet the administration may just get the hypothetical foot (read paws) in the door.

So many kind and well-intentioned individuals want to help those in need. Unfortunately, another frustration is when these people do not recognize stress in their dogs or push their dogs to do this type of work when they clearly do not enjoy it. For these people, there are many other ways to assist. Crisis organizations, like HOPE Animal-Assisted Crisis Response, have Team Leader positions where individuals support crisis dog teams but do not work with their own dog.

Undeniably, the life expectancy of dogs is the most difficult fact to cope with. Rather than focusing on this sad reality, I try to recall all the wonderful work and interactions, all the people's lives the dogs have touched, and how they have enriched my own life and career.

Advice and Words of Wisdom

Integrating dogs into your career can be challenging, but it definitely offers a multitude of rewards and benefits! For those considering work within the human-animal interaction field, there are many things that can be done to prepare.

Shadow therapy dog teams in various settings to see what they do and how they assist those in need. Contacting organizations to see if they have a therapy dog program is a great place to start; many hospitals, nursing homes, and residential facilities have therapy programs. Additionally, finding a mentor who can guide you and offer support during your journey is invaluable.

Volunteering within human service organizations is also helpful to gain valuable experience interacting with others. Some organizations may welcome a volunteer to assist in activities or accompanying therapy dog teams. If you have a dog that loves people and is well-behaved, you could consider becoming a therapy dog team and volunteering your time. National therapy dog organizations, including Pet Partners and the Alliance of Therapy Dogs, even have options for junior/younger handlers. As mentioned earlier, HOPE Animal-Assisted Crisis Response has volunteer Team Leaders who coordinate responses to crises and disasters while providing support to the canine teams. This is a great way to work with dogs, obtain additional training and experience, and help others.

Additionally, seek out education! There are many valuable resources out there, including books, free online webinars, human-animal bond conferences, and special certificates and degrees in this area. If this is what you want to do, forge ahead, develop a plan, and follow your dreams!

63
HOW I GOT HERE

Kayla Holland Baudoin

High-pitched neighs echoing in the wind on a brisk winter morning, the smell of hay in the air, gentle, warm kisses of my "guard" dog licking me awake as the sun rises, and the soft fur of the cat rubbing against my legs as I stumble to the kitchen for breakfast is how I remember typically starting my day. My love of animals was instant; I do not remember a time that I was not surrounded by dear companions.

My appreciation and curiosity related to humans grew as I worked within my mother's private social work practice. This curiosity led to my Bachelor of Science in Psychology and Master's in Social Work (MSW) through Louisiana State University (LSU) and to my Licensed Clinical Social Work certification.

During my MSW program, I selected an internship within the LSU School of Veterinary Medicine (LSU Vet Med). It was through my interactions with veterinary students and clients of the animal hospital that I discovered my love for working with graduate students and those who cherish the human-animal bond. This solidified my decision to practice veterinary social work (VSW) within a joint academic and clinic setting.

I will never forget my first client, who described the grief she experienced after the loss of her avian companion of 20 plus years. In fact, her story broadened my view of what a companion animal was. Before this client, I was unsure how someone could express the same feelings of sadness, guilt, and appreciation for a bird as others did for the loss of their loyal dog. This, among other experiences, expanded my knowledge and compassion for all animals and the connection they develop with their human counterparts. To me, a companion animal is any creature that brings joy and becomes part of the social fabric of a family.

"Average Day"

In 2021, I was hired as a Wellbeing Manager embedded within LSU Vet Med. My focus is on wellbeing initiatives for the LSU Vet Med community, providing consults and referrals for faculty, staff, and clinical students and offering counseling for clients of the small and large animal clinics in relation to anticipated grief, end-of-life decisions, and grief and loss of companion animals. The dynamic part about my position is an average day does not exist. Each day, week, and month provides new opportunities. For example, one day I may provide wellbeing rounds for our house officers (interns/residents) to allow them a space to express frustrations, challenging cases, and discuss mental health issues while another day I might see a grieving client one hour, offer continuing education units to veterinary nurses another hour, and conclude the day with a departmental conflict management workshop.

Rewarding Experience and Its Challenges

One of the most incredible parts of this position entails validating the emotions and grief that a client experiences after the loss of their companion animal. The societal shift to understanding the grief process for the loss of a pet has not quite caught up to the needs of many. Thus, providing a safe space where someone can grieve without feeling judged for mourning their companions or being a burden to friends and family is invaluable.

Another rewarding component is advocating for cultural change within the academic environment. Faculty and staff are often overworked, relying on house officers and students to compensate for those who often feel exhausted and burned out. It brings me joy when I contribute to policy changes that enhance wellbeing and impact cultural shifts to positively influence the work environment.

While there are several positives, challenges do exist. Due to overlapping (dual) roles, one must be extremely delicate when advocating for change with administration—whether that be in relation to policies or culture or how faculty feedback is managed. Providing perspective while maintaining confidentiality can be challenging. It is important to consider how even generalized information can inadvertently break confidentiality and do a cost versus benefit analysis.

When I work with clients of the clinic, I start where they are in their grief journey. I work to ensure I notice the potential for my personal bias rising to the surface and remember to keep that in check. Be careful not to manage a client's needs as you would want done for yourself. Just because you want something done a specific way does not mean the same is true for your client.

Skills Needed for Veterinary Social Work

Aside from completing an MSW from an accredited program and becoming licensed within your state, the following are helpful for those pursuing veterinary social work:

- Be knowledgeable about various theories on the grief process and how grief presents.
- Understand compassion fatigue vs. burnout and how to combat. Self-care is key.
- Be proficient in communication skills, active listening, conflict management, and providing constructive feedback.
- Be able to manage expectations through boundary setting.
- Be knowledgeable about suicidal ideation, your obligations, how to create a safety plan, and available resources.
- Be flexible, resourceful, and proactive.
- Develop your own self-care plan; do as you teach.

Conclusion

One of the best parts about social work is you do not work in a silo. You have a mountain of support from fellow mental health professionals. Utilize that. We are here for you.

64
PAW AND HOOFPRINTS ON MY CAREER PATH

Angela Lavery

I suppose my beginning started out as it does for many of us, with an incredible love of animals from a very early age. Although I was one of those kids who found ways to adopt many different kinds of pets, it wasn't until my 30s that I truly understood how much I wanted to foster human and animal connections for others as well. I learned of the therapeutic power of animals when I worked as a Hospice Social Worker and Bereavement Care Coordinator. In this role of providing end-of-life care, I learned of a certified therapy dog team at our hospice agency. What a gift it was in my life to witness how this volunteer and her beautiful golden retriever provided much needed connection at a critical point in the lives of those at the end of life. As I assessed for and then arranged these visits with our interested hospice patients and caregivers, I saw the magic unfold. I witnessed first-hand what the presence and touch of a dog can bring, whether it was inside a long-term care nursing facility or a bed within the home of a hospice patient.

One story changed everything for me as a gerontological and end-of-life care social worker. We had a hospice patient who had been transferred from her independent living apartment to a long-term care nursing facility. Since her admission to the facility, we suspected that some of her decline and change in speaking and interacting was not only due to her terminal diagnosis but was due to the grief and loss around the transition from the familiar independence of her own quiet apartment to a bustling care facility. Each time we would visit this older hospice patient, she would not speak and kept her head down and body hunched over while sitting in her wheelchair. Her family noted the change and wondered how much of this sudden change was related to her diagnosis. After talking more with the family, I learned that this woman grew up on a cattle ranch where she was surrounded by animals and had her own pets throughout her life. We were able to arrange a visit by our therapy team. We watched as the golden walked over to her wheelchair and were thrilled to witness the older woman slowly pick up her own head and then reach out her hand and pet and stroke the beautiful soft blonde coat of the dog. We delighted in getting to hear her begin to talk about pet dogs she had during her life. It was the first time any of us had heard her speak. Her adult daughter was present and was filled with joy. This was truly one of my favorite days in my work in end-of-life care.

Later in my career, I decided to return to school to pursue a PhD. I chose to study in a Social Work program that had both experts in the field of gerontological social work as well as human animal interactions and interventions. I began studying for my PhD in Social Work at the University of Denver (DU) in the fall of 2010. DU's Graduate Social Work program had its own Institute for Human and Animal Connection. What an honor it was to observe the work of leaders within the field of human animal bond and interactions. Despite my full-time studies within the PhD program, when time allowed, I attended events and programs offered by the institute. Following graduation from the PhD program, I moved to the east coast and began working at West Chester University of Pennsylvania's Graduate Social Work Department. Here, I am able to collaborate with other colleagues who feel passionate about and study the human-animal bond.

A Day in My Current Life

When I am not teaching graduate social work and gerontology courses, I work on a project that involves older adults and equine interactions. There is a dearth of information on older adults and their lives with horses. This project includes not only asking about older adults' perceptions of their interactions and lives with horses but also explores what possible oppressive factors such as ageism and paternalism may impact their ability to participate or enjoy equine activities at this point in their life.

In addition to sharing about their lives with horses, these older adults have shared what they would like others to know about supporting their ongoing equestrian-based activities. Some of the older adult participants have chosen to create a "digital story" highlighting their life with horses. This is an intergenerational activity, where the older adult is paired with a college student to create the video. The video is then given to the participant to have as a keepsake.

Best/Most Rewarding Parts of Your Job

The most rewarding part of my research is getting to see how much older adults appreciate being asked about their work and interactions with horses.

We have so much to learn about the roles of older adults within families and communities, from which both humans and animals receive and benefit. The critical resources that older adults provide can thrive and strengthen our lives and communities, as long as we resist and confront ageist attitudes and stereotypes and foster supportive environments where folks of all ages continue to benefit from our connections to animals. I am thrilled to be part of this endeavor.

65
CRITICAL ANIMAL STUDIES AND ONE HEALTH IN SOCIAL WORK

Atsuko Matsuoka

I am a university professor who is passionately interested in expanding the scope of social work education and practice to include human-nonhuman animal relationships and concern for nonhuman animals. I teach an MSW course on social work and animals using Critical Animal Studies (CAS) as my theoretical basis. CAS allows us to examine relationships at the interpersonal level as well as the social, political, economic, and cultural structural processes by employing concepts of speciesism and anthropocentrism and by promoting intersectional analyses (e.g., Adams, 2000; Matsuoka & Sorenson, 2018; Nibert, 2002, 2017; Nocella et al., 2014; Sorenson, 2014).

When social workers make assessments or try to understand people's lives in order to support them, we tend to focus only on human relationships, although nonhuman animals are present and often play significant roles in people's lives. For example, ecomap and intake assessment tools include(d) only humans and human-related organizations. Yet, nonhuman animals provide steady emotional support for many people. Such support can come not only from companion animals (or 'pets') but from urban wild animals, e.g., pigeons and squirrels. At the same time, we often fail to acknowledge that humans' lives are dependent on other animals as sources of food, health, labour, research and entertainment/education (circuses, aquariums, vivisections and zoos to name a few). Increasing awareness about the abuse and exploitation of other animals and the significant positive influences of non-human animals on human health has led to ethical and political decisions to be vegan or limit the use of nonhuman animals. Meanwhile, social workers have begun to explore ways to better understand the everyday lives of people we work with, including their significant relationships with nonhuman animals.

Existing social work and related literature clearly show a growing interest in the use of other animals in social work practice, such as animal-assisted therapy (Gee & Mueller, 2019). When it comes to 'using' others (including other animals), social workers must examine power relationships between the users and the used. Therefore, I encourage students to re-examine such relationships, realizing nonhuman animals are sentient beings entitled to fair treatment and justice. My course helps them to realize justice is not limited to humans alone, rather we need to consider justice across and beyond species. I call such justice 'trans-species social justice' (Matsuoka & Sorenson, 2014).

I also encourage students to consider all our relations (not limited to human relations) and critically examine different approaches, for example, the strengths and limitations of the One Health approach as they apply to social work. A strength of the One Health approach is that the term itself clearly describes how human health is intertwined with the health of other nonhuman animals. Thus, the concept of One Health is easy to relate to and helps convince others to consider nonhuman animals in the social work framework. However, the most serious limitation of the One Health approach if it is used in social work is the unquestioned anthropocentrism and speciesism. The concept of One Health emerged as a part of controlling zoonotic disease (i.e., infectious disease transmitted from animals to people). Many are familiar with the news of destroying a large number of farm animals when zoonotic disease is widespread among livestock. Such measures to control disease based on the One Health approach are beneficial for human health but destroying healthy animals ignores the rights of sentient beings. Applying such drastic measures should call for moral and ethical debate. Knowing this, social workers should be aware of such challenges using the One Health approach in social work.

Limitations are not always negative because by addressing them we can explore a better way. This is one of the most rewarding parts of teaching. I recommend that we start by examining power relationships within human and nonhuman animal relations. First, we critically examine taken-for-granted anthropocentrism and speciesism within our relationships and in our practice assumptions. By doing so, social workers can assess whether the One Health approach is appropriate or whether it perpetuates unchecked oppression, including anthropocentrism and speciesism, along with classism, racism, ableism and sexism. Such an analysis provides a better understanding of intersectional oppression (including speciesism, sexism, ableism, racism and classism). Addressing such intersectional oppression holds the key to decolonization. Those interested in learning more about Critical Animal Studies and the kinds of projects that my colleagues and I are involved in can learn more at the "Animals and Social Work" website: http://animalsandsocialwork.info.yorku.ca/.

References

Adams, C. J. (2000). *The sexual politics of meat*. Continuum.

Gee, N., & Mueller, M. (2019). A systematic review of research on pet ownership and animal interactions among older adults. *Anthrozoös, 32*(2), 183–207. https://doi.org/10.1080/08927936.2019.1569903.

Matsuoka, A., & Sorenson, J. (2014). Social justice beyond human beings: Trans-species social justice. In T. Ryan (Ed.), *Animals in social work: Why and how they matter* (pp. 64–79). Palgrave Macmillan.

Matsuoka, A., & Sorenson, J. (Eds.). (2018). *Critical animal studies: Toward trans-species social justice*. Rowman & Littlefield. https://www.rowmaninternational.com/book/critical_animal_studies/3-156-8606c11f-3a7d-4a69-9f66-b5ab28e57336.

Nibert, D. A. (2002). *Animal rights/human rights: Entanglements of oppression and liberation*. Rowman & Littlefield.

Nibert, D. A. (Ed.). (2017). *Animal oppression and capitalism*. An Imprint of ABC-CLIO, LLC.

Nocella, A. J., II, Sorenson, J., Socha, K., & Matsuoka, A. (Eds.). (2014). *Defining critical animal studies: An intersectional social justice approach*. Peter Lang Publishing.

Sorenson, J. (2014). *Critical animal studies: Thinking the unthinkable*. Canadian Scholars Press.

66
HOSPITAL VETERINARY SOCIAL WORK IN THE CANADIAN CONTEXT

Sarah Bernardi

Growing up in a small town in Northern Ontario, Canada, I had never stepped foot in a specialty and emergency veterinary hospital. My experience was limited to bringing our family dogs to their regular veterinary clinic. Like many, my love for animals started young. My first companion was our family dog Sparka-lee (named by me at 5 years old). Sparka-lee was in our lives for 17 years. My mom and dad made the decision to euthanize her after her quality of life declined significantly. For my brother and I, this was our first experience witnessing euthanasia and losing a pet, we had no idea what to expect. That entire process was gut-wrenching. To this day, I have never seen my family collectively so devastated. For some time afterwards, we struggled to navigate the tremendous grief and emptiness that followed our loss.

Fast forward three years later, I had just graduated with my MSW. I was at my parents' home searching for jobs online when "Veterinary Social Worker" (VSW) appeared on screen. It was for a private specialty and emergency hospital. The decision was easy, I have always loved animals and they are an important part of my life, so I sent in an application. Two months and three rounds of interviews later, I began my first VSW job in the hospital.

This role was a massive learning curve for both me and the hospital, I was their first VSW on staff. All at once, I was learning staff roles, getting to know specialty departments, and trying to figure out where I fit in. Integrating a VSW position into the hospital was an ongoing process of trial, error, and boundary setting. A guiding light during this time was a Canadian VSW who worked in a hospital in another province. This person became my lifeline and support as I tried to navigate this environment. Every step was a new, but exciting challenge. I developed intake/consent forms, resources, policies, and procedures and taught staff how to engage with the service.

DOI: 10.4324/9781003335528-72

I have since left the private setting and now hold the VSW title at the Ontario Veterinary College and Health Sciences Centre (OVC HSC), a teaching hospital. I provide support to clients whose companion animals are being treated at OVC HSC. Day-to-day, my role includes facilitating client decisions about medical treatment and end-of-life issues; case debriefing, emotional support, and stress relief strategies for clients and staff; assisting clients in processing difficult decisions for their pet's treatment, including surgery and euthanasia options; connecting with clinical leads and staff through daily interactions like rounding and departmental meetings; and provision of grief counseling to clients.

It is an exciting time for VSW in Canada, recently three new VSW positions opened in hospital settings, and it is expected that these opportunities will continue to grow. However, despite this growth, Canadians entering this field will still face unique challenges. Canada's population is smaller, and the physical space is larger, we don't have nearly as many emergency/specialty hospitals compared to countries like the United States (US). In addition to this, the landscape of social work is incredibly different from the US, so while invaluable insight comes from VSW practitioners in the US, Canada is still carving its own path—our VSW community is smaller (but mighty!) and more dispersed. For those entering the field and looking to create a sustainable job, you may consider the following:

- Define your role clearly! Many clinics have not had a VSW presence, be prepared to share information on what social work is, and more specifically, the scope of your practice. Do you provide services to clients, staff, or both? What are your service limitations? If you are expected to provide direct counseling services to staff, you must have a strong sense of boundaries and your management team should respect and reinforce these.
- Be aware of isolation! Often, animal care teams will only have one VSW on staff, which may become overwhelming and lonely. First and foremost, access to clinical supervision is necessary for professional accountability and ethical practice. You can connect with the professional VSW community for additional peer support, the International Association of Veterinary Social Workers (IAVSW) is a great place to start.
- Don't get hung up obtaining the VSW specialty! Please note that you do not require this specialty to practice with this demographic. There are schools in the US that offer this specialization, but it is not always a realistic or accessible option for Canadian citizens to obtain a degree from these institutions. The social work skills and education you receive in your province are transferable to a VSW role, and there are many ways you can bolster your knowledge about this area of social work.

To summarize, VSW is a role that has been created with recognition that there is a human component to veterinary medicine. My passion is getting to work with the incredible staff, students, and faculty to provide support and care to the animals and their humans. In particular, the grief work I do with clients is something I love—this role has allowed me to reflect upon my own loss and I feel a deep connection with those who are experiencing anticipatory grief and grief after the death of their companions. These animals are part of our family systems, the bond shared with them is unlike any other—and it deserves to be validated and acknowledged. I am incredibly grateful to share this experience with others and look forward to seeing this field shift and change.

67
BRINGING VETERINARY SOCIAL WORK INTO A ONE-HEALTH MODEL

Augusta O'Reilly

My journey began when I graduated with an undergraduate degree in psychology with plans to enter the field of animal behavior. I had wanted to work with animals since I was young and veterinary science did not align with my schooling. After graduation, I became a veterinary assistant because I still felt the call to work in a veterinary setting in some capacity. I spent several years working directly with animals but found myself drawn toward utilizing my understanding of the human mind in my work. As a veterinary assistant, I was placed in the intensive care unit, where I often volunteered to support human family members when they visited their non-human family members or assembled paw print memorials after a pet's passing. I enjoyed connecting with both clients and colleagues within the veterinary clinic, and my co-workers saw this and would seek me out for support.

One day, the veterinarian I worked with mentioned that at her veterinary college, the University of Tennessee, Knoxville, they offered human support that was available to both staff and families. She believed I would fit well into the program. That night I went home searched for "mental health at UTK Veterinary College" and found "veterinary social work (VSW)." I applied that week! Originally, I had applied with the hopes of using the program to grow my understanding of how to operate a therapeutic farm for at-risk youth, but over the course of my training and work experience, it led me to another path that felt just as right as the day I discovered the veterinary social work program.

I graduated from the University of Tennessee, Knoxville with a master's in social work and a certification in VSW in May of 2018. I completed my hours to become a fully licensed clinical social worker (LCSW) and after a few years working in community-based mental health with at-risk youth and chronically mentally ill adults, I became aware of a job that would lead to me my current position and passion. A leader in the VSW field had posted a job for a veterinary social worker at the University of Tennessee, Knoxville Program for Pet Health Equity (PPHE). It is a program that focuses on the barriers and community-wide support needed for lower socioeconomic families to access veterinary care. It was work that I had never experienced before but with my understanding of community-based mental health, training with trauma-informed care, and a passion to help both animal care professionals and families, I applied and was offered the position.

As Director of VSW with PPHE, a growing and evolving program, my day-to-day schedule can look different, but the focus is always on program development. One component of my job is helping to grow and develop the One-Health Program: AlignCare. AlignCare is a community-based program that aligns professionals from animal welfare, public health/mental health, and veterinary clinics with low-income families who have a sick or injured pet. Within the AlignCare program, I oversee the veterinary social workers who provide direct support to families. A typical family interaction consists of connecting families with community resources, helping mediate between the family and service provider, and providing support around grief and end-of-life discussions. I develop and present educational materials for animal care professionals working with marginalized families and the role that a VSW has in the animal-welfare sector. I present at private workshops and conferences throughout the year. I work alongside the PPHE Director of Operations to develop educational material for Doctor of Veterinary Medicine curriculum to add insight on how lack of veterinary care access can have a negative impact to the humans who are experiencing it, both the providers and families. I also work alongside the Associate Director of Research for PPHE to develop research proposals that will grow the understanding of the mental health impacts of the human-animal bond, the impact of access to care, and the effects of working with veterinary social workers. I also provide training to professionals around de-escalation techniques, how to implement trauma-informed care, and how to connect and build relationships with community members. I also attend and speak about the benefits and the implementation of VSW at different community information sessions.

It has been very rewarding to connect with communities across the country that are supportive and believe in the work that VSWs do. I have learned numerous transferable skills and created a number of connections to help grow the VSW field within the access to veterinary care scope. While the rewards greatly outnumber the challenges, one of the hardest challenges is developing a program with limited resources. One skill that has been pivotal in doing this work is being flexible and resilient and being able to pivot when one plan doesn't work out and being able to create and attempt another plan.

My advice for others who want to work in this arena is to be open to any job that sparks your interest, even if it doesn't exactly match your degree. Many skills can be transferable and learned on the job. I started off thinking I only wanted to do clinical work and now I am doing macro-level work and it has been so rewarding. I give credit to networking and getting involved in listservs, discussion boards, and other platforms in my area of interest. This can lead to finding unique positions such as mine, jobs that are often posted on smaller forums. Stay open-minded and enjoy the path.

68
SOCIAL WORK AND HUMAN-ANIMAL INTERACTION IN AN ACADEMIC SETTING

Lisa Townsend

About Me

My love of animals began at the age of 5 when our family adopted a sweet little Westie who saw me through my childhood. Crystal taught me how freely I could love another being – she was playful, funny, non-judgmental, and empathic. She fostered my sense of responsibility, sparking my first feelings of care and protectiveness. This early relationship inspired a commitment to living with and caring for animals. My work is an extension of this – I chose social work as a career in recognition of the complex interrelationships between people and the spheres in which they live – families, schools, neighborhoods, workplaces, and other social systems that challenge or foster their growth.

A Day in My Life

I am an academic clinical social worker – I provide therapy services and conduct research. I work with youth and adults who struggle with chronic suicidal ideation and self-injury, a group that often faces marginalization from education, employment, and social relationships. My current research examines changes in inflammatory cytokines in response to animal-assisted intervention (AAI). I work at the Center for Human-Animal Interaction (CHAI) in the School of Medicine at Virginia Commonwealth University (VCU). Directed by Dr. Nancy Gee, the Center focuses on the tripartite mission of increasing human-animal interaction (HAI) knowledge through interdisciplinary research, improving health and well-being through AAI, and educating others about the benefits of HAI. Readers can visit chai.vcu.edu to find out more about CHAI. My role there is to develop and supervise clinical programming and monitor our randomized controlled clinical trials, which examine psychological and physical health outcomes of AAI in hospitalized adults and children.

I broaden my HAI knowledge by shadowing our Dogs on Call (DOC) teams as they visit throughout the hospital. DOC teams are human and canine volunteers who visit patients and staff in the VCU Medical Center and help provide the animal-assisted interventions for our research. Seeing the dogs at the Center always brightens my day!

Training 101

The role I have is ideal for someone who loves reading and spending a great deal of time writing. The clinical part of my job requires obtaining an MSW or equivalent degree followed by two years of supervised clinical practice to achieve independent licensure. The academic part of my position required completion of a PhD – I loved my graduate program and count those years as some of the best ones of my life. Full-time MSW programs take two years to complete and PhD programs require four years – a substantial time commitment, but well worth it if academic social work is your calling. I came to HAI much later in my career when I connected with Dr. Gee, our center director, through our mutual interest in mental health. I quickly realized the need to bolster my knowledge of HAI through specific coursework, which I completed online through a program at Oakland University. As with any work involving other living beings, my HAI education is ongoing and I often shadow our DOC teams to gain real-world HAI experience.

Daily Treats

My biggest treat of the day is having dogs greet me in the office. Our DOC teams often stop by the Center on their way to or from the hospital. We will close the Center doors and play games of fetch or tug with the dogs, giving them (and us) a chance to play and relax.

A more sobering, yet profound benefit is walking alongside our teams as they provide comfort to patients and staff. Our teams visit people hospitalized with serious illnesses, injuries, and psychiatric disorders as well as the staff who care for them. They also help us with our research studies in the main hospital and in a local long-term physical rehabilitation facility. Emergency medical staff and outpatient units receive love from the dogs too.

Daily Challenges

Balancing many roles – therapist, researcher, dog-mom – is my greatest challenge. The desire to do it all is strong and yet there are only so many hours in a day. For me, the concept of balance has morphed into the idea that we must flex to meet the shifting demands of our roles – some days, my clients need more of my time; other days, writing takes center stage. Flexibility asks us to step away from guilt-based responding and toward a sense of acknowledging overall progress. My future goal is to work with my own therapy dog to provide mental health care for my clients, enhancing my clients' engagement in our sessions while bolstering my own well-being.

Finding Your Niche

HAI work looks different for everyone. Some people volunteer with their therapy dogs, some teach, and others counsel or respond to crises with their animals. If you are interested in social work and HAI, link with others who share your interests. Ways to connect include certificate programs in social work and HAI; some of these require in-person coursework while others are virtual. Joining an HAI association is a good way to find other HAI providers – the Association for Animal Assisted Intervention Professionals is one such group, as is Pet Partners and the Alliance of Therapy Dogs. If you have your own companion animal, find an in-person, positive behavior-based training facility that provides training classes as well as fun options for enhancing your bond. You could also check out nose-work, agility, or swimming groups. Alternatively, if you do not have a dog, you can train to be a secondary handler for someone who has a therapy animal. Local humane societies/animal shelters always need volunteers – this can be a way to care for and learn about animals while building your HAI skills. I encourage you to gain hands-on experience – nothing substitutes for experiencing the human-animal bond firsthand.

Final Tidbits

My wish is that you love many roles during your career. Allow yourself the flexibility to try new things, challenge yourself to do things you think you can't, and remember that we are all important threads in a much larger universe.

INDEX

academia, human-animal interaction 191–230; critical animal studies 219–220; designing diverse social work career 204–206; dog person, at work 199–200; dream jobs 210–212; inclusive communities 201–203; instant love story 213–215; paw and hoofprints on 216–218; pit bull puppies 196–198; professional and personal meaning through 191–195; social work 228–230; supreme dogs 210–212; veterinary social work (*see* veterinary social work (VSW))
Acri, M. 205
Advanced Practice Social Worker 23
advocacy: animal 56–58; human-animal interaction 13, 138–140; policy 46–50
Ahimsa Fellowship 57
AIDS epidemic 112
Alaska Animal Rescue Foundation (AARF) 200
AlignCare 226
Alliance of Therapy Dogs 31, 101, 212
alternative academic (alt-ac) 63
American Humane Association 164
American Humane Society 113
American Rescue Act 49
Americans with Disabilities Act 202
Amovita International 132, 133

AniCare 55
animal abuse 5, 18, 53–55, 91, 92
animal advocacy 56–58
animal-assisted activities (AAA) 29–30, 79
animal-assisted intervention/interaction (AAI) 29–30, 228; aspect of 80–81; challenge 74; clinical work within disability community 79–81; equine-assisted services 85–87; forensic interviews 113; human-animal interaction 91–93; in juvenile justice 100–102; pandemic pups 97–99; Pandora's Peter Bear 95; paws for play 88–90; paws in play 82–84; power of paws 71–75; professional practice around 78; shelter pets and kids 100–102; therapy dogs (*see* therapy dogs); unexpected implementation 172–174
animal-assisted play therapy 83–84, 88, 141–143
Animal Assisted Play Therapy (VanFleet and Faa-Thompson) 143
animal-assisted social work (AASW) 100, 123
animal-assisted therapy (AAT) 42, 71–74, 79, 127, 179, 220; challenges of 84; clinical work within disability community

79–81; counseling program 83; dogs 88–90; Human-animal bond In Ministry 184–185; in Israeli psychiatric hospital 186–188; lessons learned and shared 80–81; in private practice 80; psychotherapy 76–78, 106–108; in research 80; rewards of 84; in schools 80
Animal Behavior and Conservation 71
Animal Husbandry and Dairying 57
animal organizations 29, 193; human and (*see* human-animal interaction (HAI)); national therapy 31
Animal Studies 63–64
animal welfare 37, 63–64, 73, 78, 112, 162, 167, 226; advocacy 6; community-based 164; and ethics 83–84; issues 182; practices in 153–156
APPA National Pet Owners Survey (2023–2024) 111
applied behavioral analysis (ABA) therapy 147
Association for Play Therapy 83
Australian Association of Social Workers 11–12

Bachelor of Social Work (BSW) 20, 155, 203
Bardach, E. 48
Bereavement Care Coordinator 216
Bexell, S. 147–149
bilingual home-based therapist 123
biophilia hypothesis 67
Brace, J. 3
Brooklyn District Attorney's Office 53
burnout 22, 24, 78, 83, 104, 118, 180

CABI's Human-Animal Interactions Journal 122
Caldwell, P. 197
Canada, veterinary social work 222–224
Canadian Veterinary Medical Association 145
canine *see* dogs (canine)
Care & Empathy Officer (CEO) 144
careers: current snapshot 121; designing diverse social work 204–206; humane education 148–149; in One Health 123–125; paw and hoofprints on 216–218

caring, human-animal interaction 184–185
Carlsson, C. 67
CAT Continuing Education 60
Center for Human-Animal Interaction (CHAI) 228
Centers for Human-Animal Bond Conference 86
Certified Animal-Assisted Intervention Specialist 202
Certified Animal Assisted Play Therapist™ 88
Certified Humane Educational Specialist 147
chasing impact, human-animal interaction 56–58
cherished pets model 11–13
Child Advocacy Center 139
Child and Family Studies 179
Child Centered Play Therapy (CCPT) 141
Cleveland State University 158
client support 23–24
Clinic Support Service 14, 15
cognitive behavioral therapy (CBT) 85, 123, 179, 205
College Counseling Center 210
college of veterinary medicine (CVM) 36–37, 86
Colorado State University's School of Social Work (CSU) 191
community dogs 62–63
Community Health Board 60
Community Investment 158
Community Mental Health Center 210
Community Practice service 36
community services: cherished pets veterinary social work 12; human-animal interaction 61–64
companion animal (CA) 111–113
Companions and Animals for Reform and Equity (CARE) 169, 170
compassion fatigue 5, 22, 24, 34, 78, 83, 104, 118, 121, 123
conflicts: human-animal interaction 61–64; management 5
Council on Social Work Education (CSWE) 6, 130.169, 169, 192, 202
COVID-19 182, 192; epidemic 32; pandemic 63, 99, 112, 130, 181
CP Foundation (CPF) 11
Crisis Pet Retention (CPR) program 167
critical animal studies 219–220

Dalhousie University 60
Deakin University Field Education 11
de-escalation techniques 226
Delta Society 29, 127
dialectical behavior therapy (DBT) 123
Director of Veterinary Services 144
disability community, animal-assisted therapy 79–81
The Doctor of Social Work (DSW) 67, 72
Dog Game 104
dogs (canine) 88–90; academia (*see* academia, human-animal interaction); canine-assisted therapy (CAT) 60; canine-assisted trauma therapy (CATT) 95; Canine Companions 139; Canine Good Citizen (CGC) 101, 107; Canine Good Citizen-Advanced (CGCA) 107; community 62–63; co-therapists 76–78; facility 81, 113, 139–140; family members, human-animal interaction 61–64; free-ranging 62; person at work 199–200; in play therapy 88–90; rabid street 63; service 59–61, 71, 106–108, 176, 193, 199–202; social work (*see* social work); stray 62; supreme, academia 210–212; therapy (*see* therapy dogs)
Dogs on Call (DOC) teams 229
Dumb Friends League 164

Educational Policy and Accreditation Standard (2022) 192
embedded social worker, in veterinary medicine school 8–10
emotional support animals (ESAs) 202
Employee Assistance Program (EAP) 9
employee support, veterinary social work 24
environmental justice 48, 202
equine (horse): animal-assisted intervention 85–87; of different color 35; Equine Assisted Mental Health 205; equine-assisted service (EAS) 65, 67, 85, 86; overarching benefit of 67; psychotherapy 73; social work 65–67; Therapeutic Riding Instructor 65–66; veterinary social work 35–37, 157–159

evidence-based practice 46, 85, 120, 133, 205
eye movement desensitization and reprocessing (EMDR) 123

Faa-Thompson, T. 88, 143; *Animal Assisted Play Therapy* 143
facility dogs 81, 113, 139–140
Fair Housing Act 202
A Fair Shake for Youth 75
Family and Children's Services 144
Fieldstone Farm Therapeutic Riding Center 158
forensic interviews, animal-assisted intervention 113
free-ranging dogs 62
Fry, N.M. 207

Gandenberger, J. 207–208
Gautam Buddha 58
Gee, N. 228, 229
Gestalt psychotherapy 60
Golden Retriever Lifetime Study (GRLS) 135–136
Graduate School of Social Work 135, 163, 207
grief: animals to help heal communities 179; hospital veterinary social work 224; human-animal interaction 112; veterinary social work 5, 18–22

Hanrahan, C. 60
Harris, T. 132–133
Healing Paws LLC 158
help, human-animal interaction and 166–168
High Hopes Therapeutic Riding Center 157
Historically Black Colleges and Universities (HBCUs) 170–171
Holmquist-Johnson, H. 192
hoofprints, on academia 216–218
HOPE Animal-Assisted Crisis Response 103, 210–212
Hope Animal Hospital 182
horses *see* equine (horse)
Hospice Social Worker 216
hospital veterinary social work (VSW) 26–28; Canadian context 222–224
Human and Animal Connection 217
human-animal bond (HAB) 47, 72, 123–125; animal health in

112–113; positive impact of 139; power of paws 71–75
Human-Animal Bond in Colorado (HABIC) 86, 191
Human-animal bond In Ministry (HIM) 184–185
Human-Animal-Environment Interactions in Social Work (HAEI-SW) 207–209
human-animal interaction (HAI) 11, 175–177; within academia 191–230; advocacy and pawprints 138–140; animal-assisted intervention and 91–93; animal welfare, practices in 153–156; canine family members 61–64; caring 184–185; challenges 60; chasing impact 56–58; community 61–64; conflicts 61–64; daring to dream 117–119; elevation 163–165; equine-assisted social work 65–67; grief and loss related to 112; help and 166–168; integrated approach 120–122; interprofessional practice skills 127; law enforcement 175–177; non-profit organization 192; Pandora's Peter Bear 95; police social work 178–180; policy advocacy 46–50; practice 111–149; program evaluation 46–50; programs and policies 41–45; puffy's pet boarding 51–52; services 181–183; social worker's learnings from 160–162; Sprout 59–61; therapy dogs 175–177; tripartite mission 228; veterinary social work 13; violence 5, 53–55; well-being 169–171
human-animal studies (HAS) 197–198
human-animal support services (HASS) 112, 114
human-canine interaction (HCI) 164, 201–202
humane education careers 148–149
Humane Education Practitioner Certificate (CHEP) 147–148
human-non-human-animal interactions 57, 92–93, 120, 165, 197, 219–220
Huston-Tillotson University (HT) 170–171

inclusive communities, human-animal interaction 201–203
Institute for Human-Animal Connection (IHAC) 148, 164, 207–208
Institute for Salivary Bioscience Research 158
integrated approach, human-animal interaction 120–122
interdisciplinary team 32, 154
intergenerational activity 217
International Association of Veterinary Social Workers (IAVSW) 160, 223
International Consultant 133
International Institute of Animal Assisted Play Therapy® 89
International Society for Animal-Assisted Therapy 60
internship program 24, 205; DU's Institute for Human-Animal Connection 135; with HOPE Animal-Assisted Crisis Response 103; in hospice setting 191; within LSU Vet Med 213; play therapy studies 83; possibility of 21
interprofessional systems approach, VSM 3–7
intersectional oppression 147, 220
intimate partner violence (IPV) 53–54
Isle of Dogs (2019) 62

juvenile justice, animal-assisted intervention in 100–102

Kent State University 30
Kingdon, J. 47
Kitten Kindergarten 101
Kogan, L. 192
Koret School of Veterinary Medicine 185

Lantzy, M. 147–149
law enforcement, human-animal interaction 175–177
Lawrence Humane Society (LHS) 167
licensed clinical social worker (LCSW) 32, 95, 141, 213, 225
LifeLearn Animal Health 145
Louisiana State University (LSU) 213; LSU School of Veterinary Medicine (LSU Vet Med) 213, 214

macro social work 46, 201, 202
Maritime Service Dogs 60
master's in social work (MSW) 9, 17, 23, 36, 61, 71–72, 77, 79, 127, 154, 155, 164, 179–180, 186, 207, 208, 213, 219, 222, 229; *see also* veterinary social work (VSW)
Maternal and Child Health 166
Mayor's Office of Animal Welfare 181, 182
medical negligence 5
mental health, and veterinary medicine 8, 15
Michigan Humane 153, 155
Ministry of Fisheries 57
Morris Animal Foundation (MAF) 135, 136
My Dog Is My Home 182

NASW Code of Ethics 66
National Association of Social Workers 78, 122
NATIONAL Crisis Response Canines 95
networking organizations 31
New York University: Langone Health Hospital 205; Silver School of Social Work 72
non-human animals 6, 8, 62, 91, 92, 111, 136, 163, 197, 219, 220
North American Veterinary Licensing Examination (NAVLE) 3
Nova Scotia Health Authority 60
Nova Scotia Mental Health and Addictions 60
Nova Scotia Service Dog Act 60

One Health 30, 111; academia (*see* academia, human-animal interaction); careers in 123–125; critical animal studies and 219–220; evidence-based practice 46; health and wellbeing 144–146; human-animal interaction (*see* human-animal interaction (HAI)); limitations of 220; social work (*see* social work); strengths of 220; veterinary social work into 225–227
Ontario Veterinary College (OVC) 223; OVC and Health Sciences Centre (OVC HSC) 223

Packman, W. 192
pandemic pups, animal-assisted intervention 97–99
Pandora's Peter Bear 95
PATH Certified Riding Instructor 205
pawprints: on academia 216–218; human-animal interaction 138–140
paws, animal-assisted intervention: and play 82–84, 88–90; power of 71–75
Pet Assistance & Wellness Program (PAWS) 194, 200
pet loss support group 9, 18, 24, 28, 121
Pet Partners therapy 29–31, 74
Pets Plus Us 144, 145
PETS® supervision models 133–134
physiological homeostasis, in children 113
pilot program 45, 77, 200
Pioneer Pet Clinic 144
play therapy 95; animal-assisted 82–84, 141–143; dogs in 88–90
police social work 175, 178–180
policy advocacy: compelling narratives 49; creativity 49; evidence 49; human-animal interaction 46–50; strategy 48; timing 49
Prairie View A&M University (PVAMU) 170–171
Professional Wellness Group 145
Professor Paws Project 201–202
program development 77, 181; activities 161; human-animal interaction (*see* human-animal interaction (HAI)); Program for Pet Health Equity 226
program evaluation, human-animal interaction 46–50
Program for Pet Health Equity (PPHE) 226
psychology, and social work 103–105
psychotherapy, animal-assisted 76–78, 106–108
puffy's pet boarding 51–52
Puppies Behind Bars 75

Quackenbush, J. 43

Recreational Therapist 29
Registered Play Therapist 141, 142
Reining in Anxiety (RiA) 85, 205

relief veterinarian 35, 36
Residential Crisis Stabilization Program 77

self-care 15, 21, 25, 78, 84, 98, 103–105, 142, 177, 180, 209
Senior Heart Rescue and Renewal 178
service dogs 59–61, 176, 193, 199–202; animal-assisted psychotherapy 106–108; psychiatric 71
Shaw, G.B. 142
shelter pets and kids 100–102
Shin Rin Yuki 67
Shoemaker, Louise 42–43
Silver School of Social Work 72
Skid Row, Los Angeles 182
Slippery Rock University (SRU) 103, 175, 179, 211
Social Service Administration 196
The Social Side of Practice 144
social work: academia 204–206, 228–230; critical animal studies and 219–220; equine-assisted 65–67; human-animal-environment interactions 207–209; human-animal interaction (*see* human-animal interaction (HAI)); police 175, 178–180; practice 111–149; psychology and 103–105; responses 112; teaching in higher education 129–131; Ten Grand Challenges 206; weaving humane education into 147–149; *see also specific social works*
social workers: in agencies 42; embedded, veterinary medicine school 8–10; human-animal interaction: caring 184–185; inclusive communities 201–203; learnings 160–162
Social Workers Advancing the Human Animal Bond (SWAHAB) 44
Society for the Prevention of Cruelty to Animals (SPCA) 59
Spit Camp 158
Sprout 59–61
Stephens, R. 132–133
Stewart Little movie 178
Strand, E. 158
stray dogs 62
street dogs: clandestine killing 62; rabid 63

supervision models: evidence-informed 132–134; PETS® 133–134
supreme dogs, academia 210–212
Surrey Hills Sanctuary 72
systems change 13, 53, 55

Tedeschi, P.: *Transforming Trauma: Resilience and Healing Through Our Connections With Animals* 164
telehealth 98
therapy dogs 83–84, 104, 106–107, 173, 211, 216, 230; animal-assisted intervention (*see* animal-assisted intervention/interaction (AAI)); in forensic interviewing 113; handler teams 77; human-animal interaction 175–177; national organizations 212; programs in child welfare 113; shadow 212; wellbeing 89
Therapy Dogs International 74
Toronto Humane Society (THS) 161
Transforming Trauma: Resilience and Healing Through Our Connections With Animals (Tedeschi) 164
Triangle model 123
Tuskegee University 171

University of Chicago 196
University of Connecticut 157
University of Denver (DU) 30, 100, 123, 135, 163, 205, 207–209, 217
University of Guelph 144
University of Tennessee 8–10, 15, 17, 225; College of Veterinary Medicine (UTCVM) 3
University of Waterloo 144
University of Wisconsin 23
Urban Resource Institute (URI) 43

Van der Kolk, B. 96
VanFleet, R. 88, 143; *Animal Assisted Play Therapy* 143
Veterans Association (VA) 199–200
veterinary medicine 5; human medicine to 32–34; mental health and 8, 15; school 8–10
Veterinary Research Assistant 135
veterinary social work (VSW): in Canadian context 222–224; challenges 9–10, 24–25;

cherished pets model 11–13; effective supervision for 132–134; grief 5, 18–22; horses and 35–37, 157–159; in hospital 15, 17–18, 26–28; human-animal interaction 13; interdisciplinary team 32, 154; interprofessional practice space 3–7; isolation 27; journey 14–16; kaleidoscope of 17–19; into one-health model 225–227; Pet Partners therapy 29–31; portfolio expansion 28; rewards 9–10, 25; role of 23–24; skills for 215; training in 26; from University of Tennesse 8–10
Veterinary Social Work Certificate program 158
violence: domestic 42–43; human-animal interaction 4–5, 53–55; interpersonal situation 72; intimate partner 53–54; sexual 139
Virginia Commonwealth University (VCU) 228

welfare, animal 37, 63–64, 73, 78, 112, 162, 167, 226; advocacy 6; community-based 164; and ethics 83–84; issues 182; practices in 153–156
well-being, human-animal interaction 22, 111–113, 169–171; effects on children 164; policy advocacy 47
wicked problems 149
Wilfrid Laurier University 144
World Small Animal Veterinary Association 145

Zoology Foundation 67, 135, 147

Printed in the United States
by Baker & Taylor Publisher Services